Advance praise for *Central Bank Capitalism*

"Financial globalization is the significant fact of our age. *Central Bank Capitalism* foregrounds the role of central banks in enabling this development, and the challenge that political scientists face in integrating this into their understanding of governance."
  —PERRY MEHRLING, author of *The New Lombard Street*

"Monetary theory and policy are shrouded in near-mystical language and ideas. Wullweber shines a bright light on both and in plain language reveals the interdependence of private capital markets, money markets, the shadow banking system and central banks."
  —ANN PETTIFOR, author of *The Case for the Green New Deal*

"Wullweber offers a brilliant new perspective on the role of central banks in today's global economy. With deep empirical analysis, he sees a new regime emerging governed by powerful monetary authorities. *Central Bank Capitalism* is provocative and insightful."
  —BENJAMIN J. COHEN, author of *International Political Economy: An Intellectual History*

"Central banks remain some of the most mysterious and important institutions of modern time. In this tour-de-force analysis, Wullweber unpacks their technocratic processes and shows them to be deeply political."
  —MARIEKE DE GOEDE, author of *Speculative Security*

"*Central Bank Capitalism* makes the reader understand why monetary policy is no longer boring—and why this is a problem for all of us."
  —WALTRAUD SCHELKLE, author of *The Political Economy of Monetary Solidarity*

"Everyone should try to understand how and how much central banks are crucial for economics and politics, and this book is a great place to start. Even well-informed readers who've kept up with recent financial developments will have a great deal to learn from Wullweber's comprehensive vision of global financial politics."

—ROY KREITNER, author of *Calculating Promises*

"Recommended reading for anyone who wants to understand the workings of contemporary finance capitalism and the central role that central banks play in its perpetuation."

—CASPAR DOHMEN, Deutschlandfunk

"Wullweber takes us deep into the engine room of central banks—the institutions decisively responsible for steering today's economy. The great strength of his book lies in the fact that he does not stop at a (critical) description of financial market developments. Instead he points out why the situation evolved as it did, either because of inaction, mostly on the part of Western governments, or because of financial market deregulation."

—*pro zukunft*

CENTRAL BANK CAPITALISM

CURRENCIES

New Thinking for Financial Times

STEFAN EICH AND MARTIJN KONINGS, EDITORS

Central Bank Capitalism

Monetary Policy in Times of Crisis

JOSCHA WULLWEBER

STANFORD UNIVERSITY PRESS
Stanford, California

Stanford University Press
Stanford, California

Printed in the United States of America on acid-free, archival-quality paper

Library of Congress Cataloging-in-Publication Data

Names: Wullweber, Joscha, author.
Title: Central bank capitalism : monetary policy in times of crisis / Joscha Wullweber.
Other titles: Zentralbankkapitalismus. English
Description: Stanford, California : Stanford University Press, 2024. | Translation of: Zentralbankkapitalismus | Includes bibliographical references and index.
Identifiers: LCCN 2023058052 (print) | LCCN 2023058053 (ebook) | ISBN 9781503638969 (cloth) | ISBN 9781503639621 (paperback) | ISBN 9781503639638 (epub)
Subjects: LCSH: Banks and banking, Central. | Monetary policy. | International finance.
Classification: LCC HG1811 .W79 2024 (print) | LCC HG1811 (ebook) | DDC 332.1/1—dc23/eng/20240327
LC record available at https://lccn.loc.gov/2023058052
LC ebook record available at https://lccn.loc.gov/2023058053

Cover design: George Kirkpatrick
Cover art: iStock

To Hanne, Junar, and Mika

Contents

Preface

This work is a translated and revised version of the third edition of my German book *Zentralbankkapitalismus*. The English edition has been expanded to keep pace with the complex challenges of our times and their implications for global finance and central bank policy, notably the resurgence of inflation since 2022, and the worsening climate crisis compounded by so many other dilemmas facing the world today in a multiplicity of interrelated emergencies aptly referred to as the polycrisis of capitalism (World Economic Forum 2023).

In 2022, inflation made a spectacular comeback on a global scale. After having largely disappeared for fifteen years, at least in Western industrialized countries, it returned with an unexpected vengeance. Indeed, until very recently, the focus was rather on deflation, as Western central banks struggled to prevent prices from falling. But then, in a matter of mere months, prices rose to levels not seen for forty years, and central bankers came under pressure to react. The plea for central bank intervention was not surprising, considering the high priority accorded to price stability as a stated objective of monetary policy. After some hesitancy, central banks around the world heeded the call to hike key interest rates in the most comprehensive tightening of monetary policy in decades (Romei and Stubbington 2022; Tooze 2023a). There was good reason for their initial reluctance: Only a few months after raising key interest rates in 2011, the European Central Bank (ECB) was forced to reverse its decision because of the euro crisis. In 2019, just a year and a half after moderately increasing its benchmark interest rate to 2.5%, the Fed was similarly required to backtrack and cut interest rates when the US money and capital markets began to stumble. More important still, central bankers were well aware that the problem they were facing was not one which could be solved by raising key interest rates. Such a measure makes sense in an overheated economy and when a wage-price spiral leads to inflation. This was not the case in 2022 and 2023. On the contrary, most economies were still struggling with the effects of the COVID-19 pandemic and overall wage developments were modest.

The rise in prices in 2022 and 2023 can rather be attributed to supply-chain problems caused by the pandemic and the high cost of fossil energy, especially in the wake of, but not solely owing to, Russia's war of aggression in Ukraine. Other factors include extreme events such as crop failures due to the climate crisis (Weber and Wasner 2023) and the practice of price gouging that has led to record profits for corporations in a variety of sectors (Schnabel 2022). Even the president of the European Central Bank, Christine Lagarde, called attention to this type of exploitation, known as "greedflation": "In some sectors, firms have been able to increase their profit margins on the back of mismatches between supply and demand, and the uncertainty created by high and volatile inflation" (quoted in Allenbach-Ammann 2023). Key interest rate hikes have no influence over such factors. Instead, they can very likely stall the recovery of economies from the COVID crisis, because when key interest rates increase, loans become more costly for businesses and households. They therefore borrow and invest less. In addition, because central bank bond-buying programs (called *quantitative easing*) have also been scaled back, debt has become more expensive for the state, which, in turn, has tightened public budgets (austerity policies).[1] This has made the fight against inflation even more difficult: In order to bring down energy prices and suppress the increase in prices due to climate-related crop failures in the medium term, it is absolutely necessary for governments to invest extensively in green and sustainable transformation. Higher borrowing costs caused by an increase in the key interest rates, however, reinforce the reluctance of states, but also of private actors and households, to make the necessary investments. Finally, just to touch briefly on an issue that will be discussed later in the book in greater detail: High interest rates combined with the scaling back of quantitative easing destabilize the shadow banking system, and therefore the global financial system as a whole. Short-term funding markets are particularly sensitive to this type of change (Pozsar 2022). The UK gilt market turmoil of September 2022 was the first crisis to become visible after these policies were adopted (Plender 2022). The regime of rising rates, however, was felt most severely in the traditional banking sector. The beginning of 2023 marked the failure of the US banks Silvergate Bank, Silicon Valley Bank, and Signature Bank, followed by the implosion of First Republic Bank, which was taken over by JPMorgan. In Europe, Credit Suisse collapsed (Jenkins 2023; Masters et al. 2023).

Calls for central banks to intervene to control rising prices are based on the hope of returning inflation to tolerable levels. Central bank intervention, however, comes at a huge price. To produce the intended effect, the increase in key interest rates must be high enough to slow down investments and the overall economy. As a result, fewer jobs are created, less people are hired, and more employees become redundant. This can lead to an economic recession, or even worse a recession accompanied by high inflation; in other words, stagflation (IMF 2022). Instead of leaving it up to central banks to fight this very special form of inflation, governments themselves can address the problem far more directly and in a more differentiated and effective way than is possible via key interest rates: They could, for example, launch large investment programs that would greatly reduce dependence on fossil fuels and overall energy consumption (Neuhoff 2022). In the medium term, such an investment policy would already reduce inflation by half. They could introduce a windfall profits tax to siphon off excessive war earnings and impose price controls to prevent companies from making high and undeserved gains from supply shortages. This would further significantly reduce inflation. In the short term, they can protect the most vulnerable social groups from rising prices by introducing price caps (Weber 2021; Ehrhart, Schlecht, and Wang 2022; Editorial Board *New York Times* 2022). Indeed, countries such as France, Italy, Spain, and Norway that have subsidized retail energy and food prices experience significantly lower inflation rates than countries that have not (Sandbu 2022a; Arnold and Jopson 2023).[2] Many more policy options exist to combat inflation. However, they are not being exploited, or only very hesitantly.

Instead of taking action, governments and political parties in most Western countries have rejected responsibility for economic developments. They prefer to leave economic matters to market forces while remaining committed to austerity. Indeed, virtually all advanced economies have cut public spending for investments over the past two decades by an annual amount equivalent to almost two trillion US dollars (Sandbu 2022b). Except for a brief interruption when fiscal aid was provided during the first two years of the COVID pandemic in 2020 and 2021, this trend has only worsened (Mackenzie 2023). With governments shying away from strong fiscal policies and the market unable on its own to restore stability shaken by financial and economic crises, central banks are left to fix the problem. Welcome to the world of central bank capitalism!

Acknowledgments

This book would not have been possible without the generous assistance of many people with whom I have shared innumerable hours of discussion and debate. I am particularly grateful to Christoph Scherrer for his invaluable guidance and inspiration over more than a decade of collaboration. It was Christoph who first introduced me to the issue of money and the global financial system. Throughout my academic career, whenever I needed help or advice, I could rely on his keen sense of analytical reasoning. I am also very fortunate to have had the opportunity of collaborating with Rainer Voss. I remain especially grateful for the countless occasions when we have exchanged ideas around diverse and often controversial issues relating to the financial system and financial market dynamics. With his experience and expertise as a former investment banker, Rainer has challenged me with a formidable perspective "from within" to complement my academic and analytical approach "from without." The occasional clash between theory and practice has always proven highly productive for bringing the two dimensions closer together, which would not have been possible without his valuable insights. I also wish to express my sincere appreciation for the many fruitful discussions with those members of financial and central banking community who prefer to remain anonymous. The extensive comments offered by one of these kind individuals on the entire manuscript of this book were especially appreciated.

I am especially indebted to the editors of the thought-provoking series "Currencies: New Thinking for Financial Times"—series editors Stefan Eich

xvi Acknowledgments

and Martijn Konings and SUP editor Caroline McKusick—for their insightful and encouraging consideration of my manuscript. Their expertise and constructive feedback, together with that of the three anonymous referees, greatly aided my revision process.

My first encounter with the theme of the book began many years ago as a PhD student with an invitation to a discussion group around the topic of money. The sessions generated such lively interest that the group continued to meet regularly for several years. Those meetings were a primary source of my motivation to probe the inner depths of the financial system and the mechanics of financial capitalism. For this I owe my sincere gratitude to the entire group, and especially to Jenny Simon, Halyna Semenyshyn, Christian Möllmann, İsmail Doğa Karatepe, and Shuwen Bian. I would also like to thank everyone who participated in the stimulating and inspiring discussions at our many doctoral and postdoctoral workshops, as well as during the meetings of the Critical Finance Network and the German Research Foundation's research network Politics of Money.

My sincere appreciation also goes to Oliver Kessler for critically reviewing and commenting on the first draft of the German version of this manuscript, and for organizing the many captivating workshops and conferences that I have had the pleasure of attending. The sharp intellectual wit that he brings to science is always a breath of fresh air. Ulrich Brand gave me the opportunity to engage in the intellectual life of the University of Vienna, where I enjoyed a semester as visiting professor. For many years, Uli has been a remarkable academic advisor, motivator, and idea generator. My gratitude also extends to my new colleagues at the Department of Politics, Philosophy and Economics at the University of Witten/Herdecke, where I have been honored to join the faculty with a Heisenberg professorship. Particular recognition is due to my research team—Nicolás Aguila, Paula Haufe, Judith Wehmeyer, Riccardo Baioni, Simon Schairer, Janina Urban, Jan Fichtner, and Teresa Jakovlev. The synergy of their knowledge-producing hub demonstrates how important and exciting, but at the same time how much fun, research can be. It also shows that despite, or perhaps because of, all the differences, the creation of knowledge is always a collective affair. I am delighted to be able to continue my teaching and research in such an exciting environment. With the founding of [tra:ce]—the International Center for Sustainable and Just Transformation—of which I am currently director, we have taken a proactive step toward strengthening research to confront the climate and environmental crises and to support a just transformation of society, economy, and the state. I would like to thank Perry Mehrling very much for his critical review of the manuscript—his Money View was a major inspiration for this book. Many thanks also to Brigitte Young for her critical and constructive feedback on portions of my manuscript. Likewise, special thanks to Vanessa Redak for reviewing sections of my book through the expert eyes of a central banker at the Austrian Central Bank (where it incidentally surprised me to learn that money is not accepted in their canteen as payment for meals—neither in the form of cash nor credit cards!). Also a big thank you to Marieke de Goede, Jerry Cohen, and Ann Pettifor; the discussions with them and their very different approaches and publications were extremely important for my intellectual career.

Loren Samlowski has done an incredible job in proofreading and editing this manuscript. Her revisions and comments, which went far beyond mere questions of grammar and style, have helped to make a complex subject matter more readable. I am also indebted to Nicolás Aguila, Paula Haufe, and Ajla Rizvan for their valuable recommendations for revision in the chapter on high frequency trading. Teresa Jakovlev is to be commended for her exacting research of raw data and skillful execution of the book's graphs and illustrations. I am indebted to Tobias Pforr for many discussions on how central bank capitalism has changed in recent years. Daniela Gabor contributed valuable insight with her suggestions, comments, and critical questions on parts of my original manuscript. Daniela was the person who led me to realize the significance of repo transactions while consistently emphasizing the complexity of money creation. Jerry Cohen and Marieke de Goede also made important comments on different sections of the manuscript. I am indebted to Benjamin Wilhelm, Nina Boy, and Timo Walter for their collaboration in the workshops we conducted together and our many engaging and controversial discussions. My appreciation further extends to the German publishing house Suhrkamp and in particular to my German editor, Christian Heilbronn. Along with his discipline and knowledgeable precision, his professional editorial skills helped me to streamline my text, while making it more accessible to a wider audience.

Sincere thanks to the German Research Foundation (DFG), which, by funding the Heisenberg professorship, has enabled me to strengthen my research focus. Gratitude is also due to the Volkswagen Foundation, whose generous assistance made it possible to finance the intensive program of sessions, presentations, and discussions conducted at two conferences in 2015 on "Financial Crises as Global Challenges" and 2023 on "Crisis Capitalism," which took place at the Herrenhausen Palace in the German city of Hanover. My deep sense of gratitude to my students is not just an empty phrase. Their critical and inquisitive questions that lead to lively, sometimes even heated, discussions provide valuable stimulus for research, challenging me to rethink my perspective, break down complex issues into basic units, and explore the interrelationships. Working together with them is always a mutually enriching experience.

I am deeply indebted to my parents, who contributed in so many ways to paving my academic career, and especially, from the bottom of my heart, to my mother, Helga Wullweber, who always found time to discuss my ideas with me, and who up until her death read all of my texts, including the original manuscript of this book. Her critical but constructive reflections always helped to crystallize my thoughts. Our conversations are irreplaceable and remain deeply missed. Claudia Lichter deserves special recognition for relieving me of so many of my day-to-day organizational duties, especially after the death of my mother, and giving me more time to focus on my writing. Wholehearted thanks to my family and friends and especially to Faride Schubert, Colja Schubert, Irmela Kuhlmann-Causin, Mechtild and Uwe Glunz, Thorsten Hinrichsmeyer, Jörg Rohwedder, Martin and Steffi Wollschläger, and Jürgen Kraus, for accompanying me along this at times rocky journey with all your help and encouragement. My most important thank you belongs to my amazing family: Time and again Junar and Mika manage to put me back on my feet. And nothing in the world can outweigh what I owe to Hanne for her unwavering support and counsel and for the countless ways in which she always serves as my mainstay. The laughter we share in our family is precious. I am fortunate to be taking this journey with you.

CENTRAL BANK CAPITALISM

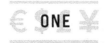

ONE

Introduction

Central Banks and Power

The more widely we interpret our mandate, the greater the risk that we will become entangled with politics and overburden ourselves with too many tasks. As a consequence, our independence might be called into question, and rightly so.
—Jens Weidmann, German Federal Bank President, 2020

The unconventional is now the conventional.
—Julia Coronado, former Fed economist, during the Federal Reserve meeting at Jackson Hole, Wyoming, 2020

There are times when we need to go big and go fast.
—Andrew Bailey, Bank of England Governor, 2020

THE TERM *CENTRAL BANK CAPITALISM* is a pointed, perhaps even somewhat provocative reference to a fundamental transformation that is taking place in present-day capitalism. It highlights an ongoing process that became apparent during the global financial crisis, but whose beginnings trace back to the early 1990s—a process that is radically and profoundly altering the nature of Western economic and financial systems. In brief, and leaving aside the complexity of the issue for the moment, it can be said that the global financial system and contemporary capitalism in Western industrialized countries are no longer capable of functioning without the permanent, highly unconventional, extensive, and in some respects extreme interventions on the part of central banks. Suspending these central bank interventions would mean the collapse not only of banking systems but also of global financial systems and economies around the world.

At the beginning of the pandemic, in March 2020, a large part of the global economy had come to a standstill. Possibilities across the globe for cushioning the economic impact of a lockdown were highly uneven. Low-income countries in particular had difficulties in raising the necessary financial resources to buffer the economic consequences of the pandemic (World Bank 2022a). But there were also considerable differences among industrialized countries. Even in the eurozone, Member States acted in a poorly coordinated manner and were not able to develop an overall strategy to overcome the coronavirus outbreak. While Germany managed to mitigate the consequences of the downturn with a set of mechanisms designed to lend support to struggling businesses (short-time working arrangements, special credit lines, and a variety of other economic and social policy measures), countries such as Italy and Spain, both of which were hit much harder by the pandemic in 2020, had no comparable financial schemes or buffers (ECB 2020a). Rather than working together to alleviate the economic and social repercussions of the COVID-19 crisis, governments took separate and unilateral action. The European Commission proved to be a toothless institution without the competences required to provide anything in the way of assistance aside from warnings and exhortations. During the first few months, as the pandemic spread across Europe, instead of providing mutual support, EU Member States argued over the feasibility and form of joint solutions and financial support.[1] This only exaggerated the already existing differences across Member States. Indeed, it looked as if there would be a flare-up of the dispute that had been triggered during the euro crisis over possible measures of aid and support for individual EU countries. The deep rifts between Member States that had opened up toward the end of 2010 began to widen. Even die-hard Europe advocates began to doubt the European project (Münchau 2020). Increasingly it seemed as though the coronavirus crisis would accomplish what even the global financial crisis of 2007–9 and the subsequent euro crisis had not brought to pass: the breaking apart of the European Union.

At that point, in March 2020, when all other European institutions seemed paralyzed, or simply incapable of mobilizing adequate financial resources, the European Central Bank (ECB) stepped in with all its might. In an unprecedented campaign in mid-March 2020, it launched its 750-billion-euro Pandemic Emergency Purchase Program (PEPP). The funding instrument, designed mainly to enable the ECB to purchase euro area sovereign bonds, was later more than doubled to 1.85 trillion euros. In addition, the ECB expanded its Asset Purchase Program (APP) from a monthly figure of 20 billion euros to a massive 140 billion euros per month (ECB 2020b, 2020c). The new president of the central bank, Christine Lagarde, has had to navigate a steep learning curve since retracting an ambiguous remark that caused confusion early in her term. In March 2020, she issued the following unequivocal statement: "Extraordinary times require extraordinary action. There are no limits to our commitment to the euro. We are determined to use the full potential of our tools, within our mandate" (Christine Lagarde via Twitter on 19 March 2020).[2] The ECB is still the only institution willing and able to effectively counteract a breakup of the euro area (Wullweber 2020a; Quaglia 2023).

The situation in the euro area is special. At the same time, from what we have seen in the United Kingdom and other leading industrial countries, and especially in the United States, central banks can and do intervene quickly and consistently in the financial market and the economy (World Bank 2022a). When on 9 March 2020 financial markets around the world plunged, the US Federal Reserve (the Fed), which plays a pivotal role in the global financial system, took immediate action and used all of its power to stabilize financial markets, above all the money and securities markets. Simultaneously, the Fed set up a historically unique emergency program and provided a total of 2.3 trillion US dollars in credit to support the economy. Similar programs were launched by the Bank of England, the Bank of Japan, the Swiss National Bank, and the Bank of China (Boyarchenko et al. 2020).

I

The measures undertaken by these central banks during the COVID-19 pandemic were not exceptions to the rule: We are living in an age of central bank capitalism. In the years since the global financial crisis, central banks have become much more powerful and unconventional in their approach. They can—and must—react to crises much more quickly and forcefully than other institutions. At the same time, their monetary policy instruments are not subject to parliamentary debate or voting procedures. This raises questions about the democratic legitimacy of their measures.

The implication behind central bank capitalism is that to an increasing extent it is the central bank, on the basis of technocratic processes, that has to make critical decisions with far-reaching economic and political implications. Elected governments tend to shy away from actively shaping and steering the economy with strong fiscal policy (Carney 2016). Even during the COVID-19 pandemic, the main concern in government circles had merely been to stabilize the economy. Only very cautiously was there even a hint of programs that would actively steer investments. As soon as the economic crisis triggered by COVID-19 seemed to have passed its peak, most governments returned to a regime of austerity, a fiscal policy committed to tightly balanced budgets while largely refraining from strong fiscal impulses, financial guidance, and measures of support.[3] De facto, this policy implies an immense reduction of state spending. As governments continue to hesitate, even in the face of a growing climate crisis with catastrophic economic consequences and costs,[4] their central banks must intervene more than ever before in order to prevent the collapse of the entire financial system. Nevertheless—to introduce an aspect that will be examined more closely later in this analysis—central banks share responsibility for making the system unstable. For years they have been strengthening one of the prime instigators of instability: the shadow banking system. Since the global financial crisis, the balance sheet figures of the world's most important central banks have accordingly increased many times over. From 2004 until mid-2022, the ECB's balance sheet had expanded more than tenfold—from approximately 800 billion euros to over 8,700 billion euros (St. Louis Fed 2022a). In a similar manner, by mid-2022, the Fed had increased its 2007 asset balance of 850 billion dollars to almost 9,000 billion dollars (St. Louis Fed 2023a).

As the following chapters will show, increasing the volume of balance sheets is not necessarily a problem. Under central bank capitalism, the difficulty, in fact, is rather balance sheet reduction, so-called quantitative tightening, because it tendentially increases the crisis vulnerability of the system. Theoretically speaking, there is no natural limit to the amount of money that central banks can create in their own currency. This applies in particular to the leading central banks of industrialized states and high-income countries (practically speaking, however, limits are eventually reached, for instance in the event of rampant domestic inflation that diminishes the external value of the currency or erodes confidence in its stability). The enormous size of central bank balance sheets, however, is an expression of a deep crisis that has spread throughout the financial system and the world economy since 2007.

To stabilize the financial system, central banks have come to use monetary policy instruments that until recently would have been inconceivable in terms of their scope as well as their incisive and radical nature. At the same time, these instruments have come debatably close to exceeding central bank mandates. In former times, central banks were allowed to issue credit only to traditional banks. Since the outbreak of the COVID-19 pandemic, however, it has been possible in the United States as well as in the United Kingdom for struggling businesses and municipal authorities to take out loans through central bank facilities (Milstein and Wessel 2021). Moreover, the Bank of England has been allowed to purchase government bonds directly from the government. Another example involves schemes known as quantitative easing (QE) that have enabled central banks to engage in the large-scale purchase of assets, especially government bonds (indirectly on secondary markets). These schemes exist in a gray area that arguably verges on government financing, a practice forbidden for many central banks. Until the expiry of the QE program in mid-2022, however, the Bank of England had bought nearly 50% of all British government bonds. By comparison, prior to the global financial crisis, the share of UK government bonds held by the Bank of England was negligible. The situation has been more extreme in the euro area. By 2020, the ECB had bought up 70% of all government bonds issued by euro area Member States. In Japan the figure stood at 75% (Gabor 2020). Despite all the problems associated with QE programs, it should not be overlooked that central banks did stabilize the government bond market and, in turn, the financial market, making it easier for governments to finance the necessary measures.

Such developments have been blurring the boundary between monetary and fiscal policy, a boundary that until recently had marked a red line of market liberal policy that was not to be crossed under any circumstances.[5] In the meantime, the conditions of modern capitalism have been increasingly demonstrating that some of these red lines are no longer tenable without risking the collapse of the entire system and jeopardizing the welfare of a large part of the population. It was becoming increasingly clear—not least during the COVID-19 pandemic—that maintaining a stable economy requires not just intervention on the part of central banks but also a broader interpretation of their mandate. Central bank capitalism, however, also implies that the powerful shifting of roles in the shaping of monetary and fiscal policy should attract as little media attention as possible. Neither governments nor central banks like to publicly debate the new developments that are intermingling the two areas of policy and the resulting need for institutional changes to address the issue.

The idea behind the term *central bank capitalism* is to call attention to the complexity of the current situation with all its contradictions and paradoxes that will be explored at length over the course of this book. In contrast to fiscal policy, which is within the remit of government, monetary policy does not normally have direct bearing on the productive economy—the so-called real economy. So far, it has to take an indirect route through the financial system.[6] This means that monetary policy measures frequently fail to achieve their intended purpose. This was the case with the interest rate hikes in 2022 and 2023, which were meant to fight inflation without overweakening the economy (in the sense of a "soft landing"). It was also the case, however, for the monetary policy measures implemented since 2008 to help set flagging economies back on their feet. For the most part, instead of serving to stimulate the productive economy, the extra liquidity created through those measures reached financial players who channeled it back into the financial system in the form of financial investments. This, in turn, has led to recurring boom and bust cycles, and on the whole to a gigantic asset inflation that destabilizes the financial system and, ultimately, the productive economy. The gains, however, in no way reflected corporate reality, the state of national economies, or the overall global economic situation. Many sectors were left struggling to survive, and their prospects are still highly uncertain. In this respect, central banks themselves are trapped in a vicious circle. To stabilize a financial system in a constant state of crisis, they have to provide permanent measures that tend to make the system even more prone to crisis.

Since 2008, the global financial system has been operating in crisis mode. When the coronavirus pandemic took hold in March 2020, it was obvious that existing structures could not even come close to containing—or at least cushioning—its economic repercussions. On the contrary, the new developments only served to amplify the weaknesses already present in the system while accelerating mechanisms such as feedback loops, downward liquidity spirals, and other such dynamics that stoke the economic downturn and impede economic recovery. Even if shock waves such as COVID-19 or Russia's war of aggression against Ukraine are not foreseeable, the weaknesses in the global financial system have long been apparent. Although various drivers of instability have been building up for years—and some for decades—other causes of crisis are inherent in our current market liberal financial system. The COVID-19 pandemic and the global financial crisis are therefore not events that occur in an otherwise stable financial system. Since the 1980s, stability is the exception rather than the rule.

II

Over the past thirty years, the global financial system has undergone a radical process of transformation. In today's global financial system, the core position is occupied by the shadow banking system. And it is precisely the shadow banking system that is a major contributing factor to the fundamental instability of the overall system. Shadow banking involves the intermediation of credit and assets outside of the banking system. It currently accounts for an annual trading volume of more than 239 trillion US dollars (FSB 2022). Nearly 50% of all credit transactions are conducted through shadow players, which include money market funds, hedge funds, and investment banks. For many investors the area is an interesting source of low-cost liquidity under terms with considerably fewer restrictions than in the traditional bank-based credit system. In addition, ever since the financial crisis, the (unsecured) interbank market—the traditional source of lending and borrowing among banks—has come to a virtual standstill: Banks simply no longer trust one another.

Repurchase agreements, or repos for short, play a central role as a credit and collateral instrument in the shadow banking system. Repos are contracts for the sale of securities and other assets at an agreed price with a commitment on the part of the seller to repurchase the same securities at the end of a set term, which frequently runs on an overnight basis but which may also have a longer maturity period. The trouble with such transactions is that they are not a crisis-proof form of security. In fact, quite the opposite is true: They add to the severity of crises. A crisis in the shadow banking system can also impact the productive economy in cases where it becomes difficult for nonfinancial actors to procure liquidity. Crisis in the financial system tends to spill into other sectors of the economy. Without a functioning global financial system, capitalism would collapse. In a profit-oriented economy, participants are required to anticipate changes in supply and demand and to invest accordingly in the future. The process of capitalist production therefore requires advance capital in order for producers to be able to invest in machines, buildings, raw materials, wages, etc., before they can produce goods on a large scale so that they can sell what they produce at a profit. Therefore, as a rule, producers need to take out credit to finance their undertakings. Credit is available through the financial system, and here, increasingly, through the shadow banking system. The productive economy and the financial system are therefore closely interrelated and mutually dependent (Amato and Fantacci 2012). One of the many paradoxes inherent in central bank capitalism is the fact that the world's leading central banks themselves have assumed an active role in strengthening the shadow banking system and are therefore party to a destabilizing system.

Also implicit in the concept of central bank capitalism is the idea that the shadow banking system has come to occupy a central position in the financial system. It is impossible to comprehend the two major financial and economic crises of the early twenty-first century without looking at the dynamics of the shadow banking system. In the years following the financial crisis, central banks were compelled to radically expand their repertory of monetary interventions and their scope of action. They now conclude transactions not only with traditional banks but also with shadow bank players, for whom they have come to act as dealers of last resort. And this amounts to direct intervention in the shadow banking system. Central banks are no longer merely a source of liquidity. They now also operate as dealers and market makers. In the words of Mark Carney, former governor of the Bank of England, they are "open for business" (Carney 2015: 8; Birk and Thiemann 2020). Ultimately, they are in the unique position of being able to decide which financial players can access central bank money and government bonds (so-called safe assets), who can sell their assets to the central bank at par, or close to par, and on demand, and under what conditions. This means they can determine who gets access to financial liquidity and market liquidity. When the COVID-19 crisis erupted,[7] central banks were ready to take prompt action. The dramatic situation made it necessary for them to expand their inventory of instruments beyond the range of traditional measures such as lower key interest rates, more liquidity provision and lender of last resort credit lines, and even beyond the already existing unconventional measures such as quantitative easing, dealer of last resort, and international currency swaps. They began to extend credit to nonfinancial actors. And in the United Kingdom, to make sure that the British government had access to enough liquidity, the Bank of England began to purchase UK government bonds directly from the primary market, crossing another red line into previously forbidden territory.[8]

III

Central banks hold a position of enormous political and economic power. And yet, they have long been viewed as apolitical institutions. Until recently, monetary policy was considered to be mainly a matter of technocratic decision-making based almost exclusively on mathematical formulas. To a large extent, the failure to recognize central banks as autonomous political agents lies in the widely held conviction dating back to the 1980s and 1990s that they should be independent from government and preserve a position of neutrality in political matters of the day (McNamara 2002). Many scholars have overlooked the fact that financial players and their strategies in the global financial system have been guided not only by the regulatory system but also, to a decisive degree, by political and economic structures, the logics of profit and questions relating to the generation and securing of liquidity. And in this respect, central banks play a prominent role (Baker 2006; Hall 2008). At least theoretically speaking, the central banks of major industrial countries have unlimited financial resources at their disposal. The firepower that they possess is unique and by and large crisis-resistant. Consequently, without a firm grasp of the role played by central banks and their monetary policy, it is futile to try and understand the governance of the financial system under present-day capitalism.

During former times of relative price stability and steady growth, central banks were expected to function in a more or less predictable manner. The exercise of monetary policy was mainly a question of adjusting key interest rates. In the years between the 2007–9 financial crisis and 2022, however, key interest rate policy all but lost its efficacy. At leading central banks—especially the so-called C6 (the Fed, the ECB, the Bank of England, the Bank of Japan, the Swiss National Bank, and the Bank of Canada)—key interest rates had been hovering around, or just above, the zero percent mark. Consequently, during this period they ceased to fulfill their steering function. The approach that has meanwhile taken center stage is based primarily on balance sheet policies— the strategic creation (and destruction) of massive amounts of money, and the purchase and sale of assets. A firm grasp of these monetary policies in this sense is the key to understanding the qualitatively new approach to financial crises and the fundamental transformation that has taken place in the governance of today's financial system: "Several major central banks reached milestones using their balance sheets as active tools for providing monetary policy accommodation" (Potter 2017a; ECB 2015a; Logan 2018). In 2022, interest rate policy made a comeback (Romei and Stubbington 2022). Central bankers were well aware that raising policy rates is the wrong answer to global inflation. Climbing interest rates are clearly strangling entire economies. It would have made more sense for central banks to refrain from hiking interest rates, leaving it up to government bodies to more directly tackle inflation (see the preface). But central bankers obviously preferred to live up to their reputation as guardians of price stability (Gopinath 2023). The price that has to be paid for this is high. It is called economic recession (Duguid and Smith 2022). This is all the more surprising as central banks have been extremely creative over the past twenty years when it comes to stabilizing the financial system.

IV

The year 2008 was a watershed in the history of governance in the international financial sector. It marked a radical break with the previously existing system of regulation. When interbank markets came to a standstill after the Lehman Brothers insolvency in September of that year, the world financial system was brought to the brink of financial collapse. At that point, the Fed stepped in with a historically unique response: It created a series of monetary instruments, or facilities, allowing itself to conclude repurchase agreements with nonbanks in order to give them access to the Fed's balance sheet. Since the creation of these new facilities, various shadow players such as investment funds, money market funds, security dealers, and asset managers have been able to use them to tap Fed accounts. Before then, only commercial banks were permitted the privilege of concluding such transactions with the Fed.

The new strategy bears no comparison to previous crisis intervention strategies. It follows an entirely new kind of governance rationality involving a transformation in the exercise of statehood. It is neither the resurgence of the Leviathan in opposition to financial markets nor the re-embedding in society of unchained market forces (Polanyi 1957). To conceptualize state and market as opposing entities, for example, in the form of state versus capitalism, or state versus financial markets, misses the point and does not measure up to reality. The state-market nexus is rather a constitutive and conditional relationship and not a dichotomy. Finance is embedded in state relations and vice versa (Wullweber 2020b).

In this vein, a number of recent studies establishing a connection between security, state, and the financial market explore how these factors are interrelated (Boy 2017; de Goede 2017; Langley 2017). Three different directions can be identified in this context (de Goede 2010: 101–103): The first examines possible instrumental relationships between the financial system, monetary policy, and security. Studies in this category focus on topics such as early twentieth-century dollar diplomacy in the United States (Rosenberg 1999), the issuance of war bonds (Aitken 2003), the relationship between foreign capital investments / foreign investment positions and foreign political interests, as well as the use of military force to defend financial interests (Van der Pijl 2006). Various studies argue that the accelerated trend toward liberalization after the collapse of the Bretton Woods system (see chapter 2) led to a power shift as a result of which nation-states have grown increasingly exposed to the structural constraints of the global financial markets (Helleiner 1994; Strange 1986; Pauly 1997). Some of these studies view the states as responsible for this change (Strange 1986), while others consider the financial markets to be the driving force behind the development (Cohen 1996).

The second line of research highlights security aspects in the financial system. It focuses on the underlying question of how the financial system creates certain forms of security and insecurity. In addition to facilitating the creation of credit, it is the basic function of the financial system to provide, produce, and trade securities used as collateral. It was at a coffeehouse by the name of Lloyd's where the insurance market Lloyd's of London got its start. Like other similar establishments, Lloyd's Coffee House was a popular meeting place for merchants and business people. They gathered to find partners who were interested in taking risks, for the most part in international import and export trade and commercial maritime shipping. Before a ship could set sail, enough funds had to be raised to cover the cost of the expedition and the risks involved. Financiers willing to share those risks signed their names to the bottom of a document detailing the specifics of the journey. This practice came to be known in the insurance world as underwriting (Lobo-Guerrero 2011).

The motivation for this kind of risk trading is of course the prospect of earning a profit. For risks to be tradable, they have to be assessed and rendered comparable. The mathematical assessment and trade of risks is possible only if the risks are quantifiable. This accounts for the massive importance attached to rating agencies and mathematical risk assessment models (MacKenzie and Millo 2003; MacKenzie 2006; Sinclair 2005). Illiquid and nontradable assets such as mortgages can be made tradable through the practice of securitization (Gorton 2017: 564–65). The consequence of securitization, however, is that the securitized instrument detaches the risks from the goods it secures, and in this way delocalizes and depersonalizes the creditor-debtor relationship (Martin 2007: 31–33). This became evident during the global financial crisis. Loans and mortgages were securitized for the sake of risk-shifting (off the balance sheets of the lending banks), to reallocate, redistribute, and thereby conceal their risks. According to de Goede (2010: 104–5), the security/insecurity dynamic is an ongoing theme throughout the history of the modern financial system: "Simply put, if financial technologies and profit are premised on the provision of security, the commercial logic of the markets is to identify more and more insecurities to be hedged."

The third line of approach views the relationship between the financial system, the state, and security not as instrumental or causal (in the sense of security and insecurity as produced by the financial system), but rather as being closely and inextricably intertwined. In this context, the logic of finance is the *security's economic double* (de Goede 2010: 106). Scholars who take this approach argue that the emergence of modern states is closely linked to national debt not least in order to raise the funds needed to finance wars: "[T]he founding moments of all modern nation-states are identical to the funding of their debts" (Brantlinger 1996: 29, as quoted in Boy, Burgess, and Leander 2011: 116; see also Germain 1997; Boy and Gabor 2019). As pointed out by Boy, Burgess, and Leander (2011: 116), the epistemological origin of both security studies and economics after World War II can be traced back to *Theory of Games and Economic Behavior* by John von Neumann and Oskar Morgenstern (von Neumann and Morgenstern 1944). Game theory plays an important role not only in the field of economics but also in the domain of international relations (IR) and international political economy (IPE). Algorithmic decision-making models are utilized both in finance and the military (Der Derian 2001; Martin 2007).

From a Foucauldian perspective (2009) it can be argued that the logic of finance and security is premised on governmental practice that relies less on prohibition and the containment of insecurity than on productive power (Dillon 2007, 2010). Foucault himself has variously shown how crucial economic knowledge is for security practices (Foucault 2009). Other studies emphasize the amalgamation of the entrepreneurial self with the securitization of specific subjectivities based on financial responsibility and rationality (Langley

2007; Campbell 2005). Boy, Burgess, and Leander (2011: 115) also stress the connection between the logic of finance and the logic of security: "[F]inance and security share a claim to universal applicability in (all) other social spheres, resulting in various forms of financialization and securitization." At the same time, in regard to this financialization of everyday life and the constant expansion of securitization to social domains, they make the following critical observation: "The past 30 years have seen the tendency of both finance and security to 'colonize' almost every other sphere of social life" (Boy, Burgess, and Leander 2011: 116). Based on the vision of all-encompassing markets, every conceivable uncertainty can be hedged at a price corresponding to the degree of uncertainty (de Goede 2001). In brief, in both of these areas it is a matter of dealing with future uncertainties. Even more, it is about how anticipated hazards and risks influence the way the here and now is governed: "The imagination of the uncertain future shapes and constrains action in the present, both in the realm of finance and in the realm of security" (de Goede 2010: 107).

V

My analysis of central bank capitalism and the changing nature of the relationship between the state and the financial system is guided, in particular, by the governance perspective in the third line of approach (Langley 2013, 2015; Wullweber 2019a). As an analytical framework, this perspective permits the detailed identification, examination, and evaluation of the various rationalities of governance and government processes. Considering the radical transformation that has taken place in the rationality of central bank policy, the analysis of central bank capitalism as it relates to the two major financial crises that occurred during the first quarter of the twenty-first century needs to examine the question of "how sovereign monetary, fiscal, and regulatory techniques were dynamically transformed in order that they could be put to work in the governance of the bust" (Langley 2015: 8). Until the financial crisis, there was a strict separation of fiscal and monetary policy. Central banks were expected to conduct their policy measures in accordance with fixed rules and quasi-scientific criteria (Clarida, Gali, and Gertler 1999; Conti-Brown 2016). The approach taken in this study makes it possible to go beyond the mere observation that financialization processes have led to a loss of state influence. It permits a more nuanced examination of the transformation that has taken place in the way the state governs the financial system. Moreover, it facilitates an in-depth analysis of how the relationship between state and market has shifted. In this context, a close look is taken at how certain facets of the logic or rationality of governance have developed and changed over time. The concept of governance in this study is understood in the comprehensive sense conveyed by the term *governmentality* as employed by Michel Foucault (Foucault 2008, 2009). It encompasses not only the politics of specific governments but also, in general, the leading of those who are led, as well as the governing of self. It focuses on the "exercise of political sovereignty" (Foucault 2008: 2); in other words, on the mode of reflection about the best possible mode of regulation. The concept of governance therefore makes it possible to capture the complexity of monetary policy.

The various forms of governance—the means by which social problems are dealt with (strategically) and how political intervention is structured—should be understood here in the sense of Foucault's concept of power structures. Following Foucault's reasoning, it is possible to distinguish three different types of governance. *Sovereign power* stands for a hierarchical type of governance that tends to be more territorial, centrist, and juridical by nature. His *disciplinary power* is based on a form of governance that is more ideological in the sense of individual self-discipline achieved through a continuous process of monitoring (Foucault 1980: 146). The third type of power, *security power*, stands for nonhierarchical forms of governance in the sense of "governing at a distance" (Rose and Miller 1992: 173). It relies more on mechanisms of regulated self-regulation in which nonstate actors interact in relatively autonomous spaces, but without total retreat on the part of the state. The rationality of security power is peculiar to a market liberal approach. This includes the notion that the promotion of laissez-faire "will itself entail precisely its own self-curbing and self-regulation" (Foucault 2009: 41–42). The mechanisms and apparatus of security aim, above all, at securing circulation: "[I]t was a matter of organizing circulation, eliminating its dangerous elements, making a division between good and bad circulation, and maximizing the good circulation by diminishing the bad" (Foucault 2009: 18). Sovereign power and disciplinary power encompass, above all, the more or less direct control of political and economic processes. They seek, as far as possible, to eliminate uncertainty. The logic of the security power, on the other hand, regards uncertainty as a productive and potentially profit-generating force (Langley 2015: 19–22): "It is simply a matter of maximizing the positive elements" (Foucault 2009: 19).

According to Foucault, all three modes of governmentality are always present, but in differing degrees. Western societies have registered a steady shift in the direction of the rationality of security power, a trend that has increased since the 1970s. Although the other types of power mechanisms are still present, it is especially the line of reasoning behind security power that has come to shape the market liberal (neoliberal) rationality of governance. Here the question is not "one of how a space can be found within an existing State for a necessary market freedom, but of how to create a State on the basis of an economic freedom which will secure the State's legitimacy and self-limitation" (Burchell 1993: 270). It provides market forces with the greatest possible leeway: "These innovations involved a shift of policy implementation to markets, but not a retreat from the state's role in managing the economy" (Krippner 2007: 478, Krippner 2011; Mirowski 2014: 56–57). People, goods, and financial flows are supposed to be entitled to circulate largely without restriction, although market liberalism can and, in fact, does lead to an increase in state structures (Vogel 1996; Knafo 2013). Risks are not understood as a danger but rather as an opportunity and a source of profit, a fact that is also evident from the trading with risks that takes place in various forms on financial markets: "[R]isk relies on actuarial-like data, modelling and speculations that do not simply call for the elimination of risk but develop strategies to embrace it" (Aradau, Lobo-Guerrero, and Van Munster 2008: 148; Amoore 2011). What is more, risk-taking is viewed as a prerequisite to economic success (Lemke 2001; Kessler 2008).

Based on these theoretical considerations, the question is not whether the state or the market has become more powerful. It is rather the state–market *relation* as a hybrid constellation; in other words, the form and modes of governance that are changing. In this vein, the various monetary policy measures adopted for the purpose of crisis intervention—instruments such as key interest rates, lender of last resort, and quantitative easing—can be regarded as dynamic mechanisms of market liberal governance. September 2008, however, was a game changer. The crisis intervention measures undertaken when the global financial crisis escalated marked a clear break with former types of governance. The nature of this break is not compatible with the classic conception of security power, which relies, in particular, on flat hierarchies and self-control. Central banks have rather embarked on a course of unprecedented might. At the same time, their interventions can also be understood as an ongoing search to stabilize a financial system that tends to be more and more unstable. As the following chapters will show, these altered modes of governance lead to a paradox that lies at the heart of central bank capitalism: To maintain free financial markets and, ultimately, to preserve the logic of the market liberal system on which they are based, central banks have had to break in part with that very same logic. Alongside this development, the shadow banking system has been growing steadily more important. In today's version of capitalism, therefore, two diverse trends are gaining ground: both market liberal rationality *and* state intervention. Central banks are caught in the middle of this paradox as they try to stabilize this complex constellation with all its contradictions and crisis-prone tendencies. Considering how cautious governments are when it comes to fiscal and regulatory policy—barring the brief interval during the COVID-19 pandemic when Keynesian stabilization policies experienced a revival—central banks and their monetary policy continue to be "the only game in town" (Carney 2016: 12).

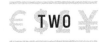

The "Boring" World of Central Banking

Monetary Policy Prior to the 2007–2009 Global Financial Crisis

EVEN AS FINANCIAL CRISES BECAME more frequent once the Bretton Woods international monetary system came to an end in the 1970s, central banks essentially kept their repertoire of monetary policy measures limited to the adjustment of key interest rates and the creation of lender of last resort facilities. With the onset of the global financial crisis, and then again when the COVID-19 pandemic struck, however, they had to significantly expand their potential for intervention. With the rise of the shadow banking system, the existing security structure, which was designed by central banks, mainly for traditional deposit-funded banks, lost its efficacy. And yet, the monetary policies presented in this chapter are still part of the basic policy repertoire of central banks. In general, central banks have a variety of monetary policy instruments at their disposal depending on the legal framework of their respective country, or in the case of the ECB, on European Union law. The need on the part of commercial banks for central bank money, the need on the part of financial players for safe collateral in the form of government bonds (safe assets),[1] and the purchase and sale of securities are ultimately the levers on which monetary policy relies.

2.1 The Mission of Central Banks

Most central banks were founded some time after the rise of nation-states. They were granted the privilege of being the only state-recognized institution to issue legally guaranteed means of payment as a securitized liability to economic entities (companies and private households).[2] Interestingly, the belief persists that central banks are not state institutions. This is probably due to the fact that during the middle of the twentieth century, around half of all central banks had private shareholders. By 2019, the figure was only about 5%, but it included some of the world's major central banks such as the Fed, the Bank of Japan, and the Swiss National Bank (Bholat and Martinez Gutierrez 2019). This does not alter the fact that central banks are still state institutions. The role of private shareholders in central banks has evolved historically and is not comparable to the role of private shareholders in companies with share capital (joint stock companies, for example). Central bank shareholders have no rights or opportunities to help shape central bank policy. Nor can they exercise any influence on the central bank as a state institution. In the United States it is even required by law for commercial banks to own a certain amount of shares in the Fed in order to be part of the Federal Reserve System. Unlike business enterprises, central banks are not profit-oriented. Any net profits that they earn are transferred to the finance ministries of their respective countries.[3] Shareholders only receive a fixed payment on their shares (similar to coupon payments on bonds). Also, where financial behavior is concerned, central banks that have private shareholders do not operate any differently from those that do not (Bartels, Eichengreen, and Weder di Mauro 2016). Although a small number of central banks do operate on the basis of a hybrid system with both private and state shareholding, this does not affect their status as independent agencies of the executive branch of their respective countries (Bholat and Martinez Gutierrez 2019). It does not follow from this, however, that governments can shape monetary policy. On the contrary, most central banks are by law independent institutions; in other words, they are not subject to directives from any other authority.

Originally, one of the chief functions of central banks was to provide the state with funds in the form of loans. Until the 1980s, most central banks were subordinate to ministries of finance (Dow 2015; Mehrling 2015; Ugolini 2017). The Bank of England, for example, was created in 1694 to allow King William III to borrow the money he needed to finance his war with France—in particular to build a powerful navy.[4] Other state central banks were set up in response to banking and financial crises. In the United States, it took a major economic meltdown for the government to realize that a financial system in crisis needs a trustworthy lender of last resort to prevent the collapse of that system and to cushion the inherent instability of the banking sector. In October 1907, when the so-called Bankers' Panic broke out, the United States did not have a central bank. The financier J. P. Morgan, then one of the most influential men on Wall Street with close ties to the real economy, stepped in and helped to stem the crisis with an initiative to back the banking system. In 1913, in order to avoid the repetition of such a situation, and not least to ensure the state's power to act in financial crisis situations, the Federal Reserve System was established.

Early in their history, the predominantly private central banks tended to see themselves as commercial banks, albeit with close and special ties to the state. They managed state funds and provided their governments with credit. It soon became clear, however, that they differed from all other banks in one particular sense: They were protected by the state and could therefore act as a bank for other banks. It was a reciprocal relationship in which the state was liable for the security of central bank assets while the central bank made money available to the state: "The central bank was thus the lender of last, if not first, resort for the government" (Dow 2015: 231). Especially in times of crisis, private banks turned to the central bank for liquidity. Central banks assumed this role as lender of last resort in the nineteenth century (Goodhart 1991; Mehrling 2011: 18–21).

Over time, the monetary policy of central banks has undergone significant change, in part because the financial system itself is always changing, but also because the goals pursued or the means to achieve them have also changed (Hall 2008; Eichengreen 2008; Krippner 2011). One of the most important tasks of central banks was, and still is, to ensure stability in the value of money. Considering that a natural value cannot serve as the basis for the unit of value, since there is no such thing as natural value, how is value of a currency maintained? The simple answer: The value of money remains stable when confidence in its currency is firm (Cohen 1998). This confidence is based on the ability to keep the nominal value of the currency, its purchasing power, reasonably stable in both crisis and non-crisis times. Money is accepted as a unit of value only if there is trust that it will remain relatively stable over a longer period of time:

"Money works best when it is taken for granted, when its value, negotiability and neutrality can simply be assumed" (Carruthers and Babb 1996: 1556).

Over the course of history, a variety of approaches have been taken to avoid major fluctuations in the value of money. For a while, the fiction of tying currencies to a precious metal, particularly gold, proved to be relatively successful. The *gold standard* meant that a banknote represented the holder's right to exchange it at the central bank for its equivalent value in gold. More often than not, however, the total value of money in circulation exceeded the value of gold reserves. Time and time again, laws governing the gold standard have been repealed. Ultimately, the assumption is misguided that gold (or any other asset) possesses a fundamental or intrinsic value (Knapp 1924; Ingham 2004). Since the abolition of gold backing for currencies, the use of money created by a central bank has been based solely on public trust in the state's promise to the effect that the value of currency issued as legal tender by its central bank will remain stable in the medium to long term. This makes it a future-oriented store of value, which, in turn, gives people the chance to defer consumption. This expectation of dependability is the basis for statutory mandates that bind the majority of central banks around the world to the prioritization of price stability.

Fixing the value of one currency against the value of another was a further policy approach to maintain a stable currency. This practice was particularly widespread under the Bretton Woods system between 1945 and 1971. It was based on the idea of combining the advantages of fixed and flexible exchange rates to prevent so-called currency wars, or *devaluation races*, among member states (and trading partners). At the same time, global financial flows were tightly restricted. The Bretton Woods agreement linked the exchange rates of the signatory countries' currencies to the price of gold via the US dollar. The price of the US dollar, in turn, was fixed at 35 US dollars per troy ounce of gold. Exchange rates were readjusted through a process of realignment as soon as the economies of the member states diverged and governments came under pressure to adjust the value of their currencies either up or down. The International Monetary Fund (IMF) was created to bridge the short-term balance of payments deficits. The idea was to stabilize the international monetary system and prevent the development of permanent economic difficulties in the various member states. At first, the international movement of capital was highly regulated, but over time the trend toward liberalization increased. It was the chief task of central banks to stabilize the convertibility of currencies within a given framework and, if necessary, to adjust the exchange rates to reflect changes in economic data. Since the currencies of all member countries were pegged to the US dollar, central banks ultimately had to align their monetary policy with that of the Fed.

The Bretton Woods system set a historical precedent. For almost thirty years, it succeeded in keeping the value of the various currencies at a relatively stable level. And yet, there was a flaw in the design of the system, one which was pointed out early on by the economist Robert Triffin. The conflict in the *Triffin dilemma*, as it was later to be called, has to do with the fact that the system was tied to the US dollar as the global reserve currency instead of to an artificial currency such as the one proposed by John Maynard Keynes under the name *bancor*. This necessarily led to a steadily increasing demand for dollars as a result of the rapidly growing volume of world trade. Although the creation of money made it possible to meet that demand, at the same time it was not possible to multiply the supply of gold reserves. On the one hand there was an increasing amount of US dollars, but on the other a limited amount of gold. In the course of time it became unfeasible to maintain the fixed exchange rate of 35 US dollars per troy ounce of gold. There were various ways to solve this dilemma (e.g., by not turning the US dollar into the global reserve currency, or by adjusting the exchange rate for gold, in other words, by devaluing the dollar), but these alternatives were not politically attractive. The Bretton Woods agreement failed not because of inevitable economic developments, but because the chief participating nations—especially the United States, France, Germany, the United Kingdom, and Japan—were unwilling to accept short-term disadvantages in order to secure the long-term advantage of a stable global financial system (Helleiner 1994; Germann 2014).

When in the early 1970s the Bretton Woods system came to an end, most participating countries reverted to floating exchange rates. On the whole, capital controls ceased to exist. The new situation necessarily required adjustments in monetary policy. Despite their weak economies, a number of countries decided to peg their own currency to the US dollar (or another foreign currency) so as to maintain the fiction of a constant exchange-rate standard. For the most part, this strategy proved to be unsuccessful. In the 1980s, inspired by monetarism, a theory of which Milton Friedman was one of the best-known proponents, some states directly imposed limits on their money supply. The underlying reason for doing so was the idea that it would be possible to combat inflation by controlling the growth of the money supply. At the time, inflation was very high in many countries, not least of all in the United States (in the mid-1970s, inflation there had risen to around 15% and in the UK to nearly 25%). Contrary to monetarist predictions, however, interest rates soared when money supply was restricted. In the United States they increased by as much as seven percentage points within the span of two years, and for a time even exceeded 20%. At the same time, unemployment climbed to 11%. Although inflation was down, the United States suffered a recession, and developing countries around the world experienced a severe debt crisis. In the early 1980s, the monetarist experiment was abandoned, having lasted only three years in the United States from 1979 to 1982 (Stigum and Crescenzi 2007: 375–77; Krippner 2011: 58–60, 114–16). Dubbed the *Volcker Shock* after Paul Volcker, who chaired the Fed at the time (Volcker 2008), the monetarist adventure cost then president Jimmy Carter his reelection in 1980.

Since the 1980s, most central banks have pursued the goal of price stability.[5] Their aim has been to control the level of inflation in relation to the overall economic price level rather than the amount of money in circulation. Up until the global financial crisis, this monetary policy approach, known as *inflation targeting*, worked primarily through key interest rates, meaning the *price* that banks had to pay for central bank money. The goal was not to control money *supply* but rather to manage money *demand*. Alongside inflation control, communication strategies, known as *forward guidance*, also came to be used to an increasing degree. The idea behind this practice is that early announcement of prospective monetary policy decisions influences market participants to factor expected monetary policy directions into price calculations even before any measures are implemented. In this way, simply communicating the likelihood of decisions serves as a market steering mechanism (Krippner 2007). Price stability is defined by most leading central banks as an inflation rate of around 2%.[6]

Since the 1990s, the view prevails that central banks should remain independent from their governments (Goodhart 2011; Hall 2008; Conti-Brown 2016). The institutionalization of independence was intended to prevent governments from ordering their central banks to print money (by buying up government bonds). It was argued that the resulting increase in indebtedness might lead to distrust in the stability of money value (Schnabel 2020a), the assumption being that keeping state debt within certain limits is requisite to preserving confidence in the state currency (Mirowski 1991: 580). Although this view is still accepted today, it cannot be empirically proven that independent central banks can fight inflation more effectively than those that are dependent (McNamara 2002). What is more, monetary policy measures of independent central banks are not purely technical decisions. When the focus is on inflation control and price stability, asset stability takes priority over economic growth and low unemployment. The Fed's decision in 2020 to foreground the fight against unemployment instead of focusing on price stability can therefore indeed be described as historic (Powell 2020; Federal Reserve Bank of Atlanta 2020).[7] However, the unprecedented pace at which interest rates were raised by the Fed and other central banks in 2022 and 2023 casts doubt on this decision. This is because such sharp rate hikes to maintain price stability always carry the risk of pushing the economy into recession and causing many people to lose their jobs.

Generally speaking, central banks exercise their functions in three areas. First, they are responsible for carrying out state monetary policy by influencing the conditions under which money and credit are provided (in terms of cost and availability). Second, they monitor and regulate the activities of banks to guarantee the security and stability of the national banking and financial system. And third, they provide financial institutions, the public, and the state with a wide variety of financial services through which they ensure the processing of domestic and foreign bank transactions, thereby contributing to the stability of the payment and settlement systems. Influencing the cost of borrowing through the policy rate also makes them responsible for the economy as a whole. Central banks face multiple, and at times contradictory, challenges. To ensure *price stability*, they must take steps to prevent significant inflation or deflation. As the institutions responsible for the *stability of the monetary and financial systems*, they are tasked with the duty of regulating those systems, and, in the event of crisis, of lending them support by injecting massive amounts of liquidity, if necessary, until fiscal and economic policy measures can take effect. Last but not least they are also responsible for keeping the *value of money stable*, which obliges them to ensure that trust in their currencies is maintained. These different tasks can sometimes require them to pursue mutually conflicting courses of action. At the same time, each area of responsibility is also affected by circumstances beyond their sphere of influence—factors including

the overall strength of their respective economies, existing governance institutions, and the rule of law, but also events such as supply chain problems and
climate disasters.

2.2 Key Interest Rate Policies

The most common and, at the same time, most important monetary policy instrument used by central banks is the adjustment of key interest rates. Indeed,
prior to the global financial crisis, central bank policy was therefore largely
equated with key interest rate policy (Borio 2012). And when inflation returned
again in 2022, the main response was to raise key interest rates. Basically, this
policy instrument concerns three different types of interest rates (ECB 2015b).
The first is the rate charged on the deposit facility (in the United States, the
rate of interest on reserve balances [IORB]), which enables banks to deposit
money at the central bank until the start of the next business day. The interest
rate on this facility represents the lower limit for the overnight money market
rate. A bank normally has no incentive to lend its reserves at a rate lower than
the IORB rate (Bank of England 2015: 3). The second category of interest rates
subject to change is known as the *marginal lending facility rate* at the ECB and
the *discount window rate* at the Fed and the Bank of England.[8] This rate is paid
by banks on money they borrow on short notice, as a rule until the start of the
next business day (overnight loans). The facility allows banks to borrow money
directly from the central bank outside of open market operations. Normally,
however, banks prefer to raise funds from the money market and, in particular,
from the shadow banking system, because interest rates there are lower than
the marginal lending rate.[9] Besides having to pay more interest if they take
recourse to the central bank, regular banks also face the threat of stigma when
they borrow from the marginal lending facility (Lee and Sarkar 2018).[10] The
third interest rate is called the *main refinancing operations rate* at the ECB and
the *federal funds rate* at the Fed, often simply called the *policy rate*. This interest
rate cannot be set directly. It is not an *administered rate* as is the IORB rate or
the discount window rate, but rather a target announced by the central bank
and pursued through various monetary policy instruments. It is the interest
rate that banks normally use to charge each other for the overnight lending of
reserve balances (Ihrig, Weinbach, and Wolla 2021). In the United States, the
United Kingdom, and the eurozone,[11] the policy rate constitutes the most im-

portant interest rate for guiding bank interest rates and liquidity in the money market.

When a central bank lowers its interest on reserves, private banks tend to follow suit and lower their interest rates in turn. This is a relatively reliable method for central banks to steer the direction of money market rates.[12] Accordingly, interest rates on the money market typically lie between the deposit facility rate (US: IORB), which marks the floor for interest on deposits, and the marginal lending rate, which defines the ceiling for interest on loans (Bank of England 2015: 5). Rates in the US federal funds market are usually very close to the IORB rate. As will be discussed later, there are two other instruments that have been added to reflect the importance of the shadow banking system for lending and steering the policy rate: in the United States, these are the Overnight Reverse Repurchase facility (ON RRP facility), which was introduced in 2015, and the Standing Repo Facility (SRF), created in 2021 (Ihrig, Senyuz, and Weinbach 2020; Afonso et al. 2022a). Similar facilities exist at other central banks. The Bank of England, for example, provides the Contingent Term Repo Facility (CTRF), the Indexed Long-Term Repo (ILTR), and the bilateral on-demand Discount Window Facility (DWF) (Bank of England 2015).

This type of money market control is also known as the *interest corridor system*. It is based on the plausible assumption that central banks can exert leverage on the money creation process of commercial banks by raising and lowering the key interest rate (McLeay, Radia, and Ryland 2014a: 20–21). Before central banks began providing ample reserves via QE programs, the main reason for this was that commercial banks are in continual need of central bank money to cover the public demand for cash, but, above all, to settle the balances they have with other commercial banks and also to meet any minimum reserve requirements: "For banks, the survival constraint takes the concrete form of a 'reserve constraint'" (Mehrling 2011: 13). Today, however, most banks have ample reserves, so the choice between very liquid reserves with relatively low interest rates and less liquid financial products with higher interest rates is more of an investment decision.

Changes in the key interest rate also have a bearing on the interest rate at which commercial banks lend money to one another and to private customers. This is called monetary transmission. When central banks pay virtually no interest on reserves, as was the case during the 2010s, or even when they charge negative interest rates, in the way the ECB did on its deposit facility between

2014 and 2022, the lending incentive for commercial banks is much higher. The assumption here is that other factors being equal, the lower the interest rate, the more likely it is that loans will be taken out (i.e., monetary easing). Conversely, higher interest rates are expected to decrease the demand for credit (i.e., monetary tightening), because a bank will not lend its reserves to another bank for less than the interest it receives on its reserves. Hence, the interest rate on reserves constitutes the floor for interest rates on loans. Since the global financial crisis of 2007–9, and the QE programs through which central banks provided commercial banks with ample reserves, it is no longer the case that central banks influence the policy rate by steering the quantity of reserves. Usually, it is *not* the policy of central banks to set the quantity of reserves. Normally, the volume simply follows the demand. Central banks rather seek to achieve a macroeconomic effect on lending practices by adjusting their interest rates; in other words, the price paid by banks for central bank money (McLeay, Radia, and Ryland 2014a: 21). In this way, key interest rate policy has an influence on the economy as a whole: "Changes in Bank Rate (or in expectations about future Bank Rate) therefore influence money market rates, rates paid more widely on bank deposits and loans, and financial asset prices, including the exchange rate. These impacts on financial markets and associated changes in expectations in turn affect spending decisions and inflationary pressures in the economy" (Bank of England 2015: 4). The general level of interest rates also affects the price of nonfinancial assets such as housing.

Briefly stated, by making loans more expensive and curbing investments, central banks seek to counteract unsustainable economic expansion, a trend economists describe as *overheating*. By lowering the key interest rate, on the other hand, they aim to facilitate lending to stimulate economic activity and boost the economy.

2.3 Lender of Last Resort

Central banks occupy a unique position among financial players. Even during times of crisis, their liabilities retain the status of legal tender, and, as such, are treated as the universal equivalent for all assets (see chapter 3).[13] Unlike other financial institutions, central banks have no liquidity problems, at least not in the currency of their own country. They can create money at will and bring it into circulation by purchasing assets, for the most part government bonds of their own respective countries.[14] In this respect, during times of crisis central banks are able to function as lenders of last resort and—at least theoretically—to give the financial system access to a potentially unlimited supply of money (Giannini 2011: 86–88).[15] The lender of last resort option is designed as a source of funding liquidity in situations where a basically solvent credit institution has sufficient ongoing revenues, but these revenues are not high enough to meet short-term debt obligations at a given point in time (see Table 1).

Table 1 shows two financial players, each with the same amount of assets and liabilities for the time period from t to $t + 3$. While players in category A are solvent and can therefore meet their payment obligations at any time, players in category B run into problems because their payment obligations at time t exceed their incoming payments. Under certain circumstances, these players may be forced to pay a high price for the funds they need in order to meet their payment obligations at time t in the event said amount is not provided by the central bank on that date. Particularly in times of crisis, however, it is difficult to differentiate between insolvent and illiquid financial players, in view of the fact that prolonged illiquidity can lead to overindebtedness and consequently to insolvency (BIS 2014: 4; Tucker 2014: 14). But even in times of noncrisis, it is of utmost importance in the financial system for financial players to be able to access funding liquidity at the right moment, considering the common practice in the financial markets to invest money over the long term and to borrow it

Table 1 *Solvent and insolvent financial players*

Solvent financial player A				
	t	$t+1$	$t+2$	$t+3$
Cash inflows	10	10	10	10
Cash outflows	5	5	5	5
Insolvent financial player B				
	t	$t+1$	$t+2$	$t+3$
Cash inflows	10	10	10	10
Cash outflows	20	0	0	0

Source: Based on Mehrling 2011: 92–97.

on short notice. From that angle, loans are nothing more than the postpone-
ment of deadlines into the future—one of the central elements of the financial
market: "borrow short and lend long" (Stigum and Crescenzi 2007: 432; Bank
of England 2015: 4).

From a market liberal perspective, the role of the state or the central banks
as lender of last resort is often discussed in connection with the term *moral
hazard* (Tucker 2014; Allen et al. 2015): The mere knowledge that the central
bank will come to their rescue if the need arises can indeed induce financial
players to accept higher levels of risk. This applies in particular to key players in
the financial system that are too important to be dropped from a systemic point
of view—the corporate giants which have come to be known as *too big to fail*
(Kindleberger and Aliber 2005: 13). As the reasoning goes, financial institutions
are not constrained by market discipline because they still have recourse to central bank money even when funding liquidity is no longer available from other
players. Some critics even blame the Fed for the global financial crisis (Taylor
2009). By the same token, central banks have been the target of criticism for exceeding the legal monetary policy framework and rescuing insolvent financial
institutions, ultimately providing too much liquidity (Humphrey 2010). And
yet, even among advocates of market liberal policy, there is hardly any doubt
since the financial crisis that the state and especially the central banks play an
important role in stabilizing the financial system. Some economists, however,
still maintain that state intervention should be indirect, and that there should
be less intervention on the whole (World Bank 2013: xiii), but it is doubtful
whether this standpoint is even realistic considering the persistent sources
of instability that have characterized the financial system since the financial
crisis of 2007–9, as well as the direction developments have taken since the
COVID-19 pandemic. When it comes to global finance, the Fed is currently
the only central bank able to act as the international lender of last resort (Mehrling 2022a, b; see chapter 4.3).

THREE

A Political Theory of Money

THE HISTORY OF MONEY, in all its many shapes and forms, goes back thousands of years. And while life without money is hard to imagine, the question What exactly is money? has long been and remains the subject of heated debates. At least as interesting as the question of what money is, however, are the questions Who is allowed to create money? and How does this money creation process work? (Chick 2013). Hence: Where does money come from? Can it be created on command? Is there a difference between the money that central banks create and the money issued by commercial banks? Are new kinds of money emerging on financial markets in the form of derivatives and so-called shadow money? What about crypto currencies? How are money and debt related, and what connections exist between money, commodities, and value? Is money tied to a tangible object like gold or something else with fundamental value? One of the reasons why money is so difficult to understand is that although it is assigned to the economic sphere, it does not originate there, but rather in the political sphere.

The fact remains, however, that the respective understanding of money decisively influences the analysis of problems and the possibilities to address them (Eich 2022). All fiscal and financial policies are based on the way money and debt is understood. Unfortunately, economics as taught in many university textbooks is based on outdated information, flawed assumptions, and faulty connections (Desan 2014; Hockett and James 2020). Consequently, various central banks have felt compelled to intervene and point out popular misconceptions in order to set the record straight (McLeay, Radia, and Ryland 2014a, 2014b; Bundesbank 2019; Ihrig, Weinbach, and Wolla 2021). This chapter therefore begins by taking a closer look at different and differing theories of money, and then goes on to develop a separate political-economic theory of money. Chapter 4 will employ the concept of security structures to discuss how this ontology of money can be applied. The theoretical framework for this discussion draws on the insights of several scholars, notably (but not only) Perry Mehrling, Daniela Gabor, Ernesto Laclau, Geoffrey Ingham, Alfred Mitchell Innes, Georg Friedrich Knapp, and John Maynard Keynes.

There seem to be many different forms of money circulating in the twenty-first century, and the ability to create money has been attributed to a variety of different agents (Cooper 2015; Bryan and Rafferty 2016). Dynamics in the shadow banking system and new money-like claims further complicate the picture. At the same time, notions about real and fundamental values continue to exist, and the value of money remains linked to the concept of intrinsic value or presumed objective value (Bieler and Morton 2008; Nitzan and Bichler 2009; Harvey 2011). With the expanding trend of financialization, and the growing importance of the financial economy, assets and financial derivatives of all kinds have come to be treated as forms of money, particularly in the years since the global financial crisis (Cooper 2015; Bryan and Rafferty 2007, 2016). Occasionally the argument is heard that no clear definition of money can be given because the forms in which it is manifested change over time, so that instead it must be understood from the perspective of microsocial practices (Zelizer 1995, 2005; Ganssmann 2012).

My conception of money differs from these interpretations. In the following pages, drawing on the political theory of Laclau (1990, 1996a, 2005), with reference to the work of political economists such as Keynes, Marx, Weber, and Schumpeter, I will explore and elaborate on the money form from a politico-economic perspective. Money from this angle constitutes a special political and economic relationship. No intrinsic value exists in money itself, or to be more precise, in the form that money takes. The object called money has value only insofar as it has been socially ascribed. The approach taken here assumes that it is not possible to understand the money form based exclusively on economic or microsociological theory. While credit between any two parties can exist in many different forms, money is a very special type of credit (money is a subset of credit). It takes on form only as the result of a social or political act (Desan

2014). In contrast to Mises (1981 [1912]), Ganssmann (2012), and the majority of scholars in the field of economics, I argue in line with chartalist theorists such as Knapp (1924), Keynes (1971 [1930]), and Ingham (2004) that the state plays a crucial role in the development of the form that money takes today.[1] At the same time I maintain that the political act involved in establishing the money form is not limited to the state (indeed forms of money existed long before states or state-like entities were created). I also take exception to those chartalist approaches that fall short by linking the form of money *only and exclusively* to the state. Even though the state does indeed have a prominent position today, the creation of the money form is not reducible exclusively to the state domain. It is rather the case, as I will demonstrate below, that money forms can also be developed independently by communities of the state (with the probably best-known example today being the cryptoasset Bitcoin).

The starting point for the following analysis is the assumption that goods do not possess any natural or intrinsic value of their own, and that the value attached to any commodity is socially assigned. From this perspective, money does not express or measure objective values; rather, it compares the relative value of one commodity in relation to another. Money acts as a general equivalent for all assets. The concept of the master signifier (Laclau 1996b; Wullweber 2019b) is used here to gain deeper insight into the nature of this general equivalent. Money is the yardstick for assigning a value that has been arrived at through a process of social negotiation. Money is itself a commodity (traded on foreign exchange markets) and, at the same time, an expression of the value relationship (unit of account) between and among all other commodities in its area of validity. In this way a particular object takes on the role of the general equivalent for all assets. Money is a hybrid of particularity and universality: It has a specific value, and it serves, at the same time, as an expression of the value of all goods in relation to one another. Money, however, is not a passive expression of commodity values. Rather, it converts an object into a commodity by assigning it a value in the first place. Money accordingly not only serves as a unit of value to define the relationship between and among commodity values. It also determines what does or does not count as a commodity. In a market economy, if an object cannot be expressed in terms of money, it cannot assume the form of a commodity. The important point here is not so much the object itself that acts as money, but the sociopolitical process that takes place in the determination of what object should assume that function and also what institution should be allowed to multiply the designated object and in what manner. In short, and in preparation for the journey that follows, the theory of money developed here intends to help the reader to

- understand the emergence of money and the different forms of money not as merely accidental but as the result, in particular, of social developments and different, sometimes conflicting interests;

- know why money is not simply a commodity among other commodities;

- see the connection and difference between money and credit;

- grasp the relation between commodity, money, and unit of account;

- be able to distinguish the different forms of money and money-creation processes, both public and private as well as institutionalized forms involving both public and private participation;

- recognize the hierarchical relationships between different forms of money;

- understand how various public and private balance sheets are interlocked, who they benefit, in what way, and why;

- gain a more serious appreciation of the international hierarchy of money;

- comprehend the context in which contemporary financial systems create the dynamics that lead to crisis and the responses that central banks have developed to address financial crises;

- acquire, last but not least, a critical awareness of the decisive role that central banks play in capitalism in general and in our contemporary capitalism in particular.

3.1 Commodity Theories, Chartalism, and Constructivism

The simplest concept of money has long proceeded on the assumption that something can take the form of money if it has intrinsic value or at least if it is tied to a material value (a view already challenged by Knapp in 1924 and by Mitchell Innes in 1913). This concept has persisted over time because, among other things, precious metals, and especially gold and silver, were (and in many cases still are) ascribed an intrinsic value. The answer to the question of what constitutes money is often reduced to the listing of its functions. These are generally grouped into three main categories. First, money acts as a medium of exchange and a means of payment. As already emphasized by Adam Smith, money facilitates the exchange of things that otherwise have nothing in common. Second, money is a store of value, an abstract purchasing power. Decisions to purchase goods can be deferred. Money, accordingly, is "a subtle device for linking the present to the future" (Keynes 2018 [1936]: 263). Third, money also represents the unit of account, a unit of value that allows all commodities to be compared with one another. This abstract unit of value makes it possible to calculate prices, costs, services, debts, credits, profits, and losses (Ingham 2011: 67).

The problem with these functions is that they only provide an approximation, an empirical description, but not a sufficient theoretical definition, of money. There is wide variation in the form money can take—from silver and gold coins to printed cotton paper (modern banknotes) or a figure on a bank account. Not everything that can be exchanged, however, constitutes money. Nor is everything money that is considered a store of value. This is obvious when we consider assets such as houses, objects of art, or shares. Moreover, in times of crisis and, in particular, in times of high inflation, money is a useful store of value only to a very limited degree. And finally, the value of money itself is subject to change, as is clear from fluctuating exchange rates; in other words, when the value of one currency goes up or down in relation to another. To characterize money simply by pointing out its functions, therefore, does not suffice to gain a full understanding.

Generally speaking, there are two fundamentally opposing ways to conceptualize money: One sees money as a commodity and a means of exchange, the other as a unit of account and an abstract form of value. The first school of thought is in the tradition of theorists such as Adam Smith (1982 [1776]), Carl Menger (1892, 1970), and Ludwig von Mises (1981 [1912]). Even in the field of economics, money is still mainly conceptualized as a commodity and medium of exchange (Mankiw 2017). The assumption here is that at some point in time it grew increasingly impractical to resort to direct barter (exchanging a chicken for a loaf of bread, for example, or a coat for a table). One particular commodity then proved to be especially suited as a medium of exchange. As the most efficient commodity in terms of transaction costs, it became accepted as the standard for which all other commodities could be exchanged, in other words, as money. The unit of account concept was subsequently derived from this micro-foundation model of money (Mitchell Innes 1913)[2]: "'[M]oneyness' is somewhat tautologically 'exchangeability'—that is, the most 'liquid' commodity" (Ingham 2004: 6). From this vantage point, money is just something that makes it easier to conduct economic processes which otherwise would take place in like or at least similar fashion. In this sense, money is nothing more than a *lubricant* (David Hume), a *wheel* that allows assets to circulate (Adam Smith), a *neutral veil* which itself has no impact on economic processes. Weber, however, clearly counters: "It must, however, be emphasized that money can never be merely a harmless 'voucher' or a purely nominal unit of accounting so long as it is money" (Weber 1978: 79). As critically stated by Schumpeter: "[S]o long as [money] functions normally, it does not affect the economic process, which behaves in the same way as it would in a barter economy: this is essentially what the concept of Neutral Money implies" (Schumpeter 1986 [1954]: 264). Many economic theories accordingly treat money as a negligible factor. Even today, the various branches of economics tend to sidestep questions relating to the form of money. In general, it is simply understood as one commodity among others. Many economists consider that its analysis is something that can be dealt with in existing microeconomic approaches to supply and demand. Until the mid-nineteenth century, it was assumed that the value of money (gold and silver coins in particular) was determined by its production costs. Toward the end of the nineteenth century, this assumption was replaced by Alfred Marshall's theory of marginal utility: the claim that the value of money depends on its supply and demand. This assumption continues to dominate contemporary economics in the form of the quantity theory of money.

Chartalist approaches reject these mainly neoclassical approaches, arguing that the defining criterion for money is the unit of account, and that as a value standard it requires a statutory framework: "Money is a creature of law" (Knapp 1924: 1). They claim that it would be impossible through barter for one commodity to develop a stable exchange relation toward other commodities to such a degree that it could serve as a reliable unit of value for all commodities. "Something which is merely used as a convenient medium of exchange on the spot may approach to being money, inasmuch as it may represent a means of holding general purchasing power. But if this is all, we have scarcely emerged from the stage of barter" (Keynes 1971 [1930]: 3). Exchange processes produce many relations of exchange, but they do not produce the measuring unit of the exchange itself (Ingham 2004: 15–17). In chartalist reasoning it is precisely the other way around: a genuine market presupposes the existence of an accepted abstract unit of value through which supply and demand can be expressed. What counts is the abstract nominal value of money (money of account): "The monetary unit is merely an arbitrary denomination by which commodities are measured in terms of credit and which serves, therefore, as a more or less accurate measure of the value of all commodities. Pounds, shillings and pence are merely the a, b, c, of algebra, where a = 20b = 240c" (Mitchell Innes 1913: 399). From this function, all forms and other functions of money are then derived. This approach construes money primarily as a yardstick and store of general purchasing power that is portable and durable across time and space. According to this view, gold becomes money when the relevant authorities, in particular sovereign states, fix its price to a specific monetary value (by virtue of a decree stating, for example, that one ounce of fine gold represents 35 dollars (see Knapp 1924; Keynes 1971 [1930]).[3]

In today's world it is chiefly the state that sets the value standard and authorizes a means of payment as a symbol of that value. The *validity* of money is based on the premise that the state will accept a certain form of money as legal tender (not least as payment for taxes due) and, in turn, it will use that money to cover government expenses (Wray 2004; Hockett and James 2020).[4] Keynes also highlights the significance of the state: "The State, therefore, comes in first of all as the authority of law which enforces the payment of the thing which corresponds to the name or description in the contract" (Keynes 1971 [1930]: 4).[5] And indeed, since the beginning of the modern age, states are authorized to define which abstract unit of value should have the function of money. Government policies thus play a significant role: "By passing a suitable law, a state can turn any object into a 'legal means of payment' and any chartal object into 'money' in the sense of means of payment" (Weber 1978: 167–68). In addition, at least in most cases, only the state is allowed to authorize the printing of money for use as cash.[6] While states have the power to determine the form of legal tender, they have only limited control over the value of money in the sense of purchasing power (see Knapp 1924).

The strong focus on the state, however, has led various theorists to criticize chartalist models. As early as 1922, Max Weber writes: "It does not, however, seem reasonable to confine the concept to regulations by the state and not to include cases where acceptance is made compulsory by convention or by some agreement" (Weber 1978 [1922]: 79). Neither does Keynes reduce the establishment of money to something that only the state has the power to do when he points out that "it may still have been the State or the community which determined what kind or quality of unit should be a due discharge of an obligation to pay" (Keynes 1971 [1930]: 11). He goes on to say: "Furthermore, it is a peculiar characteristic of money contracts that it is the State or Community not only which enforces delivery, but also which decides what it is that must be delivered as a lawful or customary discharge of a contract which has been concluded in terms of the money-of-account" (Keynes 1971 [1930]: 4). Accordingly, the state is only one possible, albeit prominent, agent in the establishment of the general equivalent and the creation of confidence in that equivalent (Hockett and James 2020). For cryptoassets such as Bitcoin, confidence is said to be grounded in the completely technical and mathematical process of money creation, a process called mining. It depends on several factors whether confidence in cryptoassets can reach a level of stability in the long run and maintain stability during times of crisis.[7] Konings (2015: 260) therefore speaks of a "confidence game . . . that . . . never eliminates uncertainty." In this confidence game, central banks are the chief players, considering that they not only secure (solvent) commercial banks but also the entire financial system, which accordingly reinforces confidence in the system's stability. Beggs (2017) argues that the authority that creates and legally establishes money should be distinguished from the process by which money is created. This is an important distinction, although it does not necessarily lead to a criticism of the significance of the state's role in the creation of money. Chartalists do not deny that money is also created privately.[8]

Constructivist approaches go a step further. Not only do they problematize the strong focus on the state; they also place social construction at the center of their analysis. In particular, the philosopher John Searle (1995, 2005) makes this point when he reasons that the defining characteristic of money, which he refers to as a social fact, is entirely a matter of social attribution. His theory, however, fails to explain *how* social institutions arise. Consequently, his approach remains restricted to the undeniably important claim that money is a social construction (Wullweber 2015a). He fails to address political dimensions along with issues such as domination and social power relations. This is also the case in Ganssmann's analysis, for example. Ganssmann rightly emphasizes everyday practices, but his perspective of the *actions* aspect of money—*doing money,* as he calls it (Ganssmann 2012)—is virtually voluntaristic: "After all, the issue can be brought down to the task of explaining money out of spontaneous social interaction" (Ganssmann 2004: 30).

While aptly calling attention to the importance of inscribing the notion of money within the context of everyday human life, Ganssmann's interpretation loses sight of the political dimension of money: "[I]t may be more fruitful to think of money not as a universal, as something introduced into society once and for all, but more in terms of a family of closely related practices and objects" (Ganssmann 2004: 30). Ganssmann's emphasis on microsocial practices obscures the sociopolitical dimension of money as a general equivalent. The approach taken here differs. As will be argued in the following chapters, money is more than just the exchange of some kind of promise to pay for something specific promised in return. It functions as a *general* promise of payment and therefore one that is recognized in society and politically enforceable, if necessary by means of compulsion. In this sense, the approach used here contradicts the position taken by Ganssmann, who holds that credit relations are a subset of money relations (Ganssmann 2012: 112–14). Everyday social interaction is not an adequate explanation for how something becomes money and what constitutes money. A promise to pay only becomes money if it is a generally valid promise; in other words, if it can be passed around at will from person to person (within a currency area or the area of validity), and if the persons holding said payment promise can use it to purchase any commodity available, provided that it covers the value of that commodity in the form of a price. The promise to pay must be generalized, socially accepted, and politically established. A specific promise to pay becomes a general form of money only through a political act, for which reason it is potentially a conflict-ridden negotiation process in which diverse interests and interest groups clash. Credit relations therefore are not a subset of money relations but rather the other way around: Money constitutes a particular subset of credit relations. Money is a generally recognized credit that can be passed around at will from one person to another. Only if an object is recognized as a general equivalent in a given society (or region) where it is used, can it fulfill the function of money.

3.2 A Politico-Economic Approach to the Money Form

There is no question that in today's world the state plays a prominent role in
the transformation of an object into money. But the political act of turning
something into money should not be construed as a matter that pertains only
to the state. A more fruitful approach takes a broader view of politics, thereby
permitting the integration of other forms of social negotiation processes into
the analysis (see also Weber 1978: 79–80).[9] My examination of the money form
and how it becomes established will therefore consider a variety of different
social and legal factors as well as processes internal to the financial market. To
explain their significance, I will rely on the concept of hegemony as developed
by Laclau (2005). Like in chartalist theory, the concept of hegemony emphasizes that social processes contain elements of force, and that political actors do
not have equal access to instruments of power: "Establishing the promise [to
pay] requires 'authority', which ultimately rests on coercion. . . . The monopo-
listic imposition of the money of account and a refusal to accept any other than
the approved credit tokens of the issuer go hand in hand with monopolizing of
physical force" (Ingham 2004: 76). The concept of hegemony expands the concept of authority. At the same time, following the theory of Antonio Gramsci,
it foregrounds the social struggles involved in the consensus processes that lead
to the acceptance of the money form: "The exercise of hegemony is characterized by the combination of force and consent" (Gramsci 1971: 80). As such, it
serves as a starting point for a more differentiated examination of the multi-
layered political and socioeconomic dimensions involved in the establishment
and production of money.[10] What object is to serve as the general equivalent of
money, what assets can be traded for money at par value upon demand, and
what institutions are entitled to create a specific form of money are all matters
that are determined in conflict-ridden struggles over hegemony. The concept of
hegemony provides the basis for taking a closer look at forms of money from
a vantage point distanced from or beyond the realm of the state, while at the
same time not discounting the importance of the role played by the state in today's world. In any community, an object becomes money *the instant in which,
by virtue of a political process, it is recognized and institutionally legitimized as the
general equivalent of the assets that are traded within that community.* General
acceptance of a specific form of money is therefore a vital element in the definition of money (Wullweber 2019b; see also Bell 2001: 150–51).

Laclau's theory defines the social and political process by which value is generated (Wullweber 2010: 63–65). It holds that in any social conflict there is a struggle to establish certain ascribed values. In this highly conflict-ridden process, social actors seek to generalize their specific interests (Laclau 2004: 283–84). Laclau applies the notion of master signifier in his political theory to reflect on socially universalized meanings and general interests.[11] Through this lens, he seeks to grasp the specific expression of a particular interest that can become universalized by way of hegemonic struggles.

The more universalized a particular interest becomes—in other words, the more hegemonic it grows—the less remains of its former particularity. In hegemony theory it is especially during the transition phase from a particular to a general interest, symbolized by the master signifier, where social struggles emerge (Laclau 2005: 96–97; Wullweber 2019c). Once a master signifier attains hegemony, it is equated with various general interests. The master signifier is not a passive expression of these general interests. Rather, through the process of naming, it constitutively retroacts on the interests and the meanings associated therewith (Wullweber 2015b).

3.3 Money as a Master Signifier

Assets and the General Equivalent

Money expresses the value of a commodity or an asset in the form of a price.[12] If it were possible to express this value directly, or if it were reflected in the commodity itself, money would be obsolete.[13] There would be no need for the *detour* via money. As argued here, contrary to the perspective of substance theory, an asset does not possess any natural value (Mirowski 1991; see also Mirowski 1986; Konings 2018). In his first volume of *Capital*, Marx writes: "Not an atom of matter enters into the objectivity of commodities as values; in this it is the direct opposite of the coarsely sensuous objectivity of commodities as physical objects" (Marx 1976a: 138). The value of a commodity can rather only be determined in relation to the values of other commodities. A cubic meter of firewood has the same value, for example, as x kilograms of flour, or y liters of milk. At the same time, x and y are not constant variables, but depend on factors such as needs, available supply, preferences, quality, production capacity, culture, and other such aspects. Commodity value is therefore independent of the specific qualities of the commodity. It expresses quality—as a social relationship—only in relation to other commodities. Moreover, the value relation between and among commodities is also an expression of needs, preferences, and other social aspects, that is, variable social factors, and not objective values. Since commodity value expresses the relation between commodities, and since this relation is socially determined, the commodity value constitutes a social relation. Even though Marx ultimately traces commodity value back to abstract human labor, he still very similarly perceives the matter of value as "purely social" (Marx 1976a: 138) and states that value "can only appear in the social relation between commodity and commodity" (Marx 1976a: 727).

Assuming here that there are no fundamental values, and that the value of a commodity is socially negotiated, then prices do not "misrepresent the underlying values" (Rona-Tas and Hiss 2011: 224). Prices would instead actually reflect market values at any given point in time (provided payment is received). In market economy systems, this means that there is no fundamental difference between the value of a commodity and the price that purchasers pay for it. Price represents the social value of a thing in relation to the values of the other goods. Accordingly, it is not the case that a market economy requires the translation of values into prices (Rona-Tas and Hiss 2011). On this point I agree with the theory of marginal utility, according to which the price of a commodity corresponds to the commodity value: "Instead of continuing to differentiate between market price and value, marginal utility theory took the sweeping step of giving up on any objective measure for assessing economic value—be it land, labor, or anything else—and anchoring value exclusively in the sphere of market exchange" (Beckert and Aspers 2011: 9). It does not follow from this, however, that there are perfect prices. Nor is there any "'real' value of goods or services" (Rona-Tas and Hiss 2011: 225). Both prices and values are negotiated socially.

The relationality of assets alone, however, does not necessarily lead to the use of money. In cases where, *ceteris paribus*, only two commodities are exchanged, there is no need for money to be used. It would always be possible, for instance, to directly trade one cubic meter of firewood for half a kilo of flour. With an increasing market size, however, an exchange of this nature would become more and more complicated and unwieldy, since each commodity would have to be expressed in relation to every other commodity. With 10 commodities, there would already be 45 relations, with 100 commodities 4,950, and with 1,000 commodities 499,500. If a single commodity among 1,000 became scarce or subject to higher demand (firewood, for instance), this would not influence one exchange relation alone (in the example cited, one cubic meter of firewood could now fetch one kilogram of flour). It would affect the other 499,499 relational pairings as well. From a certain market size onward, and depending on the changing conditions of production and demand, it becomes impracticable to express value through exchange relations. The solution of the exchange problem was found in the creation of a third entity to which all commodities can be related. It is through this third entity then that the relations between and among the other assets are expressed. Since very different things and activities are related to one another, this third entity cannot be something that all assets already have in common per se. The third entity is distanced from the concrete commodities because it only expresses the value *relation* of the commodities between and among themselves. Assets are only equivalent to each other *in relation to that entity* once it is created. In other words, their equivalence is merely mediated.

The third entity, in turn, takes on a particular significance of its own. It becomes the general equivalent of things. It is this third entity, money, the universal unit of value, which then enables the exchange of commodities, while at the same time excluding everything from monetary commodity exchange that cannot be expressed in terms of this unit of value (Keynes 1971 [1930]). Money itself is a commodity and can also have a use value. Throughout history, various objects have served as, or taken on the function of, money (silver, gold, promissory notes, but also such objects as shells or cigarettes). The special feature of these objects was that, as *particular objects*, they simultaneously assumed the role of the *universal equivalent for other asset values*. In other words, they made it possible to define the relation of other commodity values toward one another. They represented the *social relation* of the asset values. Accordingly, particularity and universality were united in a single object. Nevertheless, it is not the specific properties inherent in money as an asset or its asset value that constitute its special significance, but its ability to function as a general unit of value. This property as a universal unit of value sets money apart from all other commodities: "Money is simply 'that which is valuable' . . . . All other objects have a specific content from which they derive their value. Money derives its content from its value; it is value turned into a substance, the value of things without the things themselves. By sublimating the relativity of things, money seems to avoid relativity" (Simmel 1978 [1900]: 119).

History has shown that for an object to serve as a universal unit of value, certain attributes are advantageous and probably also socially necessary. In order to function as the conveyor of universal commodity values, money must exhibit a certain degree of stability. It must be transportable and only available in limited or limitable amounts. There have always been items whose relative durability, portability, and limited availability could have made them suitable for this role. How did it happen, then, that some objects such as gold or banknotes managed to become money while others did not? First of all, it must be noted that throughout history, different universal units of value have always existed side by side, even within the same region (Zelizer 1995; Ingham 2004: 87–89). Today, it is mainly national currencies that occupy the place of this universal unit of value. The euro is special in this respect because it functions as the universal unit of value for the former currencies of the euro area. From the point in time at which the relation of value among these various currencies was definitively fixed, the value has been expressed in euros (Goodhart 1998).

Money as a general unit of value is an expression of historically specific social developments. In the course of historical processes of socialization, these developments are potentially naturalized and de-historicized (Husserl 1978; Carruthers and Babb 1996). Over time, the general unit of value is enforced and becomes established and socially accepted. Once that happens, it may seem as though the object functioning as money only serves as the general unit of value because it has always possessed a specific inherent value. This is the way people have come to perceive objects such as gold, for example: "Through all the discussions of the nature of money there runs the question as to whether money, in order to carry out its services of measurement, exchange and representation of values, is or ought to be a value itself; or whether it is enough if money is simply a token and symbol without intrinsic value, like an accounting sum which stands for a value without being one" (Simmel 1978 [1900]: 129). In reference to the gold standard prevailing at the beginning of the twentieth century, Mitchell Innes writes: "All our modern legislation fixing the price of gold is merely a survival of the late-mediaeval theory that the disastrous variability of the monetary unit had some mysterious connection with the price of the precious metals, and that, if only that price could be controlled and made invariable, the monetary unit also would remain fixed" (Mitchell Innes 1913: 400).

What counts is not the substance or materiality of money, for in that case the materiality itself would have to possess an intrinsic unit of value. The value form of money is rather detached from its substance. The assumption that the substance of money has an inherent value misses the analytical distinction between form and substance. The money form (its function as a general equivalent) is political in origin and must be distinguished from its mere substance (the concrete conveyor). It is classic essentialism to reduce the form of things to their substance: "Only to the extent that the material element recedes does money become real money" (Simmel 1978 [1900]: 198). Marx puts it this way: "If we keep in mind only this material aspect, that is, the exchange of the commodity for gold, we overlook the very thing we ought to observe, namely what has happened to the form of the commodity. We do not see that gold, as a mere commodity, is not money, and that the other commodities, through their prices, themselves relate to gold as the medium for expressing their own shape in money" (Marx 1976a: 199).

The universal unit of value finds its expression in the symbol alone—the numerical figure. *What matters is the number.* For this reason, money does not have to be something tangible. Indeed, the majority of global payment transactions today are conducted without cash. On the other hand, this does not mean that money is growing less important, but only the specific material that conveys the universal unit of value as long as it is interchangeable (Knapp 1924). In a market economy, money is indispensable to express how assets relate to one another. Today, it has merely grown more obvious—in comparison, for example, with the era of the gold standard—that money expresses a social relation, and that the material representation of this general unit of value is interchangeable. At the same time, the conveyor is not irrelevant. It becomes relevant when certain (material) conveyors have been ascribed a special significance for the guarantee of value. Money is not entirely immaterial either, as Allon (2015: 283) assumes, since the numerical value requires a conveyor that stores and transports the universal value, even if today it is just a matter of numbers on a modern-day data storage device or facility. If money were absolutely immaterial, it could be produced arbitrarily by anyone. Money without a medium to store it would be meaningless and of no value.

The Master Signifier

The question now is: How can very dissimilar commodities be made comparable? The equivalence of commodities does not emerge from a property that the commodities already have in common. To determine their commonality so as to make them comparable and give them a value, it is necessary to look for something *beyond* the commodity (Laclau 1996a: 57). The only commonality shared by all commodities comes from their being placed in a relationship with a third entity. Commodities receive their value only by virtue of their reference to something external. And that something is money.

The capacity to serve as universal equivalent or master signifier is not already embodied in the object that comes to be this third entity. In other words, the singularity of the third entity is based not on any specifically inherent property but rather entirely on its unique position as the general unit of value, the universal equivalent. But if the only property common to all commodities is their value relation to one another in terms of the universal equivalent, and if the third entity functions as a universal equivalent only because of its relation to all other commodities, it follows that any object would, at least theoretically, be able to assume the role of the universal equivalent (see also Knapp 1924: 2). An object becomes a universal equivalent the moment it becomes distanced from its specific properties.

For an object to effectively take the form of money, it must be divested of any previous value that it possessed by virtue of its relation to other assets. The cotton that goes into making a five-dollar note is worth no more than a few cents. Once a piece of cotton is recognized as a banknote, however, it loses its value as a fabric. Its material composition becomes irrelevant. In the political process that turns an object into a conveyor of general commodity value, the object acquires an entirely new meaning—one that is independent not only of its previous commodity value or use but also of all other commodity values. The object ceases to be just one commodity among others. Money is therefore not, as sometimes assumed, or at least inaccurately perceived, an abstraction or a generalization of an object's properties. It is not "a measure of abstract value" (Ingham 2004: 68). If the universal equivalent were nothing more than the generalization (i.e., an abstraction) of certain properties, it would have to be assumed that all commodities have something in common, in which case they would all share a positive characteristic that would only have to be signaled—or abstracted—by the universal equivalent (Laclau 2004: 280). That, however, is not the case. Money is not a unit of abstract value. It rather represents the unit of a universal and consequently socially accepted and enforced value that emerges not from a commodity value but through the process of social negotiation. The value of a commodity is an expression of its relation to other commodities. This relationship depends on a specific political, social, and economic context. Commodity values are therefore a reflection of social conditions. From this it follows that a universal equivalent assumes its role as the result of a sociopolitical process (Weber 1978).

As explained in the foregoing, the master signifier refers to a hybrid of particularity and universality. Money is a hybrid of this nature. It serves a dual role—on the one hand as a particularity (a specific asset), and on the other as the universal unit of value. As Marx puts it: "It is as if alongside and external to lions, tigers, rabbits, and all other actual animals, which form when grouped together the various kinds, species, subspecies, families etc. of the animal kingdom, there existed also in addition *the animal*, the individual incarnation of the entire animal kingdom. Such a particular which contains within itself all really present species of the same entity is a *universal* (like *animal*, *god*, etc.)" (Marx 1976b: 27, emphasis in the original). Like the various animals in this analogy, the object that functions as money is part of a chain of commodity values that are equivalent. But it also transcends the chain. In this sense, money can be something particular (a commodity) and at the same time something universal (the general unit of value). Only if the system of commodities and values is subverted can an object with a specific value become an object that serves as a universal unit of value.

Because of this, and because the money form is not part of the commodity system for which it serves as the universal equivalent, theories with a purely economic focus are ill-prepared to explain how the money form evolved. Nor can an explanation be derived from the commodity system alone. In like manner, theories of microsociology are not equipped to shed light on the emergence of the money form. Although practices of barter and exchange can be closely scrutinized from a microsociological perspective, approaches from this angle lack the tools to look beyond the scope of bartering to explain how the money form comes into being. Considering that the transformation of a particular object into a universal equivalent requires a sociopolitical act, a sociopolitical approach is what we need to more fully understand the money form.

The object that takes on the function of money cannot be completely universalized. It always remains something particular or specific—a specific object, a specific asset—that can be traded itself (especially on foreign exchange markets). Moreover, it is not just the universal equivalent that is a hybrid. Hybridity carries over to all other objects (commodities) in the chain of equivalence. While retaining their particularity as goods with specific properties, they each are also assigned a value independent of their particular attributes. That value is generated entirely in relation to other commodity values. Commodity value does not take into account the specific properties of an object. It expresses those properties only as a general unit of value in terms of money—a numerical representation of a certain amount of money.

The logic of equivalence universalizes the objects in the chain and transcends the specificity of commodities. Once the universal equivalent expresses the value of each commodity in relation to all others, its value is no longer defined in terms of its respective properties. Nor is it defined directly in terms of its relation to the other commodities, but only via money, which then functions as the unit of value for all commodities: "Everyone knows, if nothing else, that commodities have a common value-form which contrasts in the most striking manner with the motley natural forms of their use-values. I refer to the money-form" (Marx 1976a: 139). What gives things their value is accordingly nothing more than the universal unit of value, congealed as money, as phrased by Simmel (1978 [1900]: 330). In this way, money forms the "unified form of value" (Simmel 1978 [1900]: 412). It also defines the whole system of commodities (see Figure 1).

The concept of the master signifier in this sense very aptly captures the essence of the money form: "What was simply a mediation . . . now acquires a consistency of its own. Although the link was originally ancillary . . . , it now reacts over them and, through an inversion of the relationship, starts behaving as their ground" (Laclau 2005: 93).

Something becomes a commodity only if it can be placed in relation to other commodities via money in a specific chain of equivalence. Unless that something can be expressed in terms of money, it cannot take the form of a commodity. As a universal unit value, money not only defines the value relationship between commodities; it also determines what does or does not count as a commodity. Money expresses both commodity values as well as the limits of the commodity system: "In those cases, the name becomes the ground of the thing" (Laclau 2005: 100). From this angle it is not the case that the unit of account is determined in terms of the real commodity value. On the contrary, commodity value only becomes a value in the first place because it is expressed in terms of the universal equivalent. To conceive of money as a master signifier implies not to regard the money form as something bound to any

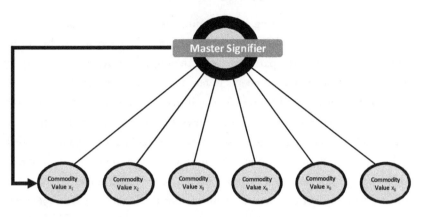

Figure 1 *Money as master signifier.*

presumed material or real value. Although history has frequently seen money tied to something material—gold, for instance—the connection was never a natural one. Ties of this nature were rather established through social and ultimately political processes. Early on, Wittgenstein criticized metaphysical and transcendental perspectives (Wittgenstein 1953). As he argued, value is neither simply *there* as a presence nor is it determined by an object's *state of being*. For Gramsci, too, there is no such thing as perfectly objective value: "It might seem that there can exist an extra-historical and extra-human objectivity. But who is the judge of such objectivity? Who is able to put himself in this kind of 'standpoint of the cosmos in itself' and what could such a standpoint mean? It can indeed be maintained that here we are dealing with a hangover of the concept of God, precisely in its mystic form of a conception of an unknown God" (Gramsci 1971: 445).

Money creates a system that would not exist without it. The present commodity system and capitalism as a whole could not exist if not for the money form that renders all kinds of different objects comparable and consequently tradable. It is the money form that creates "unity out of diversity" (Simmel 1978 [1900]: 198). At the same time, this monetary system is not self-stabilizing. Its existence is threatened when people lose confidence in it; that is, when they no longer believe that the object represented by money can (continue to) serve the function of the universal equivalent. As demonstrated earlier, the transition from a specific object to the money form always remains incomplete. Especially when times are hard—during an economic crisis, for example, or in a phase of hyperinflation or devaluation—confidence in currency tends to diminish. When that happens, the particularity of the object can resurface and again become apparent enough for people to realize that the object used as money is intrinsically worthless. This, in turn, can bring the monetary system to a collapse. The threat to the system is therefore systemic and not extrinsic. It lies at the core of the monetary system itself, in the sociopolitical relations inscribed in and constitutive of that system. The threat cannot be completely eliminated, for money always remains a hybrid: "The universal is incommensurable with any particularity but can not . . . exist without the latter" (Laclau 1996c: 35). In today's world it is up to political authorities, especially central banks and finance ministries, to sustain the myth that the value of money is stable.

3.4 A Promise to Pay: Money and Debt

Money, as demonstrated above, is a universal unit of value that expresses the relation, in terms of price, of one commodity value to others. The social relation expressed by money is stabilized by way of sociopolitical processes (such as supply and demand, or struggles over the value of labor). But what does this social relation involve?

When money is exchanged for a commodity, the seller receives payment for the relative value of the commodity in comparison with other commodities. The amount paid can then be used to buy other goods. Money makes the purchase possible because it symbolizes the (relative) value of the commodity and entails the promise that at any point in time other goods can be purchased for this symbolized value. Money is thus a promise of a future payment of a purchase—a promise to pay. A promise to pay, in turn, is a deferred payment, in other words, a credit: "The word 'credit' is generally technically defined as being the right to demand and sue for payment of a debt. . . . By buying we become debtors and by selling we become creditors, and being all both buyers and sellers we are all debtors and creditors. . . . For example, A having bought goods from B to the value of $100, is B's debtor for that amount. A can rid himself of his obligation to B by selling to C goods of an equivalent value and taking from him in payment an acknowledgment of debt which he (C, that is to say) has received from B. By presenting this acknowledgment to B, A can compel him to cancel the debt owed to him. A has used the credit which he has procured to release himself from his debt" (Mitchell Innes 1913: 392–93).

A sale in this sense is the exchange of a commodity for a credit, which can then be passed on as a debt claim in a subsequent purchase. Ultimately, this creates an unlimited amount of credit and debt relationships. Money as conceptualized above is a symbol of general value. In more concrete terms, it is now possible to grasp the notion of money as a social relationship that expresses a promise to pay. The idea of a promise to pay, which dates back to the gold standard, is still imprinted on British banknotes today: "I promise to pay the bearer on demand the sum of . . . pounds." While today this phrase may seem redundant, it actually does constitute a guarantee on behalf of the state. The owner of a ten-pound note, for instance, can rest assured that the document is not a specific credit commitment, but rather legal tender that can be exchanged at any time for central bank money.[14]

Conceptualizing money as a credit relationship, however, does not imply that all forms of credit are at once money. Money is a very special form of credit. In a narrow definition of money, it is a credit that is *universally* accepted within any given currency area (or area of application) where it is deemed valid (McLeay, Radia, and Ryland 2014b).[15] A school of thought that has come to be known as "the Money View" argues for a broader definition and takes the hierarchical character of money systems into account (Mehrling 2013). According to this approach, the answer to the questions What is money? and What is simple credit? depends on from which level in the hierarchy the question comes. From the perspective of banks, central bank reserves represent money. This is because they can only use reserves to settle their mutual liabilities. From the perspective of bank customers or the productive economy, bank deposits represent money because they are used—alongside cash, i.e., central bank money—to settle mutual obligations. Central banks, in turn, settle their liabilities in gold, at least if they do not have swap lines with each other (see chapter 4.3). Thus, for central banks, gold represents money (Mehrling 2013).

The important point is that money is not just a two-party contract, but rather a universal promise to pay for the final settlement of their liabilities among actors on the same level of the monetary hierarchy. Such a debt claim can be passed around from one person or institution to another. It is valid for everyone located on this same level as an acceptable promise to pay. Money is therefore a universally accepted promise to pay vis-à-vis other credits with specific and only limited promises of payment: "[M]oney is only a claim upon society. Money appears, so to speak, as a bill of exchange in which the name of the drawee is lacking. . . . The liquidation of every private obligation by money means that the community now assumes this obligation towards the creditor" (Simmel 1978 [1900]: 176–77). The crucial difference between credit and money lies in the function money serves as the universal equivalent for all assets. Accordingly, it is a generalized credit-debt relationship that is expressed as an abstract unit of account. In this way, the obligation to pay is transferable. It can be passed on to others. Money issuers, such as commercial banks and states or their central banks, promise to accept the very money they have issued in payment for any debts for which they themselves act as creditors. Money creation therefore implies the creation of credit. At the same time, it means that upon creation, money is offset by an equal amount of debt. In contrast to tradable goods, money can only come into being (in other words, money can only be created by central banks and private banks) with the simultaneous creation of debt.[16] By the same token, when loans, such as those created by balance sheet expansion, are repaid, money is destroyed: "A's money is B's debt to him, and when B pays his debt, A's money disappears" (Mitchell Innes 1913: 402). Banks and central banks are constantly in the process of creating and destroying money (Keynes 1971 [1930]: 20–24; see chapter 4.2). Whenever they promise to lend money to a borrower, that borrower promises to return it. The relationship between a bank and a borrower leads to a permanent creation and destruction of money.[17] Money creation by virtue of that relationship is possible today only because an institutionalized structure legitimized by the state recognizes such privately issued promissory notes as a universal equivalent for all assets, and therefore as money (this aspect will be examined in greater detail in the next chapter). Tradable promissory notes already existed in ancient Babylon more than three thousand years ago, but they were limited to the domain of commercial networks. In addition, potential payment default and bankruptcy meant that such networks were relatively unstable. Mechanisms to ensure greater security only evolved with the development of state or quasi-state structures (the Italian city-states, for example) and, ultimately, central banks.

As mentioned earlier, even though the state does play a prominent role in determining what form money takes in today's world, it does not go far enough to confine an analysis of the money form to the existence of the state alone. In fact, as will be discussed in the next chapters, the monetary system is a hybrid of public, public-private, and private forms of money. The development of contemporary monetary systems in market economies began when the systems of credit and debt in commercial trade were integrated into state money systems, and privately issued promissory notes became linked at par value with state-issued money as a result of state-guaranteed convertibility (Boyer-Xambeau, Deleplace, and Gillard 1994). In the following chapters, the concept of *security structure* is used to analytically include the political process by which selected entities are vested with the legal authority to create money. From what has been said so far, one thing is already clear: What matters more than the object serving the function of money is the political process involved in determining what object is to serve as money, but also what institution should be allowed to create it and in what way: "Money prices are the product of conflicts of interest and of compromises; they thus result from power constellations. Money is not a 'mere voucher for unspecified utilities,' which could be altered at will without any fundamental effect on the character of the price system as a struggle of man against man. 'Money' is, rather, primarily a weapon in this struggle, and prices are expressions of the struggle; they are instruments of calculation only as estimated quantifications of relative chances in this struggle of interests" (Weber 1978: 108). Since there are always alternative objects that could also function as universal equivalents, this political process is a potentially conflict-ridden struggle in which diverse interests and interest groups inevitably clash.

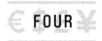

FOUR

Security Structures and Socioeconomic Layers

MONETARY POLICY DECISIONS SHOULD NOT be understood as the optimal outcome of all available policy options, because not all policy options are considered on equal footing. Rather, the choice of action takes place in an already selectively prestructured terrain in which some instruments and policies have a significantly higher probability of being chosen than others. The form of monetary policy ultimately implemented reflects the prevailing social and economic structures, institutions, norms, values, and power relations. In other words, the policy options are embedded in social layers (Wullweber 2016; Aguila and Wullweber under review). These formations are the outcome of discursive struggles over what policies are appropriate and legitimate to achieve social or economic goals, or to overcome a social or economic problem or crisis. When certain views or programs become institutionalized and universalized, they are no longer seen as specific and interest-driven but rather as universal solutions corresponding to the common good of society (Laclau 2000). The deeper a layer is situated—that is, the more sedimented it has become—the less it is politically questioned (Laclau 1990). In the resulting stratified structure, each layer selectively affects the formation of the specific texture of the other layers. Overall, the layered structure privileges "some actors, some identities, some strategies, some spatial and temporal horizons, some actions over others" (Jessop 2001: 285). Accordingly, "change is not an either-or question, because we are not operating at one level only" (Wæver 2005: 36). With the concept of stratified structures it becomes possible to "specify change within continuity" (Wæver 2005: 36). In noncrisis times, this layered structure remains largely unpoliticized and unquestioned. Change happens slowly. Crises, however, can cause one or more layers to become dislocated in a relatively short period of time (Laclau 1990). Usually, the institutional response consists of attempts to make mere "surface changes" (Wæver 2005: 37). However, major crises can also lead to the politicization and possible change in more deeply sedimented layers, or even of the entire political and socioeconomic structure. This would then result in profound institutional transformation (Howarth, Norval, and Stavrakakis 2000).

In the case of central banking, it is possible to identify different layers of accepted goals, institutional characteristics, and policies that come together to form the market liberal paradigm dominant since the 1980s. Overall, this approach is based on the idea of a dichotomy between the state and the market. The state is generally expected to refrain from interfering in market processes that, left to themselves, are supposed to achieve the socially optimal outcome. Only under certain exceptional circumstances such as market failures or crises is temporary intervention on the part of the state considered to be justified. Market liberal governance assumes the accomplishment of "policy objectives through markets" (Krippner 2007: 478). The market liberal narrative holds inflation to be an especially relevant distortion of the economy that results from an excessive creation of money, owing, in particular, to demands made by populist-leaning fiscal incumbents up for reelection. Although the surge in inflation that began in 2022 in no way fits this narrative, just as, in fact, it cannot explain the vast majority of inflationary episodes, it remains tenaciously persistent.

In terms of mandate, the market liberal approach argues that central banks should be concerned primarily, if not exclusively, with price stability (Wray 2007; see chapter 2.1). Since the financial crisis of 2007–9, many central banks also include financial stability as part of their objectives (McPhilemy and Moschella 2019; Thiemann, Melches, and Ibrocevic 2021). At an institutional level, the approach holds that the best way to pursue the objective of price stability is to keep independent central bankers shielded from the pressure of politicians (McNamara 2002; Goodhart and Lastra 2023). Similarly, central banks are not supposed to coordinate with fiscal authorities. And under no circumstances are they to engage in government financing (Hall 2008; Goodhart 2011; Conti-Brown 2016).

It is these layers of principles that form the basis of concrete monetary policy. This does not mean that they dictate policy decisions. However, they clearly limit the field of action. The concept of *security structures*, which will be discussed more specifically in chapter 8 in the context of current central bank policies, refers to monetary policies in the form of different strategies designed to ensure relative financial stability, at least for an interim phase. A security structure does not emerge by chance. Nor is it based on mathematical modeling. Decisions in favor of certain stabilization strategies are reached through a search process involving many different factors. This process is more of a balancing act than a coherent strategic plan, involving conflictually negotiated compromises between different possible forms of financial and economic stability, each with certain advantages and disadvantages. It is a constant weighing of multiple factors to determine which facilities can affect different segments of the financial system, what financial players are acceptable as counterparties, and how much funding liquidity and market liquidity is necessary to keep the system relatively stable (Mabbett and Schelkle 2019; Wullweber 2019b).[1]

The ultimate goal of all such strategies is to restore the liberal "freedom of the market" (Foucault 2008: 53). This is because liberal government logic assumes that only market freedom can establish the "natural price or the good price" (Foucault 2008: 53). As Foucault (2008: 64) points out: "Liberalism must produce freedom, but this very act entails the establishment of limitations, controls, forms of coercion, and obligations relying on threats, etcetera." The *liberal art* of central banking is accordingly about producing, organizing, manufacturing, and managing the freedom of circulation. Security structures—in Foucault's words "strategies of security"—"are, in a way, both liberalism's other face and its very condition" (Foucault 2008: 65). Accordingly, a successfully installed security structure "provides the best possible circulation, and [. . . minimizes] what is risky and inconvenient" (Foucault 2009: 19). With regard to monetary policy, there are three general types of mechanisms that provide or constrain the financial elasticity of actors or markets (Mehrling 2011): those geared toward adjusting the volume of market liquidity, those that affect access to financial liquidity, and those that influence the supply of safe assets. While these mechanisms seem simple and straightforward, the strategies used to stabilize markets in times of crisis are diverse and complex depending on the financial players involved, the markets to be stabilized, the targets of support, and the depth and extent of the crisis to be contained. A security structure can become extremely elaborate, especially in times of deep crisis.

Central bank policies have a significant impact on trading activities in both the banking system and the shadow banking system. While different circumstances admittedly demand different stabilization measures, there is no denying that the very measures used to stabilize the economy tend to benefit some players over others. Moreover, they can potentially lead to new downward liquidity spirals and new asset price bubbles, as will be shown in the chapters that follow. Briefly stated: Central bank policy interventions to stabilize markets may (and do) have destabilizing effects.

4.1 Money Creation and Security Structures

How can a state create money? Why can the state enable commercial banks to create money as well? What differences exist between central bank money, deposit money (the money that commercial banks create),[2] and other forms of money and credit? While all kinds of assets and credits can be created within the (financial) market itself, money as a stable unit of value is created only through security structures, most of which are state-run, but some of which are private. The goal of these very specific money-creating security structures is always the same: to create trust in the money form through security features and mechanisms. In the case of bitcoins and other cryptoassets, for example, this is to be achieved through the decentralized, technical, and mathematical process by which private digital money is created, which severely limits the possibility of bitcoin *mining* through the complex solution of cryptographic tasks. Any private person can theoretically mine bitcoins, but only very few actually do so because of the immense computer processing capacity needed to perform those tasks. The upper limit on the amount of bitcoins in circulation, a maximum figure of around 21 million, is a further restriction. The problem with cryptoassets, however, is that there is no security structure that would be able to maintain the promise to trade these assets at par on demand. As a result, their value is subject to wide fluctuations. In the case of repos, the process of safeguarding involves a complex set of security structures designed to protect private financial players from counterparty default. From the perspective of political economy it is interesting to note that the decisive difference between the creation of private money and state money is that private security structures are not crisis-proof. Every serious crisis so far has required intervention on the part of the states and their central banks to prevent the collapse of the financial system and/or systemically relevant private security systems such as the repo market. Indeed, it is precisely for this reason that almost every country has a central bank (Goodhart 1991).

Money-creating security structures involve complex political and institutional constellations that convert certain assets into central bank money or into assets that have a greater degree of security and can therefore be more readily traded on demand and at par (without value loss) (Wullweber 2021). These security structures encompass different levels of asset security depending on how far removed they are from central bank money (Bell 2001; from a different point of view Mehrling 2013) (see Figure 2).[3]

Figure 2 illustrates the varying levels of security for promises to trade at par (value) on demand in a hierarchy ranging from unsecured credits at the base line up through central bank money at the top. Central bank money is the only asset that remains liquid even in times of financial crisis.[4] Central bank money is also the asset that can be used to settle the liabilities exchanged between commercial banks. In general it can be said that the rank of an asset in the credit hierarchy depends on how reliable it is in terms of its par convertibility on demand: The more secure an asset, the higher it stands in the hierarchy.

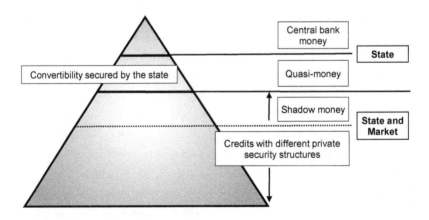

Figure 2 *State, market, and different levels of credit hierarchy (with regard to the promise to trade at par on demand).*

Ultimately, it comes down to whether or not the asset can be converted into central bank money. In other words, the higher an asset stands in the hierarchy, the more effective are its security structures, and, consequently, the more easily it can be exchanged for, or at least facilitate access to, central bank money upon demand at its original issue price. This means it can be traded at face value without incurring any significant loss. Applying the concept of security structures enables a closer look at these structures and the strategies adopted by financial players to increase asset protection. The crucial point here is the qualitative difference that exists between the various private and government protection schemes in terms of their ability to guarantee par convertibility of assets on demand.

Certain assets with a specific private security structure possess a degree of liquidity that is temporarily high enough to make it substantially easier for borrowers to use them as collateral (or securities) to access money. Securities of this kind, which contain a strong promise to trade at par on demand with government-backed money, are referred to here as *shadow money*. There is no single definition of shadow money in the literature. In this book, the term is largely equated with repos (see chapter 6.1), but the question of what exactly counts as shadow money is a subject of ongoing discussion (Pozsar 2014; Gabor and Vestergaard 2016; Michell 2016; Murau 2017a; Murau and Pforr 2020). At the core of the definition of shadow money as used in this book is the assumption that such assets promise to trade at par on demand with central bank money or government-backed private money (bank deposits). Securing that promise to the extent possible requires the provision of a private security structure consisting of a complex set of different mechanisms designed to ensure trading at par on demand (in the case of repos, examples include haircuts, margin calls, or pledged assets; for a more detailed discussion of this aspect, see chapter 6.1).

In the present conceptual framework, the category shadow money represents the highest possible level of privately generated security. The category *quasi-money*, in contrast, refers to assets for which a central bank guarantees convertibility with central bank money on demand and at par value (book value); in other words, without value loss. In this way, they become state money-like assets. Assets of this kind are deposits created by commercial banks. Quasi-money and shadow money are both money equivalents. They each represent the promise of par convertibility on demand, and in times of noncrisis are both as liquid as central bank money. However, as financial players painfully come to realize during times of crisis, neither is real central bank money (Gorton 2017). It is therefore crucial to ask who is responsible for ensuring the promise of stable value and liquidity. Quasi-money is rated higher than shadow money in the credit hierarchy. This is because in the case of quasi-money, responsibility for the promise lies with the state. In terms of liquidity, it is therefore tantamount to money (Wray 1990; Bell 2001; Mehrling 2013; Gabor and Vestergaard 2016).

When classifying assets analytically, it is important to be able to determine whether they can be traded on demand at par value through private or rather through state-institutionalized security structures, and also what kind of security they require (see also Schumpeter 1986 [1954]: 305).[5] The farther an asset is from the top of the pyramid, the less safe it is. The less safe it is, the more illiquid it becomes. As a rule, however, higher-risk assets are expected to generate higher returns: "[T]he rate of interest is the reward for parting with liquidity for a specified period" (Keynes 2018 [1936]: 146).

In times of noncrisis, the difference between shadow money and quasi-money is negligible. Indeed, during bull market phases when financial market prices are on the rise, investors on the lookout for profitable new investments and innovative sources of revenue actually prefer shadow money, precisely because it tends to be cheaper and more flexible in terms of its use (Leyshon and Thrift 2007; Aitken 2011). Financial markets on an upswing experience an overall increase in trading. When prices are high, most assets seem highly liquid, making it easier for lenders to renew private debt agreements instead of calling for repayment in cash: "The elasticity of credit thus offers a degree of freedom that relaxes the constraint posed by the scarcity of money" (Mehrling 2013: 399).

When confidence over steadily rising prices once again gives way to uncertainty, liquidity in general takes a downward turn (Gorton 2017; Moreira and Savov 2017). This causes lenders to demand settlement of outstanding debts. Under the changed circumstances, however, they no longer accept repayment by shadow money, but only by central bank money or quasi-money. Therefore, when crisis strikes, as we saw during the COVID-19 pandemic, financial players seek to liquidate as many of their debt agreements as possible and convert them into money (Wullweber 2020a). Whether or not financial players experience liquidity shortages during a crisis depends on whether they are able to access central bank money or quasi-money: "In a liquidity crisis, everyone wants money and no one wants credit" (Mehrling 2013: 401). It follows that even though during noncrisis periods shadow money created by private financial players can be backed by all kinds of security structures, it can never enjoy the same level of protection as state-created security structures (Gorton 2017: 660). The guarantee of an asset's par convertibility on demand ultimately depends on the existence of state-created security structures: "Safety is . . . an outcome of an institutional and legal framework" (Cœuré 2016).

4.2 Central Bank Money, and Bank Credit

The potential for flexibility in responding to the demand for money is specific to the nature of capitalism. Accordingly, Hyman Minsky, referring to Dudley Dillard, describes capitalism as a "monetary production economy" (Minsky 1982a: 78). Decoupling the money form from a substance such as gold with presumed intrinsic value is not the defining feature of today's monetary system because it has always been a myth that the money form can be tied to gold or some other object. Nor is the most distinguishing aspect the rising dominance of electronic money and the simultaneous phasing out of cash in its classic form. The decisive characteristic of the monetary system is rather its ability, by means of historically institutionalized security structures, to react flexibly in adjusting the supply of money so as to match demand. It is this elasticity that makes it possible during periods of economic prosperity to generate the funding liquidity needed to launch start-ups, or to foster innovation and promote the development of, among other things, education programs, workforce potential, and infrastructure projects. And in times of crisis, when the economy is weak, or when the fabric of society is disrupted by a pandemic or some other major disaster, enough money can be raised to launch appropriate responses to meet the resulting challenges.

Flexibility is possible because of the closely intertwined relationship between government and private credit systems that has developed not because of need or as a natural evolutionary process but rather in the course of a historical compromise between the state and the systems of banking and trade that enabled the integration of commercial systems of trade, credit, and debt into state-controlled monetary systems. The trade and banking sectors sought to preserve the credit systems that they had established, while states (or state-like entities) sponsored their own credit systems. Based on a process of negotiation and confrontation, state authorities allowed commercial banks to create (book) money. The state undertook to trade this privately produced debt for central bank money upon demand at par value. At the same time the state maintained the exclusive right to create central bank money through its central banks. Today's monetary system, which evolved from this historical compromise, is therefore a hybrid of state and private security structures: "Until private credit-money was incorporated into the fiscal system of states which commanded a secure jurisdiction and a legitimacy, . . . it remained . . . a dead end" (Ingham 2004: 122).

Central banks, accordingly, are not the only institutions to issue money. Although commercial banks are not allowed to create central bank money, the credit they extend in the form of deposits is recognized by the state as a valid medium of exchange. This credit therefore also counts as money. Commercial banks therefore do not need to resort to central bank money except to fulfill minimum reserve and capital requirements and settle the debt obligations that they have with each other. They are the only other institutions besides central banks that are entitled to create private credit in the form of bank deposits that can be traded at par on demand with legal tender.[6] For households and the real economy, bank deposits, although not legal tender in the strict sense of the term, are therefore largely considered to be equivalent to legal tender.[7] In return for the extraordinary privilege they have been granted to create money, commercial banks consent to comply with comparatively strict regulations that govern, among other things, the level of their equity capital and liquidity base, or their risk management practices (Ingham 2004; Murau 2017b).

Theoretically speaking, central banks can create any amount of money they choose by buying up securities. There is no objective limit to the volume of money a central bank can issue as long as trust in the value of its currency continues to hold. Confidence in the stability of money depends on various qualitative factors, including public assessment of government monetary and economic policies, perceived strength of a country's economy, education level of its people, and communication strategies pursued by its central bank. A further factor with bearing on money creation is the relative value of a country's currency in terms of other currencies (the exchange rate). By creating money on a large scale, a central bank increases the amount of currency in circulation. As a rule, this tends to decrease the value of that currency in relation to other currencies. For export-oriented countries, depreciation has the advantage of reducing export prices on the world market. It causes problems for countries dependent on imports, however, by increasing the cost of imported goods.

Quasi-money (deposit money) is created when private banks provide credit. Most branches of economics still regard it to be the primary function of banks to bring creditors and debtors together (Mankiw 2017; for a critical perspective, see McLeay, Radia, and Ryland 2014a; Bofinger 2020). According to this interpretation, banks are little more than neutral, cost-reducing intermediaries. As already pointed out by Schumpeter and Keynes, however, the money that banks pay out in credits is more than (just) the funds they take in as deposits. Above all, they create new money when they grant credits: "There can be no doubt that, in the most convenient use of language, all deposits are 'created' by the bank holding them" (Keynes 1971 [1930]: 26).[8] In its *Quarterly Bulletin* for the first quarter of 2014, the Bank of England very clearly criticized mainstream economics: "While the money multiplier theory can be a useful way of introducing money and banking in economic textbooks, it is not an accurate description of how money is created in reality" (McLeay, Radia, and Ryland 2014a: 15). Seven years later, the St. Louis Fed categorically rejected textbook explanations of how the Fed operates based on the money multiplier "theory," and clearly distanced itself from the model: "We recommend that textbook authors and teachers eliminate the use of the money multiplier concept in explaining the linkage between banks and the Fed" (Ihrig, Weinbach, and Wolla 2021).

In today's capitalist market economies, the majority of the money in circulation is created through debt contracts between banks and borrowers (see Figure 3). The private, state-secured system for creating money can thus react very flexibly to the demand for money or credit: "[W]hat the banker does with money cannot be done with any other commodity . . . for no other commodity's quantity or velocity can be increased in this way" (Schumpeter 1986 [1954]: 304–5) In other words, commercial banks can issue deposit instruments that have the same status as state money (Bell 2001: 160; Ricks 2016: 5). The mere acceptance of the convertibility of deposits into legal tender on the part of the state, however, does not suffice to stabilize the system. Chick (2013: 149–51) speaks of *convertibility risks*: "Much of subsequent history has to do with the banks learning to manage their liquidity (or their convertibility risk)" (Chick 2013: 151). Mechanisms had to be institutionalized to ensure the convertibil-

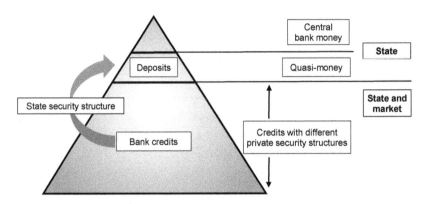

Figure 3 *Credit pyramid: Quasi-money (deposits).*

ity of bank credits. A complex institutional framework was accordingly created to guarantee the exchange of deposits at face value and to stabilize the
banking system. Measures within the framework include deposit insurance,
the marginal lending facility, and capital requirements (Goodhart 1989). In
times of crisis, central banks also act as lenders of last resort. However, the
deposit insurance system only protects deposits up to a certain limit (for example, 250,000 dollars in the United States; 100,000 euros in the European
Union; and 85,000 pounds in the United Kingdom).[9] Strictly speaking, bank
deposits above these limits no longer constitute sovereign money since they are
not covered by deposit insurance (Mehrling 2013; Ricks 2016). Accordingly,
when a bank run occurs, it becomes clear that deposit money is not central
bank money. Par convertibility of deposit money into central bank money on
demand is a promise by the bank, but it is guaranteed by the state only for
deposits up to these amounts.

In the money hierarchy, a bank credit is not on the same level as central
bank money. Commercial banks are able to create deposits (quasi-money) elastically according to need, and they do so via balance sheet entries. In contrast
to the money multiplier theory that is still taught in many university lecture
halls and classrooms, private bank balance sheet expansion is not dependent on
the availability of central bank money: Commercial banks lend their customers
privately created deposits, not central bank money or a fraction of central bank
money (McLeay, Radia, and Ryland 2014a; Ihrig, Weinbach, and Wolla 2021).

They require central bank money, however, to settle their mutual liabilities and in some countries to comply with laws. This means that they are only dependent on central bank money to a very limited extent.

Trading at face value is a government-guaranteed option rather than an obligation: "Because the central bank guarantees that demand deposits will trade at par with government currency and because they are accepted in payment of taxes, bank promises (demand deposits) are nearly as liquid as state money" (Bell 2001: 160; Mehrling 2013: 394). Aside from their minimum capital requirements and reserve requirements (that only exist in some countries), banks are not obliged to hold reserves. When a bank creates new deposits—in other words, when it grants a credit—it creates a liability against itself. Central bank money comes into play only when deposits are paid out as cash or transferred to an account at another bank. In both cases, the commercial bank must access central bank money (McLeay, Radia, and Ryland 2014a).

It has become so commonplace to use and create money and credit that it is easy to overlook the complexity and elasticity of money market processes. In order to understand how the money market and financial system work, however, and to recognize what causes financial crises, it is essential to comprehend these processes. It is therefore important to take a closer look at the institutionalized security structure between the banking system and central banks. This can be illustrated through the ideally typical balance sheets of banks and borrowers. On a bank balance sheet, the assets side lists assets (such as claims on other banks and central bank money), while the liabilities side shows obligations (including, among other things, claims from other banks and customer deposits). When a bank (Bank A) issues a credit to an account holder, the credit is entered on the asset side of the balance sheet of Bank A and at the same time as a *liability to nonbanks* on the liability side. Each transaction is always recorded twice (double-entry bookkeeping). In the case of the borrower (a), the credit increases their balance on the assets side of the balance sheet in the form of the newly created bank deposit.[10] On the liability side of the balance sheet, the loan is entered as an obligation to repay the money to the bank. The borrower's debts also increase accordingly (see Figure 4).

Since the amount borrowed must be repaid to the bank, the credit is recorded as a claim on the assets side of the bank's balance sheet. It is an IOU (I owe you), the borrower's promise to repay the bank for the credit (see Figure 5). The money created by the credit is transferred to a bank account (a demand

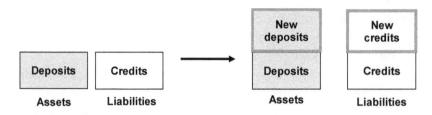

Figure 4 *Stylized balance sheet of Borrower Person a.*
Based on McLeay, Radia, and Ryland 2014a: 16.

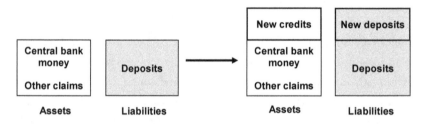

Figure 5 *Stylized balance sheet of Bank A. Based on*
McLeay, Radia, and Ryland 2014a: 16.

deposit account). If the account is held at the same bank, the deposit represents a liability on the part of the bank to the account holder: "Such a bank creates claims against itself for the delivery of money, what, hereafter, we shall call deposits" (Keynes 1971 [1930]: 20).[11] On the bank's balance sheet, the amount of the deposit increases the bank's liabilities and the amount of the credit increases its assets. When two people have an account at the same bank, and Person a transfers a sum of money to the account of Person b, the money is simply shifted from a to b. If both accounts are overdrawn (net debtor positions), the debt burden increases for Person a and decreases for Person b. From the perspective of Bank A, nothing changes. The total amount of assets and liabilities remains constant. In such a case, Bank A simply performs an intrabank transfer of funds from account holder a to account holder b. In so doing, the bank indeed merely acts as an intermediary (see Table 2).

As the Bank of England notes, however, such transactions are the exception rather than the rule (McLeay, Radia, and Ryland 2014a). In terms of total lending, the role of banks as intermediaries is negligible in comparison with

Table 2 *Transfer of deposits from Person a to Person b.*

Account of Person a		Bank A Balance Sheet		Account of Person b	
Assets	Liabilities	Assets	Liabilities	Assets	Liabilities
– Deposits			– Deposits (from Person a)	+ Deposits	
+ House			+ Deposits (from Person b)	– House	

the role they play in the creation of money through the process of lending (Jakab and Kumhof 2015). When Person a takes out a credit, Bank A does not finance the credit with funds it has on hand. Instead, it simply creates those funds: "The reality of how money is created today differs from the description found in some economics textbooks: . . . [R]ather than banks lending out deposits that are placed with them, the act of lending creates deposits—the reverse of the sequence typically described in textbooks" (McLeay, Radia, and Ryland 2014a: 14, 15). If the account of Person a has a positive balance but the account of Person b is overdrawn, a transfer of money from a to b will decrease the total amount of assets and liabilities. This is so because when a credit is repaid, money is destroyed. Conversely, in the event that Person a's account is already overdrawn and Person b's account has a positive balance when funds are transferred from the account of Person a to the account of Person b, the transaction expands the total amount of assets and liabilities, in effect expanding the money supply. This is because Person a now needs another credit, which Bank A issues by creating money (McLeay, Radia, and Ryland 2014a; Tucker 2014: 13).

When two banks are involved, the situation is as follows: To purchase a house from Person b, who has an account with Bank B, Person a takes out a loan (in this case, a mortgage) from Bank A. Bank A credits the account of Person a with the amount of the loan. The money created via the credit (in the form of a deposit) is then used to purchase the house. The amount of purchase is transferred from the account of the purchaser, Person a, and credited to the account of the seller, Person b. In return, Person a acquires the title to the property. How does this change the balance sheets of the two banks involved in the transaction? Unless the seller of the house receives payment in cash instead of through a bank transfer, the amount is normally deposited into their account. The amount that is credited to Person a from Bank A is transferred to Person b at Bank B. Bank B receives the bank deposit from Bank A, which, in turn, represents an obligation for Bank B. However, Bank B only accepts it by receiving corresponding assets, mostly in the form of central bank money. The credit remains with Bank A. Therefore, the total amount of credits on Bank A's balance sheet increases in relation to liabilities and customer deposits. This is good news for Bank A, considering that it belongs to the business model of commercial banks to charge higher interest rates for credits than the interest paid out for deposits. All else being equal, the interest margin for Bank A increases. At the same time, however, the bank has to ensure that it has sufficient liquid reserves on the assets side of its balance sheet (cash reserves, central bank balances, highly liquid securities) so as to be able, at any time, to cover liquidity shortages due to short-term outflows on the liabilities side (withdrawal of deposits) and also to meet bank supervision and regulation requirements (liquidity coverage ratio, equity backing of credits). In addition, some central banks require commercial banks to hold a minimum amount of reserves in their central bank accounts.[12] When banks need liquid resources, they can try to attract new deposits from other banks via their customers (and thereby increase their central bank balances). They can also approach the money market or the central bank directly by temporarily selling assets to the central bank (usually through repurchase agreements). Even when the money comes from the interbank market, it is, in effect, central bank money because of the increase in aggregate net lending: "[W]henever payments are made between the accounts of customers at different banks, they are ultimately settled by transferring central bank money (reserves) between the reserves accounts" (Bank of England 2015: 5).

The state-legitimized and secured lending and money creation by banks is peculiar to the nature of capitalist economy: "The *differentia specifica* of capitalism lies in banks' endogenous creation of new deposits of credit-money *ex nihilo*" (Ingham 2004: 63) Hence the term *fiat money*[13]: money created by decree (of commercial banks and central banks).[14] There is no natural restriction to this kind of money creation. Theoretically, bank credit can be issued indefinitely, for "there is no limit to the amount of bank money which the banks can safely create provided that they move forward in step" (Keynes 1971 [1930]: 23). In practice, however, a bank can reach a limit when investors lose trust in the ability of the bank to execute payments or settle its obligations. The private creation of money also finds its limits in microprudential and macroprudential regulations (such as minimum capital requirements and equity backing of risk assets) and, last but not least, in the cost-benefit analysis of the bank in question. An individual bank "must keep step with the other banks and cannot raise its own deposits relatively to the total deposits out of proportion to its quota of the banking business of the country" (Keynes 1971 [1930]; McLeay, Radia, and Ryland 2014a).

The demand and supply of money is coordinated by the money market, where money is created through the interaction between the state, its central bank, and commercial banks. It is connected with the capital market where money is converted into capital; in other words, into assets such as stocks and bonds. In this way it can be made available to the productive economy.[15] Money, or primary capital, can be acquired through the sale of stocks, corporate bonds, or other forms of assets.[16] Bank A has various options to obtain foreign currency when necessary. Before the global financial crisis, swap transactions on the short-term international money market (interbank market) made it possible to acquire foreign currencies. In the years since the crisis, however, the unsecured money market has become practically insignificant because of the substantial loss of confidence among banks (Bundesbank 2013). Its volume, compared with the figures for 2008, is only about one-twentieth of the average loan volume. Instead of obtaining foreign currency on the interbank market, Bank A can borrow money on the offshore Eurodollar market.[17] But it can also conduct repo transactions on the capital market with nonbank institutions such as insurance companies (see chapter 6.1). The interbank market, the Eurodollar market, and the repo market have come to serve the basic function of providing (profit-oriented) liquidity, with repos meanwhile being the most common way to procure funds (FSB 2021a). During noncrisis periods, interest rate spreads are not large. Repos tend to have the lowest interest rates because they are secured credits. Both the financial and the COVID-19 crisis, however, saw significant interest rate fluctuations. If financial players cannot offer acceptable collateral and have no access to reserve accounts at a central bank, they have no choice but to bid on the Eurodollar market until a counterparty accepts their offer and provides them with liquidity (Mehrling 2011: 95–98).

4.3 Political Economy of Liquidity and the Currency Pyramid

The ability of financial markets to function depends on access to and provision of funding and market liquidity. When it comes to characterizing financial markets, liquidity plays a central role. And yet, the term lacks a uniform definition. Ambiguity over how to define liquidity essentially lies in the fact that at the micro level it represents an asset's quality—how easily and quickly it can be sold and therefore converted into cash—while at the macro level it is also used as a benchmark for assessing the overall state of an economic system. Liquidity also serves as an indicator for the vitality of financial markets in terms of trading activity. As Keynes (2018 [1936]: 136) states, however, it makes no sense to speak of the liquidity of the market in general: When considered from a bird's-eye view, the market as a whole is always illiquid, because no assets are liquidated within the context of the overall system. An asset is liquidated by one trader when that same asset is acquired by another. From a global perspective, the world market always remains balanced. One country's surpluses are offset by the deficits of others, which means that "there is no such thing as liquidity of investment for the community as a whole" (Keynes 2018 [1936]: 136). The term accordingly represents an asset's potential to circulate or the velocity at which it circulates in a system. An asset is considered to have the highest degree of liquidity if its "full present value can be realized, i.e., turned into purchasing power over goods and services, immediately" (Tobin 1989, as cited in Carruthers and Stinchcombe 1999: 356). Perfect liquidity, in other words, depends on whether an asset can be traded on demand at par value.

Whether a given asset is liquid is an important (and sometimes tricky) question. But equally important is *how* liquid that asset is, and—even more important—in which way liquidity is generated. An asset's degree of liquidity depends on its demand and the ability of buyers to pay the asking price.[18] A widely used method to measure this is the so-called spread, also known as the bid-ask spread, which is the difference between the highest bidding price and the lowest asking price for the asset: the lower the spread, the higher the liquidity of the asset. Financial traders, stock exchanges, and other trading venues are generally very interested in keeping the spread for the securities they trade as low as possible. Some stock exchanges pay a bonus to market makers (traders), who secure liquidity for financial products through limit orders.[19] Degree of liquidity is also often estimated based on whether the market price of a particular asset is impacted through large-scale sale thereof, although there is no set criteria to establish what constitutes *large scale* or *impact* (MacKenzie et al. 2012: 285; IMF 2015: 49–51). What generates an asset's liquidity is confidence on the part of market players that it can be resold (for profit) at some time in the future. Liquidity is therefore a socially mediated attribute that depends on a particular political and economic context.

But how do political and economic conditions contribute to promoting and legitimizing certain financial actions while hindering and delegitimizing others? The scope for financial transactions was immensely increased, for example, by the deregulation policy of President Ronald Reagan's administration and Prime Minister Margaret Thatcher's so-called Big Bang measures. As Thatcher phrased it: "Gone are the controls which hampered success" (Thatcher 1986; see Helleiner 1994; Germain 1997; Strange 1998). In the same way, (re-) regulation can also alter the constellation of interests and influence among financial players. The 2004 Basel II Accord, which set new capital requirements for banks, significantly increased the status of rating agencies. Rather than constituting a neutral representation of the risks associated with financial products, the evaluations of rating agencies guide and structure the risk behavior of financial players (Sinclair 2005; Paudyn 2013). At the same time, the Basel Accord led to a change in investment strategies in the banking sector as banks increasingly turned to the shadow banking system in an attempt to circumvent capital requirement rules (Thiemann 2014).

It follows that the analysis of financial market liquidity must proceed on the basis of a political economic framework: "The conception of what contributes to 'liquidity' is a partly vague one, changing from time to time and depending on social practices and institutions" (Keynes 2018 [1936]: 211). Considerations that need to be taken into account include the market where assets can be sold, the buyers who are interested in assets and can afford to pay the asking price, and the legal framework for transferring rights and obligations associated with the assets to the buyer. The most liquid of all assets is cash. But there are no returns on cash. From the perspective of private financial players, the challenge is to hold on to highly liquid assets, while at the same time earning the highest possible profit. This requires traders to keep a constant eye on the balance between liquidity and profitability. The more that trading is standardized and formalized, the easier it becomes to trade, and, as a rule, the easier it is to maximize the overall liquidity of asset holdings. As Carruthers and Stinchcombe (1999: 358) point out, specific institutional and organizational conditions are necessary to create and increase liquidity. This is something that does not happen naturally without political regulation and intervention. It is in times of crisis that the underlying hierarchy of the system becomes apparent. The ultimate guarantor of liquidity is the state and, in particular, the central bank. Indeed, the close connection between the state and liquidity was highlighted already as far back as the year 1651 when Thomas Hobbes wrote his *Leviathan* and metaphorically referred to the circulation of money as the bloodstream of the body politic.[20] The cycle is guaranteed by the state, which, in turn, is dependent on money. In this sense, liquidity always involves the question of how a variety of public and private balance sheets are interlocked, who benefits from them, in what way, and why (Mehrling 2015). Accordingly, the question of which assets, institutions. and markets are granted funding and/or market liquidity is always a political issue.

Hierarchy also exists among central banks and their national currencies. The US dollar occupies a central position in today's international monetary system (Golec and Perotti 2017). It lies at the top of the credit hierarchy and remains unchallenged as the main currency for processing international payment flows.[21] The US dollar is the unit of account in which most global trade and finance is conducted and the currency used for reserve accumulation. It is the currency in which international balances are settled (Cohen and Benney 2014; Kaltenbrunner and Lysandrou 2017; Gopinath et al. 2020; Aguila, Haufe, and Wullweber 2022). This explains why "the actually existing international monetary system is very much a global dollar system" (Mehrling 2023: 1), which is an extraordinary privilege. This special status was obvious during both the financial crisis and the COVID-19 crisis, when the Fed vastly expanded its currency exchange agreements (swap lines) with other central banks (Stokes 2014). Fed swap lines facilitate the access of selected central banks to US dollars to ensure dollar liquidity (Mehrling 2015).[22] In terms of the hierarchy of central banks, the Fed is at the top of the pyramid. It is followed by the central banks that have standing swap facilities with the Fed, implying high flexibility in receiving US dollar on demand in exchange for their respective currency with low borrowing costs (see Figure 6). Currently, these are only five central banks: the Bank of Canada, the Bank of England, the ECB, the Bank of Japan, and the Swiss National Bank. Below this group follow central banks with nonpermanent Fed swap lines: the Reserve Bank of Australia, the Banco Central do Brasil, the Bank of Korea, the Banco de México, the Monetary Authority of Singapore, the Sveriges Riksbank (Sweden), the Danmarks Nationalbank (Denmark), the Norges Bank (Norway), and the Reserve Bank of New Zealand (Fed 2021). These swap lines are not permanent, but are regularly reactivated in times of crisis.

When a swap line is activated, the balance sheets of the relevant central banks are expanded and money is created. When the Fed activates a swap line with the ECB, for example, a special deposit account for the ECB is created at the Federal Reserve Bank of New York. On the liabilities side of this deposit, the ECB is credited with the corresponding amount of US dollars, which appears as an asset on the ECB's balance sheet. Conversely, euros are created on the asset side of the Fed's balance sheet, which, in turn, appear as liabilities on the ECB's balance sheet (Mehrling 2015). However, this form of currency swaps is only allowed for privileged central banks with permanent swap lines.

Below this group are the central banks that do not have a swap line with the Fed but are eligible for the Fed's foreign repo facilities (Murau, Pape, and Pforr 2023). In March 2020, the Fed announced a temporary repurchase agreement facility for those central banks and other foreign and international monetary authorities (FIMA Repo Facility). That facility became a standing facility in mid-2021 (Murau, Pape, and Pforr 2021; Fed 2022). To receive US dollars, these FIMA account holders have to pledge US treasury bonds. While central banks with swap lines can obtain US dollars just by expanding their own balance sheets, the central banks at a lower level in the currency hierarchy have to maintain enough US treasuries in stock to access dollars. The central bank of China, although part of this group, is at the level above the group's other central banks because of China's strong role as a global contender state. The international monetary system hierarchy is visualized in Figure 6.

Since the financial crisis of 2007–9, the Fed provides two security structures for the international monetary system: It can act as international lender of last resort for shortages in US dollars via its swap lines; and it also can act as international dealer of last resort, providing and buying safe assets in the form of US treasury bonds via its repo and reverse repo facilities (Murau, Pape, and Pforr 2023; for a detailed discussion see chapter 8.2 and 8.4). The fact that the Fed alone can decide which central bank gets what kind of access to US dollars gives it an extremely powerful position in the international monetary system.

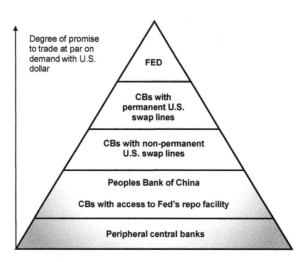

Figure 6 *The international currency hierarchy.*

Since the global money market and liquidity in the financial markets depend to a large extent on the Fed's monetary policy, there is also a responsibility and a need to constantly calibrate domestic monetary policy against its impact on the global financial system.

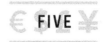

Sources of Instability in the Financial System

AT FIRST GLANCE it might seem that no market conforms as closely to the neo-classical ideal of general equilibrium theory as certain sectors of global financial markets, especially the stock markets. General equilibrium theory assumes that as long as the state does not intervene, a market with rational actors will reach equilibrium on its own through the so-called price mechanism, the natural process by which supply and demand for a particular product balance each other out and thereby clear the market. Under this assumption prices are expected to automatically adjust toward an equilibrium that is an exact reflection of the relationship between supply and demand. Following this line of thinking, it would be only natural in the case of financial markets to expect an optimal balance to be reached very quickly, especially considering how rapidly computerization and, above all, algorithmization have accelerated the speed of trading in recent years. Today's computer programs have a reaction time of far less than a millisecond. Some systems even have response times as low as 42 nanoseconds, that is, 0.000000042 seconds (MacKenzie 2021: 12). A computer can execute buy and sell orders at a speed that far exceeds the time it takes for humans to react (Beunza and Stark 2012).[1]

Market equilibrium theory has long been accepted as valid knowledge, even in government agencies (Financial Services Authority 2009). In reality, however, the shortcomings of this way of thinking could hardly be more obvious than they are in the case of the financial market. As, for example, witnessed both during the global financial crisis and the COVID-19 crisis, liquidity can spiral into illiquidity in no time at all (Wullweber 2020a). In just a matter of days after each crisis broke out, what financial players had assumed to be a liquidity glut suddenly turned into a credit crunch. In both cases, without massive intervention on the part of central banks, the global financial system would have collapsed.

5.1 Liquidity Fluctuations and Loss of Confidence

In times of rising security prices, assets of every kind seem to exhibit a high degree of market liquidity. This, however, is an illusion that rests on three main pillars (Nesvetailova 2010): the paradigm of a self-regulating financial system, the concept of Ponzi finance,[2] and a political economic structure that legitimizes new financial products, making them marketable in the process. In the years leading up to the global financial crisis, three factors contributed to the illusion of liquidity: global expansion of the private risk management industry enabled by financial innovation; the general belief that all types of credit could be bought and sold indefinitely; and a regulatory environment that made it possible to conceal shady investment practices and the accumulation of bad debts. The consequences of a liquidity illusion can be dramatic. When confidence in the future value of assets gives way to uncertainty, the liquidity of these assets diminishes and their prices decline (Minsky 1982a).

Although the probability is very high that a rise in asset prices will eventually be followed by a fall, it is impossible to tell beforehand exactly when liquid assets will become illiquid or when financial markets will experience a sharp downturn: "Liquidity is there until it is not—that is the reality of modern markets" (Amato and Fantacci 2012: 16). Generally speaking, it is only possible to say that assets become illiquid when sellers cannot find buyers. Following Pitluck (2011: 31), the liquidity assumption needs to be revised for a considerable part of financial products: "The world's stock markets are normally illiquid, filled with financial products that are, on average, challenging to trade, albeit with brief and partly predictable temporal spikes of liquidity." Especially big investors such as pension funds or investment banks are in no position to engage in high-volume asset trade, because doing so would have a direct bearing on prices. While on the New York Stock Exchange, or on Nasdaq, the largest electronic stock exchange in the United States, it is not uncommon for large US investors to place orders on the scale of 200,000 shares, only around 300 shares change hands per average order (MacKenzie et al. 2012: 283). Rather than executing high-volume orders all at once, or within a short period of time, traders split them up into smaller portions and spread the purchase over days or even months.

As long as confidence in a rising price trend holds among financial players in general, the assets traded will retain their market liquidity on the assumption that their resale will realize a profit. Once prices start to stagnate, however, the situation changes. At that point, because of the costs incurred in the transaction, the sale of securities generates a loss. Therefore, as soon as investors expect prices to stagnate or fall, they try to sell off their securities. If many financial players attempt to sell the same type of securities at the same time, or if a single player seeks to sell a large amount of a given security (or when both scenarios develop simultaneously), it will very likely cause a bottleneck in the liquidation of the securities in question. The persistence of such a bottleneck can incite panic, leading more and more investors to try and sell the product, which then leads to a massive price drop that often impacts other asset prices as well. This is precisely what happened during the last two major crises.

Liquidity is ensured as long as confidence is maintained. Confidence—*market confidence*—is therefore a core component of the financial system (Bernanke 2008; Wullweber 2016). And confidence is closely related to promises of payment: "Much financial activity involves, one way or another, the design, production, distribution, evaluation, acceptance (or rejection), enforcement, and modification of promises" (Carruthers and Kim 2011: 240). Trust in the market is founded less on the basis of internal factors and more on external factors (Amato and Fantacci 2012: 16). In financial markets it largely depends on global socioeconomic and political factors. And the most influential factors in today's world are central bank monetary policies and their security structures.

5.2 Laissez-Faire, Boom, and Bust

The two major (financial) crises at the start of the twenty-first century—the global financial crisis of 2007–9 and the COVID-19 financial crisis of 2020—were exceptional in terms of their dimension. And yet, rather than the exception, crises in the financial system tend to be the rule. Other financial crises that stand out in history include the Dutch tulip crisis of 1636–37, the British South Sea bubble of 1720 (a debt that the UK was still paying back in the 2000s) (Castle 2014), the German railway stock boom of the 1840s, and, above all, the 1929 stock market crash that led to the devastating Great Depression. After the end of Bretton Woods in the early 1970s, when the financial system was undergoing a process of liberalization and deregulation, there was a notable increase in the frequency of crises. Among the largest were the 1982 international banking and debt crisis, the 1985–89 real estate and stock market crisis in Japan, Finland, Norway, and Sweden, the 1986 US thrift sector crisis, the 1987 stock market crash, the 1994–95 Mexican peso crisis (also known as the Tequila crisis), the Asian and Russian crisis and the bankruptcy of the weighty hedge fund Long-Term Capital Management of 1997–98, the dot-com crisis of 1999–2000, and the 2001 Argentine sovereign debt crisis. A study commissioned by IMF counted a total of 147 banking crises, 218 currency crises, and 66 sovereign debt crises between 1970 and 2011 (Laeven and Valencia 2012; Kindleberger and Aliber 2015).

Economist Hyman Minsky (1982a, 2008) has demonstrated that the liberalized financial system gives rise to dynamic forces in recurring cycles that eventually end in crisis. Based on his observations of the cyclical nature of crises, Minsky developed a hypothesis of systemic risk and financial instability. His model postulates that under capitalism, as access to credit increases in an expanding financial system, there is an inherent tendency toward destabilization that neither economic activity nor government intervention can fully neutralize: "A capitalist economy generates financial relations that are conducive to instability." He therefore concludes that "as long as an economy is capitalist, it will be financially unstable" (Minsky 1982b: 36; Semmler 2011). It follows that the expectations of financial players have considerable bearing on financial market developments. The role played by economic fundamentals in building confidence, however, is limited. Expectations depend more on trust in future price trends and are subject to considerable fluctuation (Keynes 2018 [1936]: 33–35).

Minsky's work can be viewed as deriving from the tradition of classic liberal political economists such as John Stuart Mill, Alfred Marshall, Irving Fisher, and John Maynard Keynes. He regarded his hypothesis as representing a variant of Keynesianism that takes into consideration the role and dynamics of the financial system (Minsky 1982b: 14). Although his theory of systemic instability is based on liberal approaches, it closely resembles certain basic Marxist assumptions on the vulnerability of capitalist economies. David Harvey's accumulation crisis cycle, for example, which is based on the writings of Marx, is surprisingly similar to Minsky's model (Harvey 1982: 300–304).

Minsky (1982b) identifies three distinct methods to raise finance: hedge finance, speculative finance, and Ponzi finance. In hedge finance, the expected profits of business operations are sufficient to cover interest and reduce cumulative debt. Speculative finance refers to business dealings in which profits are expected to cover accrued interest, but not to reduce the debt principal, meaning that new credits must be taken out on a regular basis to finance expiring loans. The Ponzi variety of finance occurs when total income from the financed activities does not even manage to cover the interest accrued on the principal, and a succession of new credits must be taken out (or real estate and other possessions must be sold) to pay the interest on old credits. Under such circumstances, the total amount of outstanding short-term debt increases because the interest due on previous borrowings exceeds the income from the assets.

When the economy slows down due to a decrease in liquidity, hedge finance shifts toward speculative finance, speculative finance turns into Ponzi funding, and enterprises and financial players that pursued Ponzi finance become insolvent. Minsky criticizes the neoclassical economics perspective that crises can only be triggered by external factors (state intervention in particular) and cannot be caused by operations intrinsic to the economic functioning of financial markets: "Financial instability is a nonevent, something that just cannot happen, insofar as the standard body of today's economic theory is concerned" (Minsky 1982b: 13). When Reagan and Thatcher pursued a course based on neoclassical theories and deregulated the financial markets, above all in response to the demands of the financial industry, Minsky predicted that *It* could happen again—*It* meaning an economic meltdown on the order of the Great Depression of the 1930s (Minsky 1982a). And at least to a certain degree, history has proven him right.

Partly building on Minsky's work, Kindleberger and Aliber (2015) outline the different phases of a financial crisis in a model that accurately mirrors the way events evolved during the course of the two major financial crises of the present century (about the Minsky-Kindleberger connection in detail see Mehrling 2023): The first phase begins when profit expectations are fed by a promising development such as the liberalization and deregulation of financial markets, the lowering of key interest rates, a technological invention, a promising narrative such as the so-called *East Asian miracle*, financial innovations, or quantitative easing. As more and more business enterprises and individuals come to see the development as a chance to boost their profits, they begin to borrow so as to take advantage of the opportunity for gain. At this point the second phase sets in: a period of economic boom marked by the expansion of lending activities on credit markets. Demand for securities and other assets increases, causing market prices to rise. Profit margins improve, adding new impetus to the investment trend. The increase in financial investments continues to drive national income growth. This elicits positive feedback, fostering higher profit expectations and stimulating investment activity even further. And so the trend continues. Interest rates rise, obligations can be met more quickly, commodity prices increase, and the overall level of private debt climbs, causing a veritable state of euphoria: Investors buy assets in order to profit from the anticipated price increases. A follow-the-leader pattern emerges: "Investors rush to get on the train before it leaves the station and accelerates" (Kindleberger and Aliber 2005: 27). All this culminates in an asset bubble.

Eventually the cycle enters its third phase (see Fisher 1932): The economy begins to cool down, and profit expectations wane.[3] Investors become wary as uncertainty develops over the stability of economic expansion. When speculation begins to build over the likelihood of an economic downturn, financial players tend to sell more assets than they buy. Asset prices begin to drop as a result. The need to liquidate existing debts leads to the first round of so-called *fire sales* (the sale of assets well below their value). As investors struggle to procure cheap credit, their need for hard cash increases to meet ongoing obligations. In order to finance their investments, some heavily leveraged borrowers become overburdened with debt (through Ponzi finance). When falling prices prevent them from servicing existing loans, default eventually forces them into bankruptcy. As the economy continues to weaken, unemployment climbs and investors grow increasingly pessimistic about the prospects of business ventures. The downward trend may be interrupted by an occasional recovery period known as a bear market rally. During such sporadic episodes, real estate and stock prices bounce back temporarily before continuing to decline.

Finally, at some point, the fourth phase sets in: panic. During a downturn, it only takes one piece of bad news to trigger a panic—the announcement of a bank failure or a big name bankruptcy, for example, or a sharp fall in the price of certain securities. Sometimes just a few words by an influential person are enough to raise alarm. A famous example of a panic response on world markets was elicited in December 1996 by then Fed chair Alan Greenspan when he wondered during an after-dinner speech whether *irrational exuberance* on the part of investors might have led to an escalation of asset prices (Shiller 2000: 3). Although it was more of a side note in his speech, the remark was responsible for dramatic, albeit short-lived, losses on the stock markets in Tokyo, Hong Kong, London, New York, and Frankfurt. In such a situation, panic leads to the collapse of prices and an increase in bankruptcies. The liquidation of debts can no longer keep up with falling prices: "When a whole community is in a state of over-indebtedness, . . . the very act of liquidation may sometimes enlarge the real debts instead of reducing them" (Fisher 1932: 25). A vicious circle develops, forcing everyone to participate in asset sales since nearly all assets depreciate in value: "[M]ass liquidation defeats itself" (Fisher 1932: 26), causing last-minute panic. Kindleberger uses the German word *Torschlusspanik*, meaning last-minute panic over a closing door, to refer to the sense of urgency with which "investors crowd to get through the door before it slams shut" (Kindleberger and Aliber 2015: 33). What follows is a balance sheet recession of indeterminate duration. The crisis ends only when investors feel confident that asset prices cannot fall any lower, or when a lender of last resort—notably the central bank—convinces investors that sufficient liquidity is available to meet demands. As Minsky argues, however, the end of one crisis is the starting point for the gradual buildup of another. Once the economy begins to pick up, investors tend to forget past crises. They increasingly move from the relatively safe haven of hedge finance into speculative finance and then more and more in the direction of high-risk Ponzi finance. In Minsky's words: "Stability is destabilizing" (Minsky 1982b: 26).

Minsky's theory of financial instability deviates from the rationality thesis of neoclassical economics which holds that in the long term, investors will act rationally. He argues that the contrary is true, that the actions of financial market participants are often governed by irrational and emotional impulses, an observation that has since been backed by empirical evidence (Kindleberger and Aliber 2015). A similar conclusion about the impact of psychological factors has been reached in the field of behavioral finance, a very different area of study. The notion of irrational trading in financial markets, dubbed *irrational exuberance* after Greenspan's memorable remark (Shiller 2000: 3), has meanwhile gained traction in academic circles: "Behavioural economists have shown how even the most sophisticated and professional financial traders make illusory correlations, believe that unusual and unsustainable trends are likely to last indefinitely, and place too much emphasis on recent events" (Tickell 2003: 120). In other words, reactions to erroneous price forecasts can steer prices in the predicted direction: "[T]he price level is driven to a certain extent by a self-fulfilling prophecy based on similar hunches held by a vast cross section of large and small investors and reinforced by news media" (Shiller 2000: xv).

Optimism among financial players eventually turns into overconfidence with the result that risks and dependence on the effects of financial leverage are systematically underestimated: "Not only is stability an unattainable goal; whenever something approaching stability is achieved, destabilizing processes are set off" (Minsky 2008: 59). Minsky also called attention to the risk of excessive household and corporate debt. Already at the start of the twenty-first century some political economists were citing his arguments to warn that US household debt could not increase indefinitely (Bonner and Wiggin 2003). They saw the expansion of the subprime mortgage industry in the early 2000s as a gigantic Ponzi scheme. Many subprime borrowers were unable to meet their mortgage payments in a situation where mortgage protection was guaranteed only for as long as housing prices kept rising. And the fact that banks were passing on the risk of default to the financial markets signaled that they were only moderately interested in the creditworthiness of debtors (Wray 2008). In addition, an extension of the debt chain via securitization methods led to an increasingly illiquid financial system (Minsky 1982a: 174). Consequently, it was just a matter of time before the pyramid collapsed.

As Minsky predicted, the global financial crisis was followed by a recovery period: Many financial players and banks were rescued by means of state-financed bailouts. As central banks injected massive amounts of liquidity into the system through quantitative easing measures, confidence in the future development of prices began once again to grow. What followed was an unprecedented financial boom. Security prices surged to record highs and corporate and household debt rose sharply. The price development, however, was not accompanied by any robust growth in the global economy. Although the additional liquidity provided by the central banks did little to foster investments in the productive economy, on financial markets it led to asset price inflation of gigantic proportions. The slump that then followed with the COVID-19 pandemic was abrupt and radical. As central banks around the world reacted with immediate and massive intervention, however, it was only a matter of weeks before markets began to recover. Since then we have been witnessing the buildup of an even greater asset price bubble.

5.3 Financialization and the Liberal Global Order

Financial crises that have taken place over the past fifty years can be attributed to structural changes in the financial and economic system since the collapse of the Bretton Woods system, especially since the 1980s. The financial sector has been growing increasingly important, a process which is generally known as *financialization*. Financialization is a comprehensive notion that encompasses a wide range of regional and global socioeconomic developments including: the rise of the shareholder value principle as a defining feature of corporate governance; the growing dominance of Anglo-American investment banking and capital market institutions in relation to traditional loan-based banking; the steady increase in equity prices; capital reduction through share buybacks; rising dividend payouts; offshore operations; the emergence of new financial players; the rising power of financial elites; the liberalization of international capital flows; and the rapidly growing trade with ever more complex financial products (Martin 2002; Epstein 2005; Froud et al. 2006; Ertürk et al. 2008a; Van der Zwan 2014).

To a certain extent, the concept is a continuation of the discourse conducted during the 1980s and 1990s under the catchword *globalization*. The critical focus from the financialization angle, however, concentrates more on the world financial system and the logic of the financial market. It also covers the valorization and commodification of social areas and relationships that have not yet been transformed into commodities, and are therefore not yet subject to market forces or measurable in financial terms (Sassen 2009): "The bedrock of financial capitalism is not the spectacular system of speculation but something more mundane, that is, the constant searching out, or the construction of, new asset streams . . . , which then—and only then—allows speculation to take place" (Leyshon and Thrift 2007: 98).

The dynamics of financialization have made the global financial system more vulnerable and volatile in general, while in the process also increasing the vulnerability of other sectors of the economy. When, under the pressure of various political and economic interests, the Bretton Woods system collapsed in the early 1970s, exchange rates became unstable. To protect themselves from currency shifts, business enterprises had to resort to hedging strategies. In the years that followed, the US dollar lost half its value against the German mark and the Japanese yen. Owing to the high-interest rate policy adopted by the United States in the 1980s, the dollar began to recover, but without reaching its previous level. Around the same time, the currencies of many developing countries suffered sharp depreciation. And then, in the early 1990s, Europe experienced a wave of exchange rate fluctuations. Some currencies lost up to 30% of their value, especially against the German mark. In 1997, an even worse crisis emerged with the massive devaluation of currencies across the Asian tiger nations (Kindleberger and Aliber 2015). The situation led to greater fluctuations in oil prices and interest rates.

These structural changes favored the development of financial derivatives, which offered companies a certain degree of planning security. Derivatives are financial products whose value derives from other assets, indices, or interest rates. Through derivatives, investors speculate on an asset's appreciation or depreciation without actually owning the asset. Consequently, such investments are highly speculative. Options, futures, forwards, and swaps are among the best-known derivatives. In theory, however, there is no limit to the possibilities that exist for creating new variations. In his famous novel *Buddenbrooks*, Thomas Mann described speculation as practiced in a nineteenth-century setting with a type of derivatives resembling so-called forwards: the purchase of a crop at a predetermined price. Derivatives of this nature can be a wise investment for farmers who wish to protect themselves against possible crop price losses, or for traders seeking protection against future exchange rate fluctuations. Derivatives on the whole, however, are de facto betting transactions, for which reason they were long prohibited in former times by laws banning gambling in countries including the United Kingdom and the United States. Since the 1980s, however, bans have loosened, with the result that trading in derivatives has steadily expanded. In 1998, the nominal value of global derivative contracts stood at around 100 trillion US dollars. By 2007, it had already reached a level approaching one quadrillion US dollars (Stewart 2012: 300). According to the Bank for International Settlements, between 1998 and 2007, global markets in derivatives were growing at an annual rate of 25% (BIS 2007: 20).

In the 1990s, the US government under then President Bill Clinton had rejected various legislative initiatives to regulate or ban derivatives (Tett 2010: 23–25). In 1999, the Glass-Steagall Act was replaced by the Gramm-Leach-Bliley Act, which repealed the separate banking system, removing the barriers that divided bank deposit and lending operations from investment banking. By 1987, however, the Fed had already weakened the Glass-Steagall Act. A reinterpretation of the law in that year allowed banks to engage in mortgage-backed securities, commercial papers, and municipal bonds. The income from such transactions was not allowed to exceed 5% of the total turnover. In 1989, this limit was raised to 10%, and in 1997, to 25%. The Commodity Futures Modernization Act of 2000 stipulated that over-the-counter derivatives trading was no longer governed by the Commodity Exchange Act and was therefore no longer subject to the supervision of the US Treasury (Financial Crisis Inquiry Commission 2011: 48–50). Greenspan et al. (1999) argued at the time that regulation of derivatives was a barrier to innovation: "A cloud of legal uncertainty has hung over the OTC [over-the-counter] derivatives markets in the United States in recent years, which, if not addressed, could discourage innovation and growth of these important markets and damage U.S. leadership in these arenas by driving transactions off-shore."

Since that time, the prevailing model of growth around the world has been strongly led by finance. A distinction can be made here between debt-driven and export-driven strategies, the former being found primarily in Anglo-Saxon countries and the latter in countries such as China, Germany, and Japan (Boyer 2000; Stockhammer 2010). Up until the 1970s, the predominant model of growth was guided by the principles of Atlantic Fordism. Since then, there has been an increasing shift toward a finance-led accumulation regime (Boyer 2000; Aglietta 2000). The Fordist approach was based, among other things, on the idea that productivity rates could be increased by adopting an economies-of-scale strategy geared toward mass production. It held that this could be achieved by employing assembly line techniques and Taylorist organizational methods while raising real wages to enable increased consumption (a politically promoted ambition). During the 1970s, this growth regime fell into crisis. Industrialized countries have seen a variety of attempts to introduce new dynamics into the economy (under catchwords such as Toyotism, knowledge-based economy, technological innovation, information and communication technologies, to name just a few). Apart from giving impetus to a few sectors, however, these new trends have only moderately affected growth rates on the macroeconomic level (Boyer 2000; Wullweber 2010). Since the second half of the 1990s, the financial sector has come to play an increasingly important role for economic growth not only in the United States but also in countries such as the United Kingdom, Ireland, and Iceland. Nevertheless, there is a tendency to overlook the fact that the majority of small and medium-sized companies have remained largely unaffected by this process.

An estimated 30% of the total income in the United States belongs to only 1% of its wealthiest households (Fed 2023a). Against this background of burgeoning wealth, the median real income of the bottom 80% of the population has stagnated or fallen. At the same time, cutbacks continue to erode social benefits (Piketty and Saez 2003; Piketty 2014). In this situation, politicians have found themselves confronted by the problem of maintaining the overall level of social prosperity despite market-liberal economic policies.

The strategy to solve the problem, particularly in the United States, has involved integrating the working public into the financial market. Various reforms have accordingly been undertaken to facilitate access to financial markets, including deregulation of banking operations and securitization of the mortgage market. This has made household consumption more dependent on possibilities to obtain credit on a regular basis: "If wage austerity promotes higher profits, the surge of the stock market might be such that individuals perceive an improvement in their economic status, go to the bank and get credit to buy durable goods, cars and houses that they could not afford with direct wages. In other words, finance redesigns the various interests of workers" (Boyer 2013a: 7, 2013b: 99). The financing of expenses with private debt has become the motor of consumption in many countries, a development that has been referred to as *privatized Keynesianism* (Crouch 2009). The transition to private pension and retirement schemes from the welfare state pension system organized on a pay-as-you-go basis has generated a flood of capital in search of lucrative investment opportunities (Boyer 2013b: 96). Ertürk et al. (2008b: 27) speak of the *financialized masses*. This development is exemplified by the evolution of mutual funds in the United States.[4] In 1982, 6.2 million US citizens held investments in 340 mutual funds, for the most part, to finance their pensions. Already by 1998, this figure had risen to 119.8 million citizens and 3,513 funds (Shiller 2000: 35–36).

Whereas under Fordism mass consumption was based on wage increases, under the finance-led accumulation regime it is driven by the increase in private household borrowing and debt. As wage workers became more closely integrated into the financial market, they grew increasingly susceptible to Ponzi finance. They purchased houses they could not afford on their income in hopes of selling them later at a profit (Ertürk et al. 2008b: 27). This model of growth worked as long as prices for homes and shares continued to rise; in other words, as long as mounting debt was secured by increasing assets (Aglietta 2000: 153–55). Once the global financial crisis erupted, however, the post-Fordist compromise collapsed. There were warnings as early as 2000—by the economist Robert Boyer, for instance—that a growth regime of this nature was highly prone to crisis: "The more extended the impact of finance over corporate governance, household behavior, labor-market management and economic policy, the more likely is an equity-based regime to cross the zone of structural stability. The next act of the financial drama may well start on Wall Street!" (Boyer 2000: 142; see also Pettifor 2006).

Briefly put, in the years between the 1970s and the global financial crisis, the finance-led accumulation regime gained traction through a series of political decisions on how to resolve the problem of maintaining prosperity in the face of stagnating and falling real wages. This begs the question as to why the financial industry has become so important, and why it is able to assert its interests over those of other social actors. One explanation can be found in the industry's strong negotiating position and its powerful lobby. Bhagwati (1998: 10), a liberal economist, refers to the close institutional ties between Wall Street and the US Treasury Department as the "Wall Street Treasury complex." Another important factor is the *revolving door* practice, a situation involving career moves between politics and business, or between the financial industry and regulatory authorities (before Mario Draghi became president of the ECB, for example, he was employed by Goldman Sachs). This can lead to a phenomenon known as *regulatory capture*: "Regulatory capture occurs when bureaucrats, regulators and politicians cease to serve some notion of a wider collective public interest and begin to systematically favor specific vested interests, usually the very interests they were supposed to regulate and restrain for the wider public interest" (Baker 2010: 648, Baker 2015). Tsingou (2015) has introduced the notion of *club governance* in the sense of a transnational policy community separate from national politics that dominates the international regulation of the financial system in an autonomous capacity (see also Moschella and Tsingou 2013). According to Germain (2010), the strong influence of the financial industry is embedded in a neoliberal discourse that reaches around the globe. And the state clearly plays an active role in "designing, promoting, and guaranteeing the free and efficient operation of the market" (Cerny 2010: 128, 245–47). At the same time, however, various scholars have demonstrated that the financial industry is not a closed group with identical interests. Attempts have been made by some segments of this industry to divert regulatory efforts away from their own sector toward other areas (Helleiner and Pagliari 2011). Another explanation for the growth of the financial industry clearly lies in its creativity in developing new products. The evolution process is aided by the dynamic interplay between financial market regulations and financial innovations (Nesvetailova 2010). Regulatory authorities can hardly keep pace with the complex innovations. At the same time, there is a tendency among financiers to create many products specifically for the purpose of circumventing existing regulations. Back in the late 1990s, Shah (1997) dubbed this phenomenon *regulatory arbitrage*: "[T]here is an avoidance industry out there which is capable of undermining the spirit behind accounting regulations" (Shah 1997: 101). All in all, it can be said that the liberalization of the world financial system, combined with other structural developments since the 1970s, has created a breeding ground for financial vulnerability, thus greatly increasing the likelihood of future crises on a global scale.

5.4 Asset Markets and Rising Private Debt

Asset prices began to rise fairly soon after the collapse of financial markets in the autumn of 2008. The rally, however, was not a sign of well-functioning markets. And expanding asset value could not be attributed to factors such as improved economic productivity, higher living standards, growing business opportunities, or optimistic economic expectations in the years to come. On the contrary, prospects for economic recovery remained bleak. Conditions seemed far from favorable against a problematic background of political and economic developments including escalating trade wars, the ongoing eurozone crisis, fragmentation of the international community, a rising trend in inequality, the growing wave of right-wing populism, and heightened uncertainty in anticipation of the United Kingdom's exit from the European Union (Fed 2019a; IMF 2019a; Cihák and Sahay 2020).

Since the beginning of the COVID-19 pandemic, the situation has experienced a sharp deterioration. The global economy has suffered the worst recession since the Great Depression of 1929. Prospects of recovery remain uncertain. And yet, just a few weeks after the outbreak of the pandemic, financial players were once again seeking higher risks. Completely at odds with fundamental economic data, financial conditions, and historical norms, asset prices were already on the rise (BIS 2020a). The record inflow of capital in the market for junk bonds and other high risk financial products clearly shows that as early as April 2020, just a month after a financial crisis caused by the COVID-19 pandemic, financial players eager for higher returns had resumed their practice of investing in the higher risk sector (Henderson and Rennison 2020). By autumn of 2020, the indices of all major stock markets including S&P 500, Dow Jones, and the Dax had risen to record highs. A classic Minsky bubble had already formed anew.

How can this development be explained? The dynamics are complex and multidimensional. Nevertheless, various factors can be identified to provide plausible interpretations for this nearly complete decoupling of financial markets from basic economic principles. Against a backdrop of growing global inequality and uneven distribution of wealth both within and between countries, a small minority of private individuals have been amassing ever greater fortunes. At the same time, pension funds, money market funds, and other asset managers have been increasing steadily in number. These institutions and investment firms also need investment opportunities for their capital. As a result, they are constantly seeking relatively secure but at the same time profitable ways to put their money to work (Piketty 2014; Cihák and Sahay 2020). On the other hand, ever since the financial crisis, central banks have been striving to stabilize the financial system with massive amounts of funds, producing a flood of liquidity that now also needs to be invested. In a weakening global economy, money has been flowing into financial markets.

At the same time, in response to the financial crisis of 2007–9, the structures governing the global financial system are undergoing a radical and historically unprecedented transformation process. The world's leading central banks have meanwhile become the backbone of the emerging regulatory configuration (Mehrling 2017). The explanation for these developments and other far-reaching monetary policy measures lies in the failure on the part of governments in general to adopt more active fiscal policies (Arnold 2021). Instead of pursuing more formative economic policy, they have created legal frameworks based on the politics of austerity that have impeded expansionary fiscal action (Blyth 2013; Green and Lavery 2015; Konings 2016). Germany, for example, initiated the so-called debt brake to limit federal deficits. In the absence of fiscal policies capable of strengthening the economy and society, central banks have had to operate in an environment of weak economic and business activity. To encourage investment, but also to prevent a slide into deflation (or, in the case of Japan, to pull the economy out of deflation), they have introduced looser monetary policies (see chapter 8).

Liquidity has flooded the money market as a result. Central bank policies have boosted demand for government bonds. At the end of 2019, about 15 trillion dollars in bonds, including 7 trillion dollars in government bonds (30% of the outstanding stock), had produced negative yields (IMF 2019b; ECB 2020a). Corporate bond yields were also at a very low level (Fed 2019a: 11).

To generate higher returns, many financial market participants such as hedge funds, but also more cautious entities such as insurance companies and pension funds, invested in more highly leveraged and less liquid assets with higher risk profiles. As a result, those companies became more vulnerable. Some institutional investors such as fixed-income funds had invested in low-quality credit assets and had also decreased their financial liquidity buffer in the form of equity capital, for example. In a financial crisis such as the one caused by the COVID-19 pandemic or the earlier global financial crisis of 2007–9, investment strategies of this nature make it much harder to sell such assets. What complicates matters even further is the fact that in order to be able to pay interest on pension contributions and at the same time earn higher returns, retirement schemes, such as defined benefit pension funds, invest in long-term assets. This leads to even higher liquidity risks and greater volatility (IMF 2019b). The quality of credits in fixed-income fund investment portfolios has declined significantly over the past four years (IMF 2019b: 40).

In the years leading up to the two major crises, corporations from the nonfinancial private sector were able to finance themselves with cheap credit. This led to an overall increase in corporate debt. It was the loose monetary policies pursued by central banks that led them to adopt higher-risk business models. By the end of 2019, the corporate debt-to-GDP ratio was close to its all-time high (Fed 2019a). Moreover, half of all outstanding debts in the better quality classification—assets with an investment-grade rating—were classified in the lowest level on the investment-grade rating scale (triple B). This placed them in the least secure category. From 2018 to 2019, the total amount of short-term outstanding debts, which tend to be highly unstable, increased by 9% to almost 15 trillion dollars (Fed 2019a).

In short, already before the COVID-19 crisis, the volume of private debt had grown so large that for some firms (especially those financed through Ponzi schemes) repayment had become very difficult (IMF 2019b). Rising asset prices regularly go hand in hand with rising household and business debt. In times of crisis, when asset prices are elevated, their drop in value tends to be steeper. When asset prices fall, income falls, and the cost of debt service rises. Highly indebted households and businesses come under pressure. Faltering businesses need to reduce spending, and that, in turn, reduces the overall level of economic activity. Already by the end of 2019, corporations were facing a severely weakened profit outlook. Especially in the United States, loans had been used to finance special dividends for investors alongside expensive mergers or acquisitions (IMF 2019a).

When businesses encounter payment difficulties, financial players are also affected. They have to cut back on their credit lines at a time when credit is badly needed. Especially highly leveraged financial market participants lack the capital buffer they require to absorb losses. As a consequence, they are forced to cut lending and sell their assets well below their value at fire-sale prices. As the domino effect gains momentum, liquidity problems grow even more serious for the majority of corporations and financial firms, driving the cost of borrowing even higher. This is precisely what happened during the last two major financial crises. Adverse conditions such as these tend to result in heavy losses, ultimately forcing many firms into insolvency (Fed 2019a).

5.5 High Frequency Trading

The past two decades have witnessed an accelerating trend to enhance liquidity and profitability of securities through the algorithmization of trading and high frequency trading (HFT). Market making entities—which are central to the generation of liquidity in the financial markets and especially in the shadow banking system—rely heavily on computer algorithms to execute trading operations. Market making today is strictly speaking no longer in the hands of human beings. It is a task left mainly to computer programs based on algorithms. Similar to human traders, these digital market makers strive to buy securities at the lowest possible price in order to resell them at the highest attainable price, and thus to achieve the highest possible spread (profit margin). Simple algorithms, for instance, are designed to search financial markets for stocks whose value is quoted successively higher several times in a row, and to buy them in anticipation of a continuing increase in value. Other algorithms then sell those stocks on the expectation that the price will swing back to its original value. Algorithms also scan the financial market for historically correlated price patterns, e.g., between crude oil price increases and increases in the share price of oil firms, or vice versa. Since there is a frequent but asynchronous correlation between the two, fast computer programs can exploit the lag time (Adler 2012). Arbitrage opportunities can arise internally within a financial market as well as between different financial markets, or between the different prices of securities and their derivatives (e.g., stock index futures) (MacKenzie et al. 2012).

Many algorithmic computer programs are designed to execute high frequency trading. HFT involves placing and cancelling large quantities of transactions on the market in a rapid and continuous manner. Depending on prevailing market conditions, HFT can liquidate market positions so that none remain open at the end of the trading day. This has led to a narrowing of spreads in financial markets outside crisis periods (MacKenzie et al. 2012). As already mentioned, modern computing power enables frequency trading within a time frame of less than a millisecond (a thousandth of a second). At such a speed the direction of globalization tends to shift into reverse. In general, especially where financial markets are concerned, globalization is viewed as the diminishing importance of distance. In our current day and age, however, the importance of distance is increasing because of how fast computers have become. It definitely does make a difference today whether a computer program that executes buy and sell orders is situated in some outlying city, or at the New York Stock Exchange or the Chicago Board of Trade—in other words, directly at the hub of financial trading. Computers transfer trading data almost at the speed of light. Since 2011, it takes only about 4.2 to 5.2 milliseconds for information to travel from Chicago to New York via microwave relay towers. And that is significantly slower than the frequency of financial trading (Cookson 2013).[5] In this type of trading, even nanoseconds (a billionth of a second) can be crucial (Angel 2011). Reducing the time in which a trade is executed has now become an objective in the technology race (Adler 2012).

While at first glance it would seem that this could lead to an immense increase in market liquidity, Carruthers and Stinchcombe (1999: 353) argue that
one requirement of liquidity is that "everyone can know at all times what the
price is." In the case of HFT, however, this requirement is only partially guaranteed considering the clear information advantage enjoyed by traders with fast
computers in close proximity to financial markets. By the time other dealers see
the prices, they might already be outdated: "[T]raders at a large distance from
matching engines are permanently doomed to learn 'what the price is' much
more slowly than those who co-locate" (MacKenzie et al. 2012: 288). Financial
players are aware of these problems. As Natan Tiefenbrun, then commercial
director of one of Europe's leading electronic stock exchanges, puts it: "[W]e
have to abandon this idea that there is a universal truth for the best currently
available price" (Natan Tiefenbrun, quoted in MacKenzie 2012: 356).

In addition, financial markets have been experiencing anomalies for some
time now in ways that never occurred prior to the extensive computerization
and algorithmization of trading. Such anomalies involve sudden financial
market crashes with extreme price fluctuations that often stabilize and return
to normal by the end of the trading day. On the afternoon of 6 May 2010,
for example, the Dow Jones Index fell by 600 points within a span of just six
minutes, up to that point the sharpest fall in the index within a single day.
Twenty-three minutes later, the Dow Jones had made an almost complete recovery. Since then, similar events have been described as flash crashes. A study
conducted by the US Commodity Futures Trading Commission and the US
Securities and Exchange Commission (2010) concluded that the crash on 6
May was caused by the algorithm of *one* mutual fund. The only peculiarity was
the size of the trading order: 75,000 so-called E-Mini S&P contracts valued
at around 4.1 billion US dollars.[6] The dynamic interplay of feedback effects,
HFT programs, and investor behavior led to panic asset sales and triggered
a downward spiral in a reaction that has come to be known as the hot potato
effect (contracts changed hands more than 27,000 times between 2:45:13 and
2:45:27 p.m.—just 14 seconds!). When at 2:45:28 p.m. the Chicago Mercantile
Exchange halted trading for a mere five seconds, the market began to calm
down. Many automated programs shut down automatically at that point, and
to some extent trading had to be continued manually. Nevertheless, the downward spiral continued for 20 minutes and only came to a halt at 3:00 p.m. Altogether, 20,000 trading operations had been executed far below their average

starting price and were therefore retroactively reversed (Commodity Futures Trading Commission / Securities and Exchange Commission 2010).

Johnson et al. (2012) identified a total of around 18,500 events between 2006 and 2011 where strong price fluctuations, both up and down, occurred within very short time spans (less than 1.5 seconds). Over time, this averages out to one flash crash per day. And the trend is growing. Flash crashes appear to be the rule rather than the exception today: "[W]e are now in the age of the flash crash" (Oakley 2015). One of the most notorious examples of technology malfunction occurred in August 2012 when the staggering amount of 440 million US dollars was lost in only 40 minutes because of a faulty algorithm (Popper 2012). The potential for such critical fluctuations in stock prices and flash crashes expands when algorithmic programs interact with each other (MacKenzie 2014; US Department of the Treasury / Board of Governors of the Federal Reserve System; Federal Reserve Bank of New York; US Securities and Exchange Commission; US Commodity Futures Trading Commission 2015; IMF 2015; Terazono 2018). This clearly calls for a revision of the assumption that higher market liquidity means greater market stability.

Despite the speed bumps and risks associated with the use of algorithmic trading, the practice is nevertheless still growing rapidly, in no small part due to advances in the development of artificial intelligence and expanding cryptoasset markets. In 2018, for example, automated orders in the currency futures market in the United States constituted a share of 91% (Meyer 2019; Commodity Futures Trading Commission / Securities and Exchange Commission 2019). Algorithms have fundamentally altered the rhythm of markets, making their fluctuations more difficult to assess and anticipate. What is more, they are responsible for making markets more vulnerable to abrupt dislocations (Wigglesworth 2020a). As will be described in the next chapter, algorithmic and high frequency trading tends to intensify and exacerbate financial crises. After the COVID-19 crisis broke out in March 2020, a regulatory measure known as a circuit breaker was triggered on multiple occasions to curb panic sales. When prices drop to a certain level, this automatic emergency mechanism kicks in, enforcing the complete suspension of financial trading on one or more trading platforms such as the New York Stock Exchange in order to prevent algorithmic trading programs from disrupting markets to a far greater extent than would ordinarily happen without intervention.

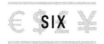

SIX

The Shadow Banking System and Free Market Capitalism

AFTER THE COLLAPSE of Lehman Brothers in September 2008, the Fed decided to embark on a historically unprecedented course. It created a variety of new facilities that gave nonbanks access to central bank money. For the first time ever, shadow banking institutions—large mutual funds, money market funds, broker-dealers, and asset managers—were able to tap into central bank funds through repo transactions. At first the facilities were only intended as temporary measures. But even before the COVID-19 crisis it was clear that without a central bank security structure it would no longer be possible to stabilize the shadow banking system—the market-liberal ideal of a free market. In September 2019, the repo market was hit by another crisis. As the interest rate for overnight repo transactions[1] rose to levels not seen since the global financial crisis, and the market threatened to collapse within a matter of days, the Fed was forced to reopen its repo facilities for regular banks and shadow banks. In this way, it created an extraordinary security structure for the shadow banking system. During the COVID-19 crisis, it once again became clear that these facilities play a major part in stabilizing the overall system (Pozsar 2014; Gabor and Vestergaard 2016; Ricks 2016; Murau 2017a; Wullweber 2021). But what is it about shadow banking entities that warrants such privileged access to central bank accounts?

With an estimated value of more than 235 trillion US dollars, the amount of securities traded annually in the shadow banking system accounts for nearly 50% of the worldwide volume of security trading. And the sector has been growing at an annual rate of around 6% to 9%, which is significantly faster than the traditional banking system, with more and more loans in the financial sector being granted by nonbank intermediaries (FSB 2022). At the same time, the two systems are closely intertwined (Aldasoro, Huang, and Kemp 2020). The Financial Stability Board defines the shadow banking system as "credit intermediation involving entities and activities (fully or partially) outside the regular banking system" (FSB 2013: ii). This definition serves as a first approximation but tends to obscure the role of traditional banks, which are important players in this field. In fact, the shadow banking system is deeply entangled with the banking system, which takes part in chains of collateral intermediation, "fragile repo funding, securities lending, derivatives trading, global liquidity creation and money market financing" (Moe 2014: 3–4). Highlighting the interplay between money and capital markets and the intermediation function, Mehrling et al. (2013: 2) define shadow banking as "money market funding of capital market lending," especially short-term funding for long-term capital market claims (see Figure 7). In addition, picking up on the discussion of money and money-like assets in chapter 4, the shadow banking system can also be characterized by the creation and distribution of money-like instruments.

The rising importance of the shadow banking system is also reflected in the general upward trend in nonbank lending and the resulting decline in the provision of funds by commercial banks (FSB 2017a, 2019; see also Hardie et al. 2013).[2] The United States continues to have the world's largest shadow banking

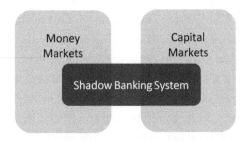

Figure 7 *The shadow banking system integrates money markets with capital markets. Wullweber 2020a.*

sector (about 40% of the global shadow banking system), followed by the euro area (which accounts for about 20%) (FSB 2017a: 48, 2021b). The main players are investment funds, broker-dealers (securities dealers), money market funds, pension funds, private equity companies, hedge funds, insurance companies, and special purpose entities (Pozsar 2014; FSB 2021b).

The shadow banking system is far less regulated than the banking system (FSB 2020a). Many policy recommendations for regulating the sector focus on ways to extend the existing regulatory perimeter for banks to include shadow banking entities. For the most part, however, such recommendations fail to grasp the role that the state and central banks play in maintaining, stabilizing, and also expanding that very system. Countries such as the United States and France but also a number of European institutions have actively supported the expansion of the shadow banking system. It should be mentioned in this connection that in contrast to the *bank-based* credit system, the shadow banking system is a *market-based* credit system (grounded in capital and money markets). In this market-based system, deposit money is not created in the act of lending as it is in the bank-based system. Shadow bank lending involves the intermediation of funds and securities via the market. Accordingly, unlike banks, market makers in the shadow system are, in effect, financial intermediaries. Through market makers, the money market becomes integrated with the capital market by financing capital market-based loans via the money market.

In the shadow banking system it is the diversity of short-term debt instruments that makes it possible to finance investment portfolios (Ricks 2016: ix). The process involves merging assets with different maturities and risk profiles (vulnerabilities): "[I]f non-bank financing is involved in bank-like activities, transforming maturity/liquidity and creating leverage like banks, it can become a source of systemic risk, both directly and through its interconnectedness with the banking system" (FSB 2017a: 5; for the historical background, see Thiemann 2018).

6.1 Repurchase Agreements (Repos)

For many financial players in today's world, the shadow banking system is a vitally important source of comparatively low-cost liquidity from entities that are subject to significantly fewer legal restrictions than in the bank-based credit system (BIS 2017). Repurchase agreements, often with a single-day maturity (called overnight repos), are the most common route to short-term liquidity. Repos are contracts to sell securities at a fixed price in order to repurchase the same securities after a set period at an agreed price plus interest. The buyer assumes legal ownership of the securities along with resale rights (a process called rehypothecation) (Singh 2017).[3] If the repo seller files for bankruptcy without buying back the securities in question, the lender has the right to sell them on the market. The securities therefore serve as collateral (see Figure 8). Technically speaking, repos are secured loans. Repo systems as a means to secure credit already existed in the nineteenth century, although at that time they were much less complex than they are today (Mehrling 2011; Gabor 2023). The Fed has been conducting repo transactions since 1917 (Bundesbank 2013: 63).

Although the asset that serves as collateral for the repo formally belongs to the creditor, the borrower continues to receive the interest accrued over the term of the repurchase agreement. This means that there is a separation between legal ownership and economic exploitation rights. As a risk control measure, one party, usually the borrower, has to pay an extra charge on the asset. This risk discount on the value of the asset is known as a *haircut*. For the sake of illustration, let us assume that to obtain a loan, an investment company concludes a repo agreement with a central bank to sell the bank a government bond with a nominal value of 100 euros. As borrower, the investment company only receives 90 euros (minus a 10% haircut in this case). The haircut is intended to ensure that if the lender defaults, the asset will still sell without loss even if its underlying market value falls. Government bonds, especially those of major

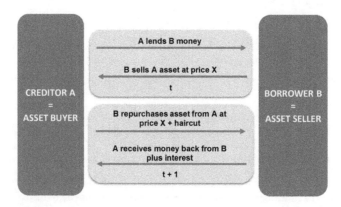

Figure 8 *Stylized repo transaction.*

industrialized countries and the euro zone, tend to have the lowest haircuts and interest rates because they are considered to be very safe and stable and therefore have less frequent margin calls (Golec and Perotti 2017).[4] The availability of government bonds is therefore crucial for repo transactions: "[H]igh-quality sovereign securities retain their liquidity in all but the most extreme circumstances" (Bank of England 2015: 6). The value of most other securities is more volatile, which is why they require higher haircuts. Repo transactions are considered to offer lenders a high level of security as a result of such privately organized protection mechanisms. Because repos promise to trade at par on demand, they are also referred to as shadow money (Pozsar 2014). Accordingly, referring back to the credit pyramid in chapter 4, repos (shadow money) directly follow quasi-money (deposits) in the credit hierarchy (see Figure 9).

If the value of the securities used as collateral for repo transactions falls, the borrower has to pledge additional collateral or take out more expensive bank loans. That leads to lower profit margins, which, in turn, results in a decrease in capital market trading. Accordingly, the availability of safe government bonds also has a direct impact on the price of other assets. Because the price of the repo transaction is based on the quality of the collateral, interest rates differ widely, depending on whether the repo is backed by government bonds or some other type of collateral. Moreover, the collateral is priced *mark-to-market* so as to protect the lender even in the event of a major loss in value. Mark-to-market means that the value of an asset or a financial product is not estimated and set at a particular point in time, but is rather adjusted on a day-to-day basis to

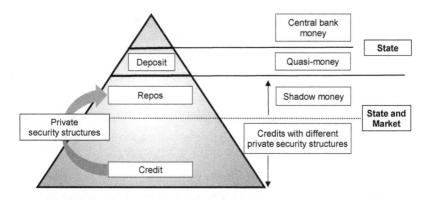

Figure 9 *Shadow money (repos) and the credit pyramid.*

reflect the market price. This, however, makes the securities considerably more susceptible to market fluctuations. In the event of a loss or gain in value, both parties are entitled to a so-called margin call that allows them to demand additional collateral (if the value falls) or additional funds (if the value increases). The cost of the repo transaction is largely determined by the amount of the haircut and the quality of the collateral (Stigum and Crescenzi 2007: 533–35; BIS 2017).

Repo transactions bring together financial players with different interests. Entities such as money market funds, asset managers, and other institutional investors or companies strive to invest their capital at a relatively low risk, which is why government bonds are preferably used as collateral: "A novel insight comes from the recognition of a fundamental demand for safety, distinct from liquidity and money demand" (Golec and Perotti 2017: 3; Bank of England 2015). At the same time, repos are highly flexible. They can usually be restructured or even extended on a day-to-day basis. On the other hand, banks, hedge funds, and other financial market participants use repos to absorb shortfalls in capital reserves, not least in hopes of making a short-term profit on the investment. Repo transactions therefore bring together market participants, who need safe but flexible and profitable investment options, and risk seekers, who use the capital to finance further financial transactions by short selling, hedging, or even reselling the collateral with the aim of generating profit: "Collateral in repos creates conditions for aggressive risk taking in a world of finance where the elusive boundary between risk *protection* and risk *production* becomes increasingly blurred" (Gabor 2016a: 972, emphasis added).

Besides giving market participants access to relatively low-cost funds, and unlike debt instruments such as secured loans, the securities used to collateralize repos can be resold. This makes them highly flexible, which also explains why the practice of reselling repos is widely seen as a positive strategy: "The re-hypothecation . . . and the re-use of collateral increase the availability of collateral, reduce the cost of using collateral, and consequently reduce transaction and liquidity costs. They also support the general functioning of markets, particularly clearing and settlement processes which rely on collateral" (FSB 2017b: 3).[5]

The reuse of collateral allows market participants to hold less collateral of their own, thereby reducing balance sheet costs. Repo transactions are growing in importance not only for economic reasons but also because of regulatory developments. The Basel III Agreement, which came into force in 2014, introduced a number of minimum safeguard requirements that can also be met with repo transactions (FSB 2017b: 3). As the Bank for International Settlements has stated: "By improving the ability of investors to settle trades and meet margin requirements, repos support the smooth functioning of derivatives markets and contribute to the resilience of the financial system and the real economy" (BIS 2017: 6). Repo transactions, according to this interpretation, stabilize the financial system because the mark-to-market valuation method forces market participants to keep a close eye on the market and to continuously factor risk into the management of their investments. In like manner, the Financial Stability Board concludes: "[R]e-hypothecation and re-use of collateral support the flow of collateral as well as funding liquidity, and therefore help to bring liquidity to where it is most needed" (FSB 2017b: 4).

The logic of financial intermediation in the shadow banking system stands in stark contrast to traditional bank lending practices. Whereas in the traditional banking system long-term loans are financed through short-term liabilities, in the shadow banking system short-term debt instruments are offset with long-term liabilities. For this reason, Pozsar and Singh (2011) speak of a "reverse maturity transformation." At the same time there is also a liquidity transformation: Nonliquid assets are rendered tradable through the practice of securitization. It is through this complex hedging system that shadow money and pseudo-safe assets are generated. This explains why maturity shifting has developed in the shadow banking system. And the combined dynamics of maturity diversification, different risk dispositions, and the practice of reusing the same securities to hedge risks have led to an overall risk transformation that is leaving the entire system increasingly susceptible to crises (Nesvetailova 2015; Bryan, Rafferty, and Wigan 2016).

6.2 Shadow Dealers

Repos can be transacted directly between two parties. As a rule, however, transactions are arranged through an agent—a broker-dealer who buys securities from one party (such as an investment manager, a pension fund, a hedge fund, or an insurance company) in order to sell them to another party (a money market fund or a central bank, for example). Broker-dealers may also trade for their own account (BIS 2017: 5–6). The repo market would not be able to function in the shadow banking system without these so-called shadow dealers (Pozsar 2014). For that reason they are also called market makers. New and systemically important players have been emerging because of the key role played by intermediaries in the repo market, which is such a critical part of the financial system (Gabor and Ban 2016: 617–18). Lehman Brothers is a good example. Before Lehman collapsed, it was one of the most important intermediaries in the shadow banking system. The firm's September 2008 breakdown was the trigger that led to the global financial crisis.

Intermediaries are clearinghouses, investment funds, and big banks such as JPMorgan, Morgan Stanley, and Goldman Sachs. While intermediation is relatively uninteresting in the traditional loan-based banking system, where, as explained earlier, most loans are provided by way of money creation, it is central to the shadow banking system. When asset owners (such as investment funds, asset managers, and pension funds) seek temporary investment opportunities for segments of their securities inventory, intermediaries make them an offer and buy up the securities at an agreed price via repo transactions. To protect the investment, the intermediaries employ mark-to-marking methods and haircuts. Then, through reverse repo transactions, they resell those very same securities (at a profit) to money market funds, while striving to keep an equal balance between repo and reverse repo positions. This is only possible in theory, however. Often referred to as matched-book trading, the practice is supposed to prevent risk exposure on the assumption that liabilities will be completely offset by assets. So *theoretically speaking* (!) matched-book traders do not need to maintain any capital and liquidity reserves (Mehrling et al. 2013). Briefly stated, financial intermediaries mediate between lenders who seek safe investment opportunities for their excess liquidity, and wealth managers, hedge funds, banks or other players who cover their liquidity needs by providing securities (see Figure 10).[6]

If necessary, banks can provide intermediaries with credit lines to bridge liquidity shortages. As a rule they do so in the form of repo transactions in which the traded securities serve as collateral. This increases need for liquidity reserves on the part of the banks. In such cases, central banks would only assume a background function. If need be, they support the granting of credit by facilitating access to financing though the expansion of balance sheet operations: "[M]arket liquidity is sustained every day because funding liquidity is elastically forthcoming in this way" (Mehrling 2011: 104). However, in today's

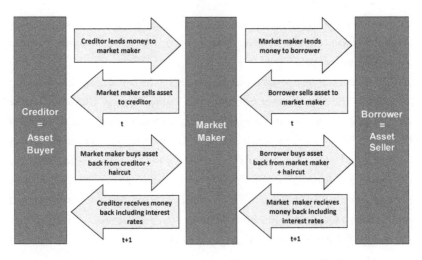

Figure 10 *Stylized repo transaction with market makers. Wullweber 2020a.*

ample reserve environment, the constraint on reserves is limited (Ihrig, Senyuz, and Weinbach 2020).

Intermediaries in the shadow banking system take on a role similar to commercial banks in the *loan-based* banking system. The decisive difference lies in the financing of intermediation and the lack of state guarantees and regulation (Ricks 2016). When a bank issues a loan or transfers money to another bank, it can create the necessary funds on its own. These options are not available to intermediaries.[7] Consequently, they have to avail themselves of other funding mechanisms and protection schemes.

6.3 The Shadow Banking System: A Perennial Trouble Spot

Repos qualify as money equivalents because, like money, they represent a promise to trade at par on demand without any loss in value. The key question here is: What kind of mechanism guarantees this promise? When times are good, repos are often held to be as safe and as liquid as money. When a financial crisis hits, however, the assets used as collateral for repos can suddenly lose their liquidity and their value. For bank credits there are special safety net structures by which the state guarantees convertibility on demand with central bank money. For repos, convertibility is guaranteed through a variety of private mechanisms and different types of collateral. This private simulation of the state protection scheme, however, only functions in noncrisis times (Gorton 2017; Wullweber 2021).

In the traditional loan-based credit system, banks take on the risk of default on a loan in the event that the borrower files for bankruptcy. They also face the risk of liquidity shortage in the event of mass withdrawals from bank accounts (Bank of England 2015: 4). While risk posed by insolvency is covered by deposit insurance and equity, liquidity risk is covered by the marginal lending facilities administered by central banks. Regular banks, which are solvent in principle, are also protected in the event of a financial crisis by their country's national central bank as lender of last resort. Through state regulations and institutions, the traditional banking system therefore enjoys a comprehensive measure of protection against systemic risks.

In the shadow banking system, the risk factors are of a somewhat different nature. In line with laissez-faire rationality, risk management is provided through a privately organized security structure. Collateral used to back repo transactions serves the same function as deposit insurance for bank accounts (deposits). Both provide protection in the event of default. The important difference, however, is that unlike in the case of collateral, deposit insurance is ultimately guaranteed by the state (Ricks 2016). In the shadow banking system, rather than operating with book credit, financial institutions hold securitized loans that are protected by interest rate swaps and currency swap transactions.[8] In other words, credit in the shadow banking system is financed not through creation of bank deposits, i.e., the state-authorized procedure whereby banks generate quasi-money, but rather through the (market-based) money market. Unlike banks, shadow banks cannot create quasi-money (deposits). Consequently, there is no balance sheet expansion when credit is issued. Insolvency risks are hardly ever buffered by cash reserves (equity capital). Instruments such as credit default swaps are rather used as protection against the risk of insolvency. Liquidity risk, on the other hand, is buffered by repo transactions that are collateralized by securities (Mehrling 2011: 118; see Table 3).

In noncrisis times the difference is insignificant, especially since the value of the collateral that underlies repos is market-based. It is subject to continual adjustment so as to reflect fluctuating prices and therefore represents a promise to pay at par value. In this respect, collateral in the market-based credit system simulates the idea of state guarantee in the traditional loan-based banking

Table 3 *Comparison of protection as provided by traditional banks and shadow banks (before central banks established their new security structures).*

	Insolvency risk	Liquidity risk	Total risk
Commercial banks (loan-based credit system)	Buffered by deposit insurance provided by the state and equity capital	Central bank marginal lending facility (discount window)	Protected by the state through statutory guarantee schemes
Shadow dealers/ market makers (market-based credit system)	Various types of securities and swaps e.g. interest rate swaps, FX swaps and credit default swaps (CDS)	Repo transactions based on securitized loans	No state protection; private securities simulate government protection

system. The difference can be crucial, however, if crisis hits and no buyers can be found for the securities that serve as collateral, or if the securities have to be sold well below the regular market price.

Before the 2007–9 global financial crisis safeguards such as state deposit insurance, marginal lending facilities (deposit windows) and the central bank function as lender of last resort had greatly decreased the risk of bank runs in the loan-based credit system. No such protection mechanisms existed for the shadow banking system, however. When the crisis took hold, the only alternative the Fed saw to stop the "run on repos" (Gorton and Metrick 2012) was to launch a variety of ad hoc facilities and thereby to create a security structure for the shadow banking system as well (see chapter 8.4). The decision was based on the reasoning that the shadow banking system, like the traditional banking system, also requires government protection. Accordingly, the decisive difference in terms of overall risk between the traditional loan-based banking system and the capital market-based shadow banking system is that until the global financial crisis, the shadow banking system had no (direct) state statutory protection and no access to central bank money (Mehrling 2011: 116–19).

In times of noncrisis, and particularly during a bull market, it becomes easy to (re)sell the majority of securities that are used as collateral in the shadow banking system. The market liquidity of those securities generally depends on the willingness and ability of traders to buy and resell them. And this depends on their access to the money market. Without a repo market, market makers would have to rely on their own capital or take out a bank loan to finance their trading activities. In this sense, market liquidity depends on *financial liquidity* (Brunnermeier and Pedersen 2009). Nowadays, securities traders finance their operations primarily through repos. They avoid borrowing money from commercial banks whenever possible and resort to bank loans only in the case of emergency. Central banks support this shadow dealer system both directly via repo transactions and indirectly as lenders of last resort for the banking system. In noncrisis times, repos therefore increase the liquidity of the entire system.

Securities that are accepted as collateral by a central bank have the highest degree of market liquidity because they can be passed on directly to the central bank from the financial intermediary through a commercial bank by means of repo transactions (Gabor 2016a). The liquidity of other securities at any given moment depends much more on the actual market situation. Other securities are also used as collateral, but mark-to-market practices make them significantly more sensitive to haircuts because of market fluctuations. The possible amount of repo transactions is limited by the market value of the securities that serve as collateral. When the *market liquidity* of securities decreases, they become more expensive to use as collateral for repo transactions (owing to higher haircuts). This causes *financial liquidity* to decline. That, in turn, leads to an overall decline in the volume of repo transactions. Financial players may then be forced to sell such securities, accelerating the downward price spiral. As the downturn affects more and more financial players, a financial crisis can occur (Adrian et al. 2017; FSB 2017b).

During an economic boom with an expanding financial market, there is a rise in the need for collateral. Since the market for government bonds is limited, traders increasingly turn to securities with higher liquidity risks. Such securities, although less expensive, must be hedged via swap transactions. This is because it is generally assumed that the price of a risk-free security (e.g., a US government bond) is equal to the price of a higher risk security plus the cost of risk insurance, interest rate swaps, and foreign exchange swaps (Mehrling et al. 2013: 6–7). Hedging of this form generates pseudo-safe assets that in times of prosperity are as liquid as government bonds that are deemed safe investments.[9] Since they are cheaper, however, and since the need for collateral during a bull market cannot be met by existing government bonds, their share of the overall volume of traded securities increases sharply (Golec and Perotti 2017: 4).[10] Before the COVID-19 crisis began, mutual funds, for example, tripled their holdings in US corporate bonds (Fed 2019a: 38). To put these numbers into perspective: In 2019, mutual funds held one-sixth of all outstanding corporate bonds and acquired one-fifth of all newly issued corporate bonds (Fed 2019a).

Repos make a well-functioning financial system more liquid by increasing the possibility of converting securities into cash. At the same time, however, repos tend to encourage highly leveraged financial practices and short-term re-financing. A few weeks before the financial crisis of 2007–9, and shortly before the COVID-19 crisis, there was a considerable rise in repo transactions. Some market participants were able to significantly raise their debt level using short-term refinancing to increase their leverage. Strategies of this nature collapse, however, as soon as profit expectations start to dwindle. Since repo transactions are generally contracts with short-term to very short-term maturities, borrowers are exposed to increased liquidity risk. At the same time, the underlying col-lateral is valued on a mark-to-market basis, making the price of repos subject to procyclical developments (FSB 2017a: 27). Moreover, because collateral for repos has no government guarantee, the repo market is intrinsically unstable (BIS 2018).

This notwithstanding, regulators have meanwhile accepted the fact that for liquidity generation the shadow banking system has come to play a central role in the financial system. Directly after the financial crisis, the Financial Stabil-ity Board and the Bank for International Settlements were still talking about reducing the size of the shadow banking sector. Since then, however, those very same institutions have come to propose the transformation of the sector into a resilient system (FSB 2015, 2017b; BIS 2019a).They have also chosen to system-atically replace the term *shadow banking* with the phrase *nonbank financial in-termediation activity* in an effort to lift the system's status "out of the shadows" into a more reputable sounding domain (FSB 2019; to retrace this development, see Engelen 2018).

6.4 Market Liberalism and International Politics

The past twenty-five years have witnessed the steady growth of the global shadow banking system, and not just because of developments in financial markets. To better understand why and how this happened, it is necessary to examine the phenomenon against the background of global developments (for a more detailed discussion of the factors involved, see chapter 5). Increas-

ing financialization has greatly widened wealth inequalities within and between countries (Adkins, Cooper, and Konings 2019; Fed 2023a). Economies
are faced with slow growth as a consequence of the concentration of excessive
wealth in the hands of a very small part of the population and a rising share of
corporate profits in relation to wage increases. This situation, complicated by
the tendency on the part of governments to shy away from strong fiscal policies
that stimulate the economy, has led to an incredibly large amount of money in
search of profit on the financial markets. The shadow banking system is supposed to overcome this paradox (Pozsar 2014).

The term *shadow banking* suggests a part of the financial system that lies
outside the purview and influence of the state. This, however, is a misleading
notion. It ignores the fact that some countries and international institutions
have actively promoted the expansion of the market-based credit system. As a
result of the separation of monetary and fiscal policy and politically enforced
central bank independence in Western states, central banks no longer guaranteed the purchase of government bonds. Consequently, bonds had to be placed
on the financial market. A situation developed in which nations stood in competition with one another over the purchase of government bonds. This is particularly the case in the euro area where member states share a common currency
but issue their own government bonds individually. Since the shadow banking
system relies on government bonds to secure lending activities, the expansion
of the market-based credit system has been very beneficial for the issuance of
government bonds (ECB 2017). This is why European institutions, led by the
European Commission and the ECB, became the driving force behind the
expansion of a European repo market that is modeled after the US repo market
(Gabor 2016a; Braun 2018).[11] The European repo market has meanwhile grown
to a size that now even surpasses that of the United States, followed by the
repo markets of Japan and the United Kingdom.[12] The strategy to strengthen
the repo market was based on the hope that it would foster a network of in-
terconnections within the various security markets in the single currency area.
Policy-makers expected that this would facilitate ECB operations and make it
easier for the ECB to communicate its decisions on monetary policy (Braun
and Hübner 2018). The idea was that an integrated European financial market
would be more receptive to ECB interest rate decisions, which, in turn, would
make it more effective than a market fragmented into national jurisdictions. In
line with this reasoning, the ECB has come to regard repo transactions as the

most important tool for implementing monetary policy decisions (ECB 2015c). What is more, the volume of repurchase agreements concluded by the ECB on a daily basis has a direct bearing on the availability of central bank money.[13] In 2002, Directive 2002/47/EC of the European Parliament and of the Council of the European Union on financial collateral came into force, creating a legal framework to simplify cross-border trading in repos with the expectation that the measure would "increase the efficiency of the cross-border operations . . . necessary for the implementation of the common monetary policy" and "balance the overall amount of liquidity in the market among themselves, by cross-border transactions backed by collateral" (European Parliament; European Council 2002). In other words, the consolidation and expansion of the European repo market involved the effort to establish an internal financial market alongside the internal European market for goods, persons, and services, where it was possible for financial players to engage not only in the unimpeded cross-border transfer of foreign currencies but also of securities.

Until 2010, when the euro crisis erupted in the wake of the global financial crisis, sovereign bonds issued by all euro area Member States were accepted by the ECB as collateral for repo transactions under the same conditions. The idea was to strengthen the Europeanization of national sovereign bonds. When the euro was adopted as the common European currency, German government bonds were regarded as secure, while almost all other euro area sovereign bonds had poorer ratings. For this reason, the policy was also intended to prevent German bonds from becoming the euro area's safe haven collateral: "Having left behind the threat of a de facto deutsche mark zone, governments worried that the Euro government bond market would become a German bund zone" (Gabor and Ban 2016: 624). To counteract this development, the ECB and major European commercial banks undertook a joint effort to encourage repo basket transactions comprising government bonds from a variety of euro area countries. Commercial banks saw this approach as a solution to the dilemma they faced from countries such as Germany, which prior to the outbreak of the COVID-19 pandemic had been on a course of fiscal restraint and debt reduction, and accordingly were not issuing enough new government bonds that were needed as collateral for the repo market. The situation was potentially aggravated by the Stability and Growth Pact, with its regulatory ceilings on budget deficit and public debt in EU countries (Gabor and Ban 2016).[14] An integrated European securities market made it possible, in effect, to use low-rated government bonds under the same financing conditions as euro area government bonds with higher ratings.[15] During the financial crisis of 2007–9, however, the fragility of the European single financial market became evident. After the onset of the crisis and the resulting euro crisis that started in 2011, the policy changed. The government bonds of countries in the euro area once again became subject to differentiated ratings, with the consequence that particularly those with higher ratings were used as collateral in repo transactions (Pozsar 2014).

Briefly stated, there are three main reasons for the growing importance of the repo market in the shadow banking system. First of all, it offers private-sector market participants a high degree of flexibility and a large variety of investment and financing options. Second, because there is a high demand among private players for assets that are suitable as collateral for repo transactions, governments can place their state bonds on the financial market under favorable terms, albeit at the same time in competition with one another. Third, central banks use the repo market as a monetary policy transmission channel. For private-sector market participants, the repo market is simply a profitable and flexible opportunity for financing and investing. For state institutions, it offers a venue to place government bonds in competition with other sovereign bonds and serves as a vehicle to pursue monetary policy. This leads, among other things, to the development of a market-oriented monetary policy that relies on measures such as regular auctions and market-based rating methods. Such practices tend to elevate the vulnerability of the financial system. In this situation, certain private-sector participants—intermediaries in particular—are becoming more and more important.

SEVEN

A Never-Ending Crisis

The Global Financial System in the Twenty-First Century

THE SHADOW BANKING SYSTEM IS central to understanding both the 2007–9 financial crisis and the financial crisis caused by the COVID-19 pandemic. Its vulnerability to crisis also plays a key role in the approach taken here to the two largest financial and economic crises that have occurred thus far in the twenty-first century.[1]

7.1 The 2007–2009 Global Financial Crisis

From 2007 to 2009, the global financial system experienced the worst crisis the world has seen since the late 1920s. Economies everywhere suffered dramatic consequences. The crisis triggered the harshest global recession since World War II, and eventually led to the European debt crisis. In the years leading up to these crises, hardly anyone realized how precarious the global economy had grown, or how close the world's financial system had come to total collapse. On the contrary, it was a widely held view among financial experts that the global financial system was experiencing a phase of stability—a long-term period of low volatility commonly referred to as the Great Moderation (Bernanke 2004): "The predominant assumption behind financial market regulation—in the USA, the UK and increasingly across the world—has been that financial markets are capable of being both efficient and rational . . . and that the overall level of prices as a result has a strong tendency towards a rational equilibrium" (Financial Services Authority 2009: 39; Galí and Gambetti 2009). This reasoning was based on the expectation that a sophisticated system of mutual private security mechanisms would effectively preclude any likelihood of a major financial breakdown. In line with this reasoning, central bank policy focused mainly on adjusting interest rates to control the money supply so as to conform to fluctuations in the economy. The security structures discussed in chapter 4 had not yet been adapted to the increasing complexity of the financial system. That only happened in the wake of the financial crisis of 2007–9.

This begs the question as to why financial experts were so impervious to even considering the possibility of crisis. During a discussion with leading economists at the London School of Economics, Queen Elizabeth II captured the essence of the matter with her widely quoted question: "If these things were so large, how come everyone missed them?" (Beattie 2008). The response of the economists was unequivocal: "The failure to foresee the timing, extent and severity of the crisis and to head it off, while it had many causes, was principally *a failure of the collective imagination* of many bright people" (Besley and Hennessy 2009: 2, emphasis added). And further: "The difficulty was seeing the risk to *the system as a whole* rather than to any specific financial instrument or loan" (Besley and Hennessy 2009: 1, emphasis added). What this means is that the meltdown caught the financial community by surprise not least because the field of economics has only recently, and very hesitantly, begun to embrace the idea that the dynamics of financial markets cannot be understood solely from a microeconomic perspective, that financial markets are not inherently stable, that instability is not just the result of external disruptive factors, that reflexive and emotional dynamics are the norm, and that in the analysis of global economic processes, it is essential to consider political factors (Baker 2017; Thiemann 2019a; Wullweber 2019d).

Housing prices in the United States stagnated in mid-2006, and then soon began to fall. Since the preceding decades had seen a steady rise in US real estate prices, the downturn came as a surprise to many. Early in 2006, foreclosure rates, and loan delinquency rates, i.e., the percentage of borrowers missing two or more consecutive payments over a twelve-month period, were both at their lowest levels since 1979, when the Mortgage Bankers Association began recording mortgage data. During the second half of 2006, however, mortgage delinquency rates saw a dramatic increase, doubling from 5% to 10%. By March 2007, the rate had risen to 13%, and by June to almost 20%, quadrupling the figure within the span of a year (IOSCO Technical Committee 2008). In March 2007, the rate of foreclosures reached its highest level since the beginning of recordkeeping in 1970. Particularly problematic were the subprime loans that were granted in 2005 and 2006. As a result of payment defaults, many small and medium-sized subprime lenders had to close or sell their operations to other institutions such as Morgan Stanley, Merrill Lynch, Citigroup, Barclays, and the Deutsche Bank. Large mortgage lenders such as Residential Capital Corporation, a subsidiary of the automotive manufacturer General Motors, also ran into financial difficulty and had to spend almost a billion US dollars to cover losses from subprime loans. In May 2007, subprime loans estimated at a value of 100 billion dollars were declared bad debts with little likelihood of being paid. Rating agencies then began downgrading loans that had previously received top ratings. As the year progressed, serious problems forced the liquidation of a number of hedge funds and special purpose entities that, as outsourced subsidiaries, had taken over the high-risk lending business for banks not only in the United States but also in countries such as the United Kingdom, Germany, the Netherlands, and Australia. The Swiss bank UBS closed a hedge fund after losing 120 million US dollars from investments in subprime loans (Kindleberger and Aliber 2015; Tooze 2018).

In August 2007, global financial markets were hit by a credit crunch (Nesvetailova 2010: 29). France's largest bank, BNP Paribas, announced that three of its mutual funds had run into difficulties and investors could no longer withdraw money from those funds. Around the world, the news caused stock prices to plummet. More and more credit and financial institutions found it hard to refinance existing loans. Because no one was aware of exactly who had what amount of bad loans on their books, commercial banks began to issue only short-term high-interest credit: "Investors are scrambling to discover which banks, hedge funds or public companies are holding potentially hundreds of billions of dollars in bad loans and subprime-related mortgage securities that are imploding" (Creswell 2007). In Germany, one important financing bank that folded because of massive losses in derivatives trading was the IKB Deutsche Industriebank, a specialist in lending to medium-sized enterprises that belonged in large part (38%) to the public development bank KfW (Credit Institute for Reconstruction). As the crisis escalated, other German banks began to falter. Among those that either applied for federal aid or petitioned for bankruptcy were the federal state-owned banks (*Landesbanken*) Sachsen LB (Saxony), BayernLB (Bavaria), LBBW (Baden-Wuerttemberg), and HSH Nordbank (majority-owned by the federal states of Hamburg and Schleswig-Holstein) but also private banks such as Hypo Real Estate Holding and Commerzbank (Financial Crisis Inquiry Commission 2011; see Scherrer 2017 for a detailed background of public sector finance).

The ECB, the Fed, and the central banks of Japan, Canada, and Australia granted emergency loans at very low interest rates in an attempt to alleviate the financial market credit crunch (Bajaj and Landler 2007). Major central banks also lowered key interest rates and concluded currency exchange agreements with the Fed (Panitch and Gindin 2014: 385). Massive central bank interventions, however, failed to stabilize the money market. Commercial banks lost their mutual trust and largely refrained from extending each other credit. Then, in August 2007, it was announced that Northern Rock, one of the largest savings and mortgage banks in the UK, was experiencing a severe liquidity shortage, whereupon its customers attempted to withdraw their savings, triggering the first bank run in the UK since Black Friday in 1866. Northern Rock eventually went bankrupt and wound up being nationalized (Nesvetailova 2010: 30–32).

In October 2007, Merrill Lynch announced the largest quarterly loss in the history of Wall Street (up to that point). In the very next quarter, that record was surpassed by Citigroup with a loss of nearly 10 billion dollars. Just weeks later, in March 2008, despite various attempts to reassure financial markets over its liquidity position, the major investment bank Bear Stearns was forced to seek emergency federal funding because such a large part of its securitized mortgage holdings turned out to be toxic. Bear Stearns was acquired by JPMorgan for 240 million US dollars. The bad bank Maiden Lane LLC created by the Fed purchased around 30 billion dollars in illiquid and high risk securities from Bear Stearns to support the acquisition (Fed 2010a). (Bad banks are state-created financial institutions that buy toxic assets and loans from struggling banks.[2]) By then nearly two million people in the United States had already lost their homes, and four million more were at risk of foreclosure (Harvey 2011: 1; Kindleberger and Aliber 2015).[3]

In September 2008, financial markets collapsed: The US mortgage market giants, Federal National Mortgage Association (Fannie Mae) and Federal

Home Loan Mortgage Corporation (Freddie Mac), suffered massive losses and wound up being nationalized. Merrill Lynch lost 23 billion US dollars on its holdings of securitized mortgages and was taken over by Bank of America. In mid-September 2008, the US investment bank Lehman Brothers became insolvent and filed a petition for what turned out to be the largest corporate bankruptcy in US history. The consequences of the Lehman bankruptcy were dramatic: "Within days the entire financial system suffered what amounted to cardiac arrest and had to be put on artificial life support" (Soros 2009: 157). As a major market maker in the shadow banking system, Lehman Brothers played a key role. Almost all other Wall Street banks and investors were counterparties to Lehman's derivatives and repo transactions. So the Lehman failure put virtually every Wall Street bank at risk of insolvency. The market for credit default swaps (CDS) collapsed. To rescue the world's largest insurance company, AIG, from insolvency, the Fed provided the firm with an emergency loan in the amount of up to 85 billion dollars.[4] Iceland wound up on the brink of economic meltdown, prompting its government to take control of the country's three largest banks. Countries such as Hungary, Brazil, Mexico, and the so-called Asian tiger states were especially hard hit, and many of their financial institutions faltered. Elsewhere—in Turkey, China, India, Australia, and New Zealand, for example—repercussions were serious although not quite as drastic. Banks grew reluctant to grant credit for international trade, and consequently, the volume of imports and exports in some sectors fell sharply (Soros 2009; Nesvetailova 2010; Helleiner 2011).

In October 2008, after rejecting the first proposal for a recovery package to rescue the US credit market, Congress approved the 700-billion-US-dollar Troubled Assets Relief Program, recapitalizing many businesses and banks with a massive set of bailouts. Major central banks cut interest rates to unprecedented lows and followed a monetary policy course of quantitative easing, making massive sums of money available through monetary base expansion (see chapter 8).

The system only regained stability, however, after the Fed began acting as dealer of last resort. When crisis hits, liquidity shortages require central banks to serve as dealers of last resort, and, in that capacity, to purchase large quantities of illiquid securities that would otherwise no longer find buyers. The establishment of so-called *bad banks* is another important mechanism employed to recapitalize banks and provide liquidity in order to prevent their insolvency. At the same time, it can also ward off a chain reaction of insolvencies that might be triggered when a faltering bank fails to meet liabilities particularly from swap and repo agreements. The crisis in the US subprime mortgage market, which was initially held to be a sector problem, soon spread throughout the world, eventually leading to global recession and the euro crisis.

The financial crisis not only made it clear that existing security structures were unable to prevent a downturn of such magnitude. It also revealed the lack of any coherent security structure capable of organizing a coordinated response. What prevailed was a microprudential regulatory approach focusing on safeguarding individual financial institutions rather than the system as a whole (Borio 2009; Baker 2017; Thiemann, Aldegwy, and Ibrocevic 2017). Nearly all regulatory powers were restricted to a national framework. The European Union had also largely refrained from setting up its own governance structures. Instead, European institutions and EU Member States were actively involved in encouraging the growth of the shadow banking system, primarily to strengthen the creation of a European single financial market. Even though various international institutions with regulatory powers existed, none were endowed with robust agency authority. For the most part, soft law standards dominated based on voluntary compliance and had been drafted by transnational and in part private institutions such as the Basel Committee on Banking Supervision (BCBS), the International Organization of Securities Commissions (IOSC), the International Association of Insurance Supervisors (IAIS), and the International Accounting Standards Board (IASB) (Tsingou 2015).

7.2 The COVID-19 Financial Crisis

In March 2020, measures to contain the COVID-19 pandemic brought global supply chains and large sectors of the economy to a near halt. The global financial system stood on the brink of collapse. Leading central banks were forced to take concerted action on an unprecedented scale to prevent a complete breakdown of the system (see chapter 8). The pandemic was responsible for causing both supply and demand shocks at the same time. Millions of people were not allowed to go to work. In large part, industrial production came to a standstill or was able to proceed only on a much reduced scale. Many businesses closed, resulting in a sharp drop in demand. Economic growth stagnated in almost every country around the globe (Bloom et al. 2020). To keep businesses from closing and help them to pay their employees, many governments launched bailout schemes and investment programs, some on a large scale (Wullweber 2020a).

Worldwide measures to control the COVID-19 pandemic led to a severe crisis in the global financial system. As demonstrated, however, even before the outbreak, the system had already shifted into crisis mode. Since the global financial crisis, a gigantic asset bubble had been building up in capital markets (St. Louis Fed 2023c). At the same time, the volume of private and business debt had surged to record levels around the world. An enormous amount of money had been invested in risky assets such as exchange traded funds (ETFs). High-frequency and algorithmic trading had become more popular than ever. What is more, the shadow banking system was experiencing steady expansion as it assumed an increasingly important role in the creation of credit and intermediation processes (FSB 2020b).

For more than a decade after the global financial crisis, capital markets experienced a steady rise in asset prices—the longest bull market in history. Just before the pandemic hit, the United States rating agency Standard & Poor's 500 Index surpassed all previous records (IMF 2020a). Asset prices rose to such extreme highs for a variety of reasons, including the growing concentration of wealth under the control of a small group of the world's wealthiest people, the increase in private pension funds in need of investment, and also the quantitative easing programs adopted by central banks to stabilize the system. To achieve higher returns, many financial players pursued aggressive strategies, investing in riskier and less liquid assets of poor credit quality. This made the financial system all the more vulnerable to market fluctuations.

At the same time, shadow banking players were reducing their liquidity buffers. In the years leading up to the COVID-19 outbreak, the traditional banking system had once again become more crisis-prone. The Basel III standards introduced in response to the global financial crisis required banks to build stronger capital buffers, and although by 2020 the banking system on the whole was actually more regulated than it had been in 2008, other factors were coming together to make the system more vulnerable (Thiemann 2019b; Birk and Thiemann 2020). Big banks kept expanding. The trend toward highly leveraged investments was growing (Blickle et al. 2020). Meanwhile, managers were receiving exorbitant bonuses and shareholders were being paid high dividends as large-scale share repurchase became a widespread practice. In 2019 alone, major banks around the world spent around 325 billion US dollars on share buybacks and dividends, weakening their capital base as a result (Bair 2020). Moreover, regulators had recently eased capital requirements and lowered stress testing standards (Systemic Risk Council 2019).

Favorable financing options in the productive economy led to a sharp increase in corporate debt (for the US corporate debt, see Fed 2023b). The very aim of loose monetary policies implemented after the 2007–9 financial crisis was to encourage higher corporate investments. And yet, the sharp increase in the volume of credit was not accompanied by rising demand. On the contrary, the economies of most industrial countries were edging toward recession. For the vast majority of people, income was stagnating or even declining. While GDP had grown since the 1970s, real income had been shrinking (St. Louis Fed 2022b). So purchasing power was decreasing instead of rising. The result was a buildup of household and corporate debt against the background of falling effective demand (St. Louis Fed 2020).

While at the beginning of 2020 empty supermarket shelves indicated that people were stockpiling over fears of possible curfews and quarantine measures, trading activities on financial markets continued at an intensive pace, reaching ever new record highs. In February 2020, the Intercontinental Exchange, which owns the New York Stock Exchange and other trading platforms, posted a daily record average of 7.6 million contracts on futures and options for that month. On Friday, February 28, 2020, the world's largest futures exchange, the US-based Chicago Mercantile Exchange Group, experienced the second busiest day in its 104-year history, with a trading volume of nearly a trillion shares (Stafford and Henderson 2020). As uncertainty grew over the impact of the pandemic, however, the long period of financial boom came to an abrupt end, reversing almost immediately into a steep decline. During the final week of February 2020, the S&P 500 stock index fell by more than 10% in its fastest drop in history, faster even than during the 1929 market crash (Stafford and Henderson 2020). European equities followed suit in the downward trend.

At the beginning of the pandemic, investors began buying up safe assets with a preference for government bonds. In early March, ten-year US Treasury yields, a key benchmark for financial players around the world, fell to an all-time low of 0.7%. Yields on shorter-term US Treasury investments even dropped below zero. Government bonds, and especially US Treasuries, count as very safe assets. As demand for Treasuries climb, their yield declines and their price increases. When a downturn occurs, fear of large, high-risk investment losses, or even default, often leads to panic sales as investors search for safer investments. As a result, prices in riskier markets tend to collapse (Cipriani et al. 2020; Smith et al. 2020b). As the COVID-19 crisis took hold, the UK's most important stock index, the Financial Times Stock Exchange Index 100 (FTSE), suffered its worst losses since the financial crisis of 2008. The German DAX initially fell by around 6% and later by more than 12%, the second largest drop in its history. US stocks posted their greatest losses since 1987 and the S&P 500 suffered the fastest reversal from a bull market to a bear market on record (Wells 2020). At the same time, US government money market funds (MMFs), which invest in safe, short-term government debt, registered their highest-ever weekly capital inflow of 286 billion US dollars, while prime funds (investments in short-term corporate debt), and municipal money market funds experienced severe outflows (Smith and Henderson 2020). Emerging market economies (EMEs) were especially hard hit by the COVID-19 crisis. Investments in EME countries were withdrawn on a large scale. As investors searched for security and liquidity, and above all for US dollars, the volume of losses surpassed even levels registered during the global financial crisis (Wheatley 2020).

In a situation where more and more enterprises become financially stressed and suffer simultaneous demand- and supply-side shocks, financial market participants in general develop a strong preference for liquidity. Financial and nonfinancial firms alike hoard cash to meet their obligations, but also to keep liquidity on hand for future investment opportunities. Investors seek to turn existing assets into money. Serious problems can result for banks when many household savers and business enterprises decide to withdraw a good part of their bank deposits at the same time. When the pandemic erupted, the situation was further exacerbated by widespread overindebtedness and highly leveraged business practices. Under such circumstances, any additional piece of bad news can trigger a run on liquidity and a market breakdown. This is precisely what happened on 9 March 2020, when members of the Organization of the Petroleum Exporting Countries (OPEC) failed to reach an agreement on output and instead of reducing oil production actually increased it. The price of crude oil experienced its sharpest decline in almost three decades (Wigglesworth 2020b). When panic struck, the prices of almost all assets decreased sharply and liquidity vanished. The stress was felt in virtually every financial market. Markets were no longer liquid. The FTSE in London suffered its worst quarter since the 1980s (Georgiadis et al. 2020).

As more and more financial players encountered liquidity problems, their uncertainty over the solvency of their counterparts grew. Since most global trading is transacted in US dollars, there was a global run on the issuers of eurodollars. This led to a dramatic acceleration of foreign exchange market activity. In such a situation, financial markets tend to become dysfunctional. Stock market circuit breakers were triggered in several instances and stock trading was suspended. The intention of a circuit breaker is to curb panic selling by interrupting the algorithmic and automated trading programs that have come to dominate today's markets (Wigglesworth 2020a). Market makers, the custodians of market liquidity under normal circumstances, either drastically widened their bid-offer spreads—in other words, the difference between the lowest ask price for a security and the highest bid price—or they stopped trading altogether. The repercussions were particularly severe for markets in corporate bonds and bond exchange traded funds (ETF). Mutual funds suffered enormous losses in mid-March 2020 (Henderson and Wigglesworth 2020). The run on security markets also had a negative impact on the credit supply to the productive economy. The disruption of credit flows led to unnecessary defaults caused by liquidity constraints.

The next phase of the COVID-19 crisis began with the meltdown of passive and algorithmic investing, the unwinding of many exchange traded funds, and the sale of even the safest of assets as market players became desperate for cash. In times of crisis, traditional correlation patterns between asset classes tend to dissolve. When stock prices fall, US Treasury prices usually rise, because in situations of market stress, investors tend to sell risky assets and buy government bonds that are considered safe. In the weeks following 9 March 2020, however, this "rule" no longer applied. The rush for liquidity in mid-March increased the volume of sales to such an extent that prices fell even for US Treasuries across the maturity spectrum. The drastic drop in security prices in general was inevitable as investors rushed to raise funds by selling assets at a time when buyers were scarce (Schrimpf, Shin, and Sushko 2020). Since hardly anyone wanted to buy securities or assets, however, a drastic price drop in prices on financial markets became inevitable. The result was a downward liquidity spiral. The pressure to sell equities spread to bond markets, and then even reached markets for completely unrelated assets such as cryptoassets. In Europe, the Middle East, Africa, and the Americas, demand for sovereign bonds, but also for corporate and financial bonds, all but disappeared, and issuance soon fell to zero (Gross

2020). Only through massive and coordinated fiscal and monetary policy intervention was it possible to break this vicious circle (Smith et al. 2020a).

Financial market participants are driven by fear and emotions. In times of uncertainty, such emotions are responsible for extreme upward and downward swings in market activity. These swings are reflected in the volatility index (VIX), which measures price movements and market expectations.[5] Toward the middle of March 2020, the mood on financial markets vacillated from one day to the next between euphoria and panic. The S&P 500 initially dropped by 9.5% but rebounded quickly, regaining 9.3% in response to strong central bank intervention. Then, over the course of next three days, it fell once again, this time by 12%. Eventually, the S&P 500 bounced back and experienced its strongest week in over a decade (Fletscher 2020). Owing to extreme volatility during this period, circuit breakers were activated on several occasions (FSB 2020c: 3).

As world financial markets were imploding, central banks decided to open the floodgates and inject vast sums of money into the financial system using a variety of facilities, some of which were newly created to facilitate access to liquidity (see chapter 8). Toward the end of March, following two weeks of severe market turbulence, there was an abundance of central bank money, but safe assets were comparatively scarce. Bond markets, saturated with funds, were quick to recover. But then, during the last week of March, in a development completely detached from the impact that lockdown measures were having on production and business activities, yields on equities rose over bond yields to levels not seen since the euro area debt crisis (Fletscher 2020). In a situation where the world economic outlook was so bleak that IMF managing director Kristalina Georgieva described the COVID-19 crisis as the worst economic crisis since the Great Depression (IMF 2020b), financial markets were euphoric, and investor risk appetite increased.

7.3 The Shadow Banking System: A Permanent State of Instability

Both the COVID-19 crisis and the global financial crisis 2007–9 can be specifically understood as crises of the shadow banking system (Mehrling 2011; Ricks 2011; Mehrling et al. 2013; Wullweber 2020a). As described in the foregoing chapters, the shadow banking system is based on a private security structure centered on repurchase agreements. The safety of the collateral used to back repos depends on its market value. Overall, the system functions on the assumption that although single securities pledged as collateral might lose their value, it is highly unlikely that all securities will lose their value at the same time. In the event of value loss, there is a risk discount on the value of the asset, called a *haircut*. If the decline in value continues, *margin calls* will apply, requiring further collateral to be posted. In addition, the price of the collateral is adjusted on a day-to-day basis (*mark-to-market*) (see chapter 6.1). In noncrisis times, repo transactions, which are the core of the shadow banking system, are therefore considered to be very safe. Experience has demonstrated, however, that confidence in the self-stabilizing ability is unwarranted. When crisis hits, the private security structure fails to work. This was clearly the case during the 2007–9 global financial crisis, but also at the beginning of the COVID-19 crisis in March 2020. The market saw rapid declines in the value not just of single securities but of virtually all assets. In the global financial crisis, security values dropped by around 1.5 trillion US dollars (Adrian et al. 2017: 5).

When times are good, repos increase the liquidity of the financial system. During times of crisis, however, the opposite is true: "[A]ll the swaps in the world cannot turn a risky asset into a genuine Treasury bill" (Mehrling et al. 2013: 8). In a downturn market, the value of repo collateral erodes swiftly because it is valued on a mark-to-market basis (MacKenzie 2012).

When profit expectations decline, security sales surge and their price falls as a result. Brokers calculate higher initial margins and increase haircuts for repo transactions when there is uncertainty over the solvency of the contracting parties. Heavily leveraged market participants can find themselves in a difficult position if they are required to provide additional liquidity and collateral that they themselves may not own. Borrowers who are forced to sell part of their securities have less potential to transact repos considering the smaller inventory of securities that they can rely on as collateral. Market players on the whole tend to become more hesitant about lending in their effort to hold on to as many liquid reserves as possible. As the sale of securities increases, their value further decreases, and that, in turn, leads to higher margin calls. More collateral has to be provided, and haircuts are increased, making liquidity scarcer and setting off a downward liquidity spiral as a consequence (Adrian et al. 2017; BIS 2017; Wullweber 2020a; see Figure 11). Bid prices rise and loans become more expensive. It becomes increasingly difficult for market participants to conduct transactions because it grows harder for them to resell securities in order to finance their own security purchases. As securities become less liquid, increased haircuts make it more expensive for financial players to use them as collateral in repo transactions. In the wake of an overall decline in financial liquidity, fewer repo agreements are transacted. Financial players in need of funds have no recourse but to sell securities below cost. This accelerates the downward liquidity spiral even more, rendering internal market security structures virtually ineffective (see Figure 11).

In this sense, the repo market tends to be a breeding ground for downward liquidity spirals. What is more, since the value of the securities is constantly being adjusted to the market price, repo prices are subject to sudden decreases. During a liquidity crisis, financial players need funds—and ultimately central bank money—to service their debts. In a global crisis, the need for funds eventually shifts from national currencies to US dollars and Fed funds (see chapter 4.3. for a more detailed discussion of this aspect). When their obligations exceed their own capital reserves, they are forced to sell their assets at almost any price they can get (Mehrling 2011: 96–98).

This is precisely what happened during both the global financial crisis and the COVID-19 financial crisis: Asset prices fell and margin calls for all repo transactions increased, triggering a higher demand for cash. And this, in turn, stimulated asset sales even further, which then led to lower prices. Mounting

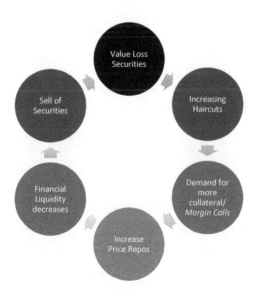

Figure 11 *Downward liquidity spiral. Wullweber 2020a.*

demands were made on dealers to add more collateral to their positions, forcing them to sell previously higher-performing assets. A vicious circle was set in motion, and, as a result, securities suffered heavy losses. When even the safest assets become more and more illiquid, market making becomes a highly risky undertaking. In both cases, market makers stopped quoting prices and failed to fulfill their market-making commitment. A vacuum occurs, as was the case in September 2008 and March 2020. After market-making activities came to a halt in almost every sector of capital markets, the breakdown spread throughout the entire shadow banking system and eventually disrupted large parts of the financial system. Central banks were the only institutions capable of filling the gap by taking on the market-making function as dealers of last resort. Stated in simpler and more pointed terms, the enormous liquidity bottlenecks that disrupted the financial system during these two major crises resulted not only from what took place beforehand, as well as during and after each crisis, but also from how the situations were handled by the world's most important central banks and regulatory bodies. The only feasible way to overcome these crises was through central bank intervention.

EIGHT

Masters of Stability

The Unconventional Monetary Policy of Central Banks

Roses are red
Violets are blue
We'll keep financing conditions favourable
'Til the crisis is through
—ECB Tweet, 14 February 2021

RECENT DECADES HAVE SEEN a major shift in the relationship between the state and the financial system. While a good part of the development was triggered by the global financial crisis and the financial repercussions of the COVID-19 pandemic, the new constellation evolved mainly as an outcome of the many years of financial deregulation, and by the prevailing market liberal belief in efficient markets and the capacity of financial markets to stabilize on their own. Prior to the global financial crisis of 2007–9 it was assumed that international supervisory and regulatory authorities were the key players in securing international financial stability. By 2008 at the latest, however, it had become clear that existing governance and security structures were in no way designed to manage a crisis or equipped to stabilize the financial system. Governments had refrained from creating robust and effective legal structures to regulate financial markets. Even after the global financial crisis, they failed to adopt effective fiscal, financial, and structural policies. Instead of taking steps to strengthen the economy and society by introducing financially sound investment programs designed to prepare economies and societies to adapt to the challenges of our times, they have actually made things worse: Rather than prioritizing sustainable investments, they have imposed comprehensive austerity measures, making economic recovery extremely difficult while generating almost no transformative steering effect. And they have shirked responsibility for sluggish growth, leaving any effective crisis response up to their central banks.

But central banks have not been prepared to deal with such situations either. They were also constrained in their options by the sedimented layers of central banking (chapter 4). During the global financial crisis, the limits of the prevailing monetary policy became apparent. It was obvious that new paths had to be taken. Central banks began implementing new monetary policies with little to no experience: "[T]hey did so without much prior theory about why it would work, and with hardly any thought about possible implications for more normal times" (Mehrling et al. 2013: 1). Moreover, as pointed out by the Bank of England, most prevailing monetary theories have proven faulty: "[T]he relationship between monetary policy and money differs from the description in many introductory textbooks" (McLeay, Radia, and Ryland 2014a: 21). Today's leading central bankers have rediscovered the nineteenth-century treatise *Lombard Street: A Description of the Money Market* (Bagehot 2006 [1873]), in which Walter Bagehot laid out principles for dealing with financial crises.[1] Certain contemporary central bank decisions can be traced directly back to Bagehot's recommendations (Bernanke 2008; Mehrling et al. 2013). Bagehot was in favor of providing as much liquidity as required in times of crisis, albeit only to illiquid but solvent institutions on the basis of safe collateral at high interest rates. He reasoned that high interest rates would prevent emergency financing from benefiting institutions not in need of funds. Regarding the use of assets to back loans, he argued against calculating the value according to prevailing market prices. He also urged the Bank of England, however, to only accept collateral deemed sound in noncrisis times.

When central banks intervened, it was therefore not a matter of following detailed emergency plans drawn up beforehand and already in place. Decisions were rather pragmatic and ad hoc, deviating more and more from prevailing and familiar monetary policy (Golub, Kaya, and Reay 2015; Kovner and Martin 2020). The measures taken by central banks were not just unconventional in terms of their nature and extent; they were historically unprecedented. When the financial system threatened to collapse during both the global financial crisis and the COVID-19 crisis, the dramatic turn of events forced central banks to radically alter their course and expand their financial instrument inventories. As already demonstrated, the shadow banking system was a major cause of the financial crisis and a key contributor to worsening the COVID-19 financial crisis. Given the magnitude of the crises and the failure of traditional central bank policy to stabilize the ailing shadow banking system, central banks revolutionized their intervention toolkit, ushering in a new era of central bank policy (Bernanke 2017; Potter 2017a). Alongside unconventional measures such as quantitative easing and lowering the key interest rate to zero percent or just above, for the first time ever, central banks assumed a financial trading and market making function in the shadow banking system. In other words, they not only acted as last resort lenders but also as last resort dealers and market makers. At the same time, they created facilities that gave shadow players direct access to central bank money. In other words, they created a new security structure for the financial system that also included the shadow banking system.

When panic breaks out on financial markets, market players are powerless to control a looming crisis. Stakeholders are deeply entangled in the markets. Their behavior is short-sighted, irrational, and driven by fear and panic (Minsky 1982a; Akerlof and Shiller 2009). Since many investments are linked to indices or specific asset or portfolio trackers, their investment freedom is limited (Petry, Fichtner, and Heemskerk 2019). Market players are often forced to execute operations according to the dictates of their algorithms, not least because they are obliged to follow investment fund guidelines (MacKenzie 2009). The various stages of the downward spiral in asset prices that sets in when panic selling begins are described in chapter 5.2 and chapter 7.3. The spiraling trend affects virtually all investments. In today's markets, most financial products are valued mark-to-market, so changes in asset prices directly impact existing contracts. Falling asset prices tend to have an almost real-time effect on practically all financial products as a result. An inevitable Minsky cycle erupts: Hedge finance becomes speculative finance; speculative finance shifts into Ponzi finance; and participants in Ponzi funding schemes go bankrupt. As the crisis deepens, prices sink even lower and finance models and investments become less and less viable. Bid-ask spreads widen, and bidding and/or offering declines or stops altogether. Chances dwindle for investors to escape from this vicious circle. Assets become unsellable and the whole system grinds to a halt.

This leads to a massive liquidity squeeze for both traditional and shadow banks alike, considering that assets—in the form of collateral—are the lubricant of repo markets, and accordingly constitute the cornerstone of the shadow banking system. As market participants draw on bank credit lines and borrow against their assets to raise funds, possibilities for new financing grow so scarce that financial markets become dysfunctional. Repo market makers are particularly vulnerable to spiraling liquidity shortages because they normally have no access to central bank money or other short-term central bank emergency lending facilities. When such institutions reduce their trading volume or even stop trading altogether, the entire shadow banking system is affected. Considering how critical the shadow banking system and the repo market have become for the financial sector, crises in these areas can cause the entire global financial system to collapse.

As demonstrated in chapter 4, central banks are the world's only institutions with no liquidity problems (in their own currency). This allows them to develop a diverse range of tools to stabilize the system in times of crisis. At the same time, since the start of the twenty-first century, central banks have had to deal with crises that are both unique in origin (the shadow banking system) and unprecedented in scale. When traditional types of emergency intervention failed to restore stability, leading central banks had to leave their familiar terrain of monetary policy and turn to new, previously unproven and unconventional means.

During the COVID-19 crisis, central banks even crossed the dividing line that had cordoned off fiscal policy from monetary policy since the 1980s. Prevailing ideology over the past three decades had not allowed central banks to directly finance government spending by buying up government bonds. The purchase of government bonds was only permitted via the secondary market. This was based on the reasoning that governments might abuse such a privilege as an opportunity to unsustainably increase public debt, and that central banks should instead remain independent from governments and serve as keepers of price stability and neutral guardians of their own currencies. The neutrality of central banks, however, has always been a political myth, making it possible to delegate complicated and unpopular political decisions regarding monetary policy to seemingly apolitical central bank technocrats (McNamara 1998, 2002; Krippner 2007; van 't Klooster and Fontan 2020). The historic effort to curb the global pandemic without destroying entire industries rendered this approach untenable. Fears of government access to central bank balance sheets were superseded, and rightly so, by the greater and more imminent threat of total breakdown that was facing global trade, a calamity that would ultimately result in the severe deterioration of economic and social conditions across the world.

The following chapters trace the process by which new central bank security structures are created in response to the new crisis dynamics.

8.1 Interest Rate Policy in Times of Crisis

The traditional crisis response of central banks is to lower key interest rates to incentivize borrowing in the productive economy, or, vice versa, to raise interest rates in times of economic overheating. Central bank interest rates influence the interest rates for private loans as well as for intercommercial bank lending. As explained in chapter 2.2, this is because private banks generally follow monetary policy rate decisions and adjust their own interest rates accordingly. The idea behind lowering interest rates is that, all other things being equal, the less it costs to obtain a loan, the higher the demand will be. Central banks seek to exert a macroeconomic effect on lending practices by adjusting their key interest rates, i.e., the price of central bank money (McLeay, Radia, and Ryland 2014a; Bank of England 2015).

During and after the 2007–9 financial crisis, leading central banks gradually cut their key interest rates (rate of the main refinancing operations) to historic lows of between 0.00% and 0.5%. Between 2016 and 2022, some central banks—the ECB included—have even charged interest on deposits, meaning that banks had to pay to keep deposits in their central bank accounts (the deposits, therefore, had a negative interest rate). A key interest rate of zero percent, or just above, is a sign of crisis. In such an environment monetary policy makers must find a different approach to steer the economy (Borio 2012).

When the COVID-19 crisis struck, leading central banks were confronted with the problem that key interest rates were already very low. It was because the global financial system had never really recovered from crisis mode, and because the economy in many countries was still weak, that key interest rates continued to hover around zero. Under these circumstances, conventional interest rate cuts exerted practically no steering effect at all. The Bank of England had slightly raised its key interest rate to 0.75%. The Fed had also lifted its interest rate minimally, fixing it at 2.5%. In early March 2020, the Fed decided to respond in a very traditional manner, cutting rates by a modest 0.5%, but to no avail. A short time later, both the Fed and the Bank of England once again lowered their interest rates to 0.25%. But even this stronger reduction failed to yield any positive results (Wolf 2020).

In 2022, central banks in the Western industrialized countries, but also in many other parts of the world, began once again to raise their key interest rates. In fact, it was the most comprehensive tightening of monetary policy in decades (Romei and Stubbington 2022). The increases were driven by rising inflation around the world. However, as explained in the preface, the problem with key interest rate hikes is that they are used as an instrument to fight demand-induced inflation, which is the case when excessive wage growth leads to price increases. This, however, was not the driver of inflation in 2022 und 2023.

8.2 Lenders of Last Resort

During the two major financial crises in the first decades of the present century, central banks were fairly quick to realize that circumstances demanded much stronger intervention than merely manipulating official interest rates. One of the most important decisions they took right from the start was to provide emergency liquidity assistance so as to prevent a liquidity crunch on financial markets: Shortly after the outbreak of the crisis in August 2007, the ECB, the Fed, and the central banks of Japan, Canada, and Australia granted the banking sector short-term, low-interest emergency loans totaling 320 billion US dollars. Although as of October 2008 the Fed had already provided 2.3 trillion US dollars in fiscal stimulus and bank liquidity, the news that one major American money market fund had failed was enough to spread panic throughout the entire US stock market. At the time, the IMF had estimated that the crisis was responsible for write-offs on US secured mortgages totaling 1.4 trillion dollars (IMF 2008: 14). By then, at the latest, it had become apparent that the crisis which Alan Greenspan referred to as "a once in a century credit tsunami" was spreading to all corners of the globe (Greenspan 2008). After the Lehman Brothers bankruptcy, nearly every Wall Street bank became insolvent: "Out of . . . 13 of the most important financial institutions in the United States, 12 were at risk of failure within a period of a week or two" (Bernanke, quoted in Financial Crisis Inquiry Commission 2011: 354). Many financial players and virtually all major financial institutions, such as Bear Stearns, AIG, Morgan Stanley, Merrill Lynch, Citigroup, Barclays, and also Deutsche Bank, had speculated extensively in financial products that ultimately turned out to be toxic securities—that is, securities which at the time were unsalable on the capital market.

The value of derivatives in general fell sharply during the financial crisis, and the securities market came to a near standstill. It was no longer possible for banks to issue securities on financial markets at that point because it was impossible to determine their price. These nonperforming assets had become virtually unsellable. To solve this dilemma, policy makers decided to create bad banks and to launch bond purchase programs. By shifting bad assets off their balance sheets, banks can restore their capital ratios. This unconventional strategy, which reverts to Bagehot's crisis toolkit, is a significant departure from the norm.

Prominent examples of financial institutions for which bad banks—in this case, Maiden Lane LLC I, II, and III—were created to help stabilize US asset markets include Bear Stearns and AIG (Kaminska 2008; Fed 2010b).[2] Central bank intervention during the past two crises, however, did not follow Bagehot's recommendations to lend funds only to illiquid but solvent banks against good collateral at high interest rates. The basket of securities used as collateral was instead substantially expanded. Interest rates were significantly reduced, and loans were also granted to clearly insolvent institutions (Tucker 2014: 19–20). Bagehot's definition of good securities, however, refers to those securities that are considered good in noncrisis times, which leaves room for interpretation (Bagehot 2006 [1873]: 57). The bailout of noncommercial banks such as Bear Stearns and AIG definitely did not conform to Bagehot's principles. What justified the rescue of such institutions was the fact that the US government had classified them as systemically important. Bear Stearns was indeed a key market maker in the shadow banking system. The fact that it was an investment bank and not a commercial bank, however, meant that financial authorities were able to rescue it only by invoking a special provision of the US Federal Reserve Act that allowed the Fed, for the first time since the 1930s, to provide emergency credit to a noncommercial financial institution (Domanski, Moessner, and Nelson 2014). Although the Fed was prepared to provide ample assistance during the financial crisis, commercial banks feared that accepting bailouts would damage their creditworthiness on financial markets. This made them reluctant to apply for short-term credit through the additional facilities—in particular through the Fed's discount window (Tucker 2014: 11). As a result, despite the massive availability of funds, the Fed's lender of last resort function had its limits as a safety net.

When the COVID-19 crisis erupted, leading central banks were quick to realize that they needed to expand their already unconventional lender-of-last-resort policies. One of their first and most important monetary policy decisions was to give financial institutions access to liquidity to ease capital shortages and prevent a credit crunch in financial markets. At the beginning of April 2020, the Fed set up a new facility to supply financial institutions with liquidity through term financing by buying up loans granted by banks to support small businesses. The program was designed to relieve banks of liquidity stress and to secure the flow of credit to business enterprises and communities (Fed 2020a). It included loan guarantees through Federal Reserve loan facilities and was intended to support the stimulus package previously passed by the US Congress. Corporate and municipal loans were purchased by the Fed under a variety of facilities, among others the Primary Market Corporate Credit Facility (PMCCF), the Secondary Market Corporate Credit Facility (SMCCF), the Main Street New Loan Facility (MSNLF), the Main Street Expanded Loan Facility (MSELF), and the Municipal Liquidity Facility (Kovner and Martin 2020).

All these policy instruments were highly unconventional. They provided 2.3 trillion US dollars in loans to support the economy and financially stressed communities (Boyarchenko et al. 2020b). Although some of these actions resembled monetary policy interventions during the financial crisis, central banks crossed another red line during the COVID-19 crisis by extending credit to the productive economy and local governments (Milstein and Wessel 2021). Central banks around the world provided massive sums of money to financial players as well as nonfinancial players in their effort to stabilize both financial systems and economic systems (Tett 2020). Intervention by the Fed even went a step further. For the first time in its history, it introduced an instrument to purchase investment-grade exchange traded funds (ETFs) in order to counter a wave of overreaction in equity trading (Ablan, Greeley, and Henderson 2020). ETFs are risky investment vehicles linked to an index or basket of assets in a market that in recent years has grown rapidly but is also very susceptible to a high degree of price fluctuation (ESRB 2019).

Another innovation in the security structure—the Bank Term Funding Program (BTFP)—was introduced by the Fed in March 2023, in the wake of the US banking crisis that unfolded in early 2023 (Fed 2023c), when Silvergate Bank, Silicon Valley Bank, Signature Bank, and First Republic were forced to file for bankruptcy. These banks had accumulated a large amount of US Treasuries in their portfolios, and the rise in key interest rates since 2022 led to a fall in the price of fixed-income assets, including Treasuries. When a considerable capital outflow in the form of deposit withdrawals forced these banks to sell a portion of their government bonds, they sustained heavy losses. At the time, the Fed estimated that US banks were holding about 620 billion US dollars of unrealized losses in their portfolios (Bloomberg 2023; Noona and Masters 2023). It was to prevent contagion that the Fed launched the Bank Term Funding Program. This program offers loans to banks, savings associations, credit unions, and other eligible depository institutions at a very low rate for up to one year. More important, under the program the Fed trades eligible collateral at par on demand, i.e., without a haircut (Fed 2023d, 2023e). This means that the risk for banks of falling Treasury prices is assumed by the Fed. Not surprisingly, the BTFP was met with an immediate and high demand for funds (St. Louis Fed 2023d). The Fed's goal in launching the program was to provide funding elasticity to the unrealized losses in banks' portfolios, preventing banks from being forced to sell their safe assets below value in times of stress.

In both crises, besides tackling the issues outlined above, the Fed had to deal with the problem arising from the fact that global trade is mainly conducted in US dollars and many business enterprises (but also countries) were struggling to meet their dollar liabilities. Between 2007 and 2010, to address this problem, the Fed set up currency swap lines with the central banks of several different countries so as to facilitate their access to US dollars and to ensure dollar liquidity (see also chapter 4.3). Swap counterparties included the Reserve Bank of Australia, the Banco Central do Brasil, the Bank of Canada, Danmarks Nationalbank, the Bank of England, the ECB, the Bank of Japan, the Bank of Korea, the Banco de Mexico, the Reserve Bank of New Zealand, Norges Bank, the Monetary Authority of Singapore, Sveriges Riksbank, and the Swiss National Bank. The swap agreements with the Fed allowed the central banks concerned to act, when necessary as lenders of last resort for US dollars. This again was a monetary policy that had not before existed in this form. It played a major role in eliminating the global shortage of US dollars (Tooze

2018). The ceiling was initially limited to a certain amount of US dollars, but was lifted entirely in 2008. In December 2008, swap transactions peaked at over 580 billion US dollars (Domanski, Moessner, and Nelson 2014: 54): "The US Federal Reserve was indeed acting as the world central bank in the context of the crisis" (Panitch and Gindin 2014: 385). In February 2010, the swap lines were closed.

In May 2010, however, because of constraints in short-term US dollar funding markets, the Fed reactivated its swap lines with the Bank of Canada, the Bank of England, the ECB, the Bank of Japan, and the Swiss National Bank. In October 2013, agreement was reached by these swap counterparties, the world's six major central banks, to convert their bilateral swap lines into standing arrangements (Fed 2013; Mehrling 2015). During the COVID-19 financial crisis in March 2020, swap lines were again extended to numerous other central banks. Under these challenging circumstances, the Fed took its policies a step further. With so many companies around the globe in dire need of US dollars, and with banks outside the United States holding nearly 13 trillion dollars' worth of dollar-denominated assets (Aldasoro, Ehlers, and Egemen 2019), it opened a temporary new facility, the Foreign and International Monetary Authorities (FIMA) repo facility, which enables foreign central banks to access dollars by using their existing stocks of government bonds to transact repurchase agreements with the Fed (Fed 2020b). In this way, the Fed not only revived its swap lines with other central banks; it also significantly strengthened the arrangements and broadened the range of eligible central banks. All things considered, the network of central bank liquidity swaps can be construed as a hierarchical international lender and dealer of last resort system for the global money market, with the Fed at the top of the hierarchy (Mehrling 2017: 113; Murau, Pape, and Pforr 2021). What this ultimately means is that the Fed has become the de facto "Sovereign International Last-Resort Lender" (McDowell 2012; Cohen 2019; see chapter 4.3). Apart from stabilizing the global financial market, the swap lines help shield the US domestic market from excessive dollar fluctuations. They thus also serve to control domestic interest rates and, more broadly, to influence domestic monetary policy (Pape 2022).

8.3 Goethe's Sorcerer's Apprentice: Quantitative Easing

In his poem *The Sorcerer's Apprentice*, Johann Wolfgang von Goethe describes a young sorcerer who, in his master's absence, uses magical power in which he has not yet been fully trained. Although the spell he casts is initially very effective, things soon spiral out of control. All attempts by the young wizard to subdue the forces he has unleashed only serve to make matters worse. Up to a certain point, this centuries-old tale contains a subtle warning for today's central bank capitalism. In an op-ed published in the *Washington Post* on 4 November 2010, then Fed chair Ben Bernanke defended the Fed's unconventional quantitative easing strategy by claiming: "We have made all necessary preparations, and we are confident that we have the tools to unwind these policies at the appropriate time" (Bernanke 2010). As the following discussion clearly shows, the measures adopted during the financial crisis have led to developments that may prove to be as difficult to reverse as the forces conjured up by the sorcerer's apprentice. The thing is, central bank capitalism has no master magician like the one in Goethe's tale who returns in time to break the spell and bring things back under control. With all the unanticipated crises accumulating in today's world, the tools that are supposed to be unwinding the unprecedented monetary policies adopted in the aftermath of the 2007 financial meltdown are only making an already critical situation more precarious.[3]

Besides acting as lender of last resort during the financial crisis, central banks shifted the focus of their monetary policy from key interest rate adjustments to quantitative easing (QE), a form of open market operations that belongs to so-called *balance sheet policies* (Borio and Disyatat 2009 ; ECB 2015c: 4, 36–38). These policies are used to make central bank money available to market participants through the purchase of securities—government bonds for the most part, but also other financial assets such as corporate bonds. As a vehicle they normally use repos.[4] Central banks finance such transactions by creating money.[5] Unlike when they adjust key interest rates, with QE they exert a *direct* impact on the amount of central bank money in circulation when they purchase government bonds from private investors (see Figure 12). The creation of central bank money (reserves) via this method is similar to the way deposits are created by commercial banks: A reserve deposit is created on the central bank account of the bank selling the securities, except that instead of a credit claim (bank loan), the government bonds are recorded on the assets side of the central bank's balance sheet (Stigum and Crescenzi 2007: 347).[6] To finance the purchase of assets (government debt in Figure 12), a central bank creates central bank money by increasing its reserves. This increases the balance of the commercial bank's central bank account (the right-hand side of Figure 14).

The liabilities side of the balance sheets shows the financial obligations that the central bank owes to third parties (the central bank money held by a bank in its central bank account). The assets side, on the other hand, shows the claims that the central bank has acquired (by extending credit to banks mainly through the purchase of government bonds). The central bank buys these assets at auctions that are held on a regular basis (in a tendering procedure), preferably from nonbank investors, such as pension funds or insurance companies (Bank of England 2015: 10). The assets are liquidated, i.e. converted into deposits, on their balance sheet (see Figure 13).

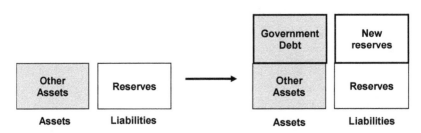

Figure 12 *Impact of QE on central bank balance sheets.*
Based on McLeay, Radia, and Ryland 2014a: 24.

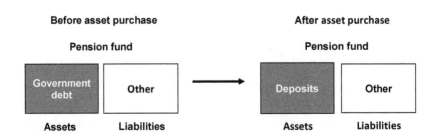

Figure 13 *Impact of QE on pension fund balance sheets.*
Based on McLeay, Radia, and Ryland 2014a: 24.

Private nonbank entities normally do not have central bank accounts. They receive money from the central bank through their commercial bank as bank deposits. Figure 14 shows what this looks like on the balance sheet of the commercial bank involved in the transaction.

The idea behind quantitative easing is primarily to loosen the money supply. First, banks receive ample reserves that reduce the liquidity constraints which can arise from the settling of balances with other banks or the withdrawal of deposits. This is because, as shown in chapter 2.2, the survival constraint for banks manifests itself as a reserve constraint (Mehrling 2011: 13). Considering that since the global financial crisis the financial system has not fully emerged from crisis mode, as evidenced, among other things, by the significant drop in interbank lending, the provision of central bank money to calm the markets is not unimportant. Second, if banks hold a large volume of central bank money that pays little or no interest, or, as in the case of ECB central bank money between 2016 and 2022, which even requires banks to pay interest, the incentive increases for them to lend money to the productive economy and to private households. As a result, bank interest rates on lending fall. Third, banks with ample and almost non-interest-bearing reserves are expected to become much more active in buying assets such as equities or corporate bonds. Fourth, as confirmed in the last decade by soaring asset prices, the value of the assets increases, which, in turn, makes it easier for business enterprises to access money on financial markets (Bank of England 2015: 10). Ideally, they will then invest in areas such as production and thereby boost the economy. Fifth, even though not an official goal of central banks, the price of sovereign bonds also rises. This, in turn, causes their interest rates (yields) to fall, relieving interest rate pressure

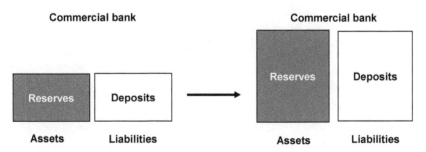

Figure 14 *Impact of QE on commercial bank balance sheets. Based on McLeay, Radia, and Ryland 2014a: 24.*

on governments and also allowing them to launch financially strong fiscal programs to support the economy. Sixth, the cumulative effects of QE are expected
to stimulate the economy, reduce unemployment, and improve income levels,
raising overall price levels in the process. After all, it was before the onset of
inflation in 2022 that QE policies were being deployed, at a time when many
Western industrialized countries were facing the threat of deflation, a far more
damaging force than (moderate) inflation. The downside of quantitative easing,
however, is that in general it almost inevitably leads to soaring asset prices. In
fact, since the end of the financial crisis in 2009, we have been witnessing a
phenomenon called asset inflation—the formation of an asset price bubble of
gigantic and historically unprecedented proportions (St. Louis Fed 2023c).

Soon after the Fed embarked on a course of quantitative easing in 2008,
central banks in the UK, Japan, and China followed suit (Fed 2015a).[7] The ECB,
however, waited until early 2015 to introduce its own comprehensive program
of quantitative easing. The reason for the late start was the strong resistance
expressed by a number of EU Member States, especially Germany (Weidmann
2013b). The ECB was facing considerable political backlash over the scope of
its limited mandate. Initially it was also permitted to buy government bonds
only to a very limited extent (but eventually the ECB did become active on the
secondary market; see Featherstone 2011). Another problem was that the ECB
viewed a failed economic and fiscal policy as the primary cause of sovereign
debt in euro area countries. Accordingly, it had always made intervention in the
government bond market contingent upon the implementation of economic
and structural reforms, as well as fiscal austerity measures. Since, at the time,
quantitative easing was far too unconventional for policy makers at the ECB,
they began expanding a variety of other monetary policy mechanisms so as
to improve financing conditions for commercial banks (Domanski, Moessner,
and Nelson 2014: 52–54). These included, among other things, extending the
term of the refinancing operations (to six months), expanding the number of
trading partners (from 140 to around 2,200), and significantly relaxing requirements for securities lodged as collateral.[8] It soon became apparent, however,
that these mechanisms were wholly inadequate. Under these circumstances,
ECB policy makers were forced to deviate from their conservative path and
venture into uncharted territory.

Generally speaking, the actions of both the Fed and the ECB are guided
by market liberal principles; in other words, by the belief that the market is an

efficient self-regulating system. While in crisis situations the Fed manages to work around this ideology in order to achieve effective results, the ECB tends to cling to a market liberal approach until it is almost too late. Decisions that the Fed managed to reach in a matter of a few days were years in the making at the ECB. In 2009, the ECB longer-term refinancing operations were extended from one to three years and again in 2014 to four years (Bundesbank 2017: 30–31). In May 2010, the ECB did launch its Securities Market Program (SMP), a bond-buying measure with a volume of close to 200 billion euros. But other financial transactions were carried out simultaneously to remove that same amount of central bank money from the market elsewhere, a practice known as sterilization. In September 2012, the SMP was replaced by the Outright Monetary Transactions Program (OMT), which enables the ECB to buy theoretically unlimited amounts of government bonds on the secondary market from vulnerable euro countries. In theory, therefore, it closely resembles quantitative easing. In practice, however, because the program requires the benefiting countries to accept the conditions of the European Stabilization Mechanism, it ultimately amounts to the sterilization of any additional central bank money created under the program. To date, the OMT has remained untapped, mainly because, after Mario Draghi proclaimed that the ECB would do *whatever it takes* to save the euro, interest rates on government bonds tumbled. More than anything, though, the transfer of the ECB presidency to Draghi, but also the legal briefs backing a wider scope of freedom for the ECB to act, finally paved the way for ECB decision-makers to embark on a course of unconventional monetary policy (Jones 2015). At the beginning of 2015, the European Central Bank finally launched a full-fledged QE program to the tune of 60 billion euros per month, an amount which at the beginning of 2016 was expanded to a monthly figure of 80 billion euros (Bundesbank 2017).

Before the outbreak of the COVID-19 crisis, many central banks (but not the ECB, which was still struggling with the euro crisis) had once again significantly reduced, or even completely phased out, their QE programs. By the time the crisis hit, however, participants in the financial market as well as enterprises in the production sector were in such dire need of liquidity that, as already mentioned, they even wound up selling their safest assets, especially Treasury bonds and other government bonds normally among the most sought-after securities, triggering "the biggest dash for cash the world has seen" (*Financial Times* 2020). Central banks around the world were quick to react and had soon revived or stepped up their QE programs. The Fed created a standing program of asset purchases, primarily for Treasuries and government mortgage-backed securities that during the first few weeks peaked at 75 billion dollars per day and over 300 billion dollars per week. For the sake of comparison, the Fed's daily purchase of assets during the global financial crisis amounted to 30 billion dollars (FSB 2020c). After the lessons it learned from the global financial crisis, the ECB wasted no time in taking unconventional action. It launched a 750-billion-euro Pandemic Emergency Purchase Program (PEPP), expanding the amount to 1.85 trillion euros later in the year. At the same time, it renewed its asset purchase program with a monthly figure of 20 billion euros (ECB 2020b; ECB 2021a). In a similar move, the Bank of England set up a term lending scheme for small and medium-sized businesses and a COVID Corporate Financing Facility to support larger businesses. In addition, it made liquidity available to the financial sector (Bailey et al. 2020).

Rising inflation in 2022, however, eventually led to the phasing out of all central bank QE programs. Most central banks switched instead to a policy of quantitative tightening (QT) and began selling government bonds. The balances held by commercial banks at the central bank shrank as a result, thereby gradually reducing the volume of central bank money. Because an exit from QE programs tends to hamper economic recovery and introduces more financial volatility and uncertainty, the move was contested (Acharya et al. 2022; World Bank 2022b). The fact that QE programs were already highly controversial made it impossible for central banks to deviate from the prevailing practices of central banking in times of inflation (see the discussion on "layered structures" in chapter 4). It is unclear, however, how QT is supposed to work without causing severe turbulence in the financial system (Wu and Duguid 2022; Jones 2023; see chapter 8.5), considering that the existing security structure is based on low policy rates and QE. To return to the start of this section and Goethe's cautionary tale: Sorcerers' apprentices who experiment with unconventional forces can wind up creating a flood of new and even more complex problems that defy simple solutions.

8.4 Dealers of Last Resort

During the two major crises in the first quarter of the present century, *financial liquidity*—in other words, the availability of money—did not translate into *market liquidity* for securities. Despite the fact that there were ample funds at commercial banks, investors were simply not trading in securities. Central banks came to realize that this was due in large part to the dynamics of the shadow banking system. What the system lacked as the crisis unfolded was a state security structure to stop the downward spiral. Central banks responded to the dilemma in a previously unimaginable fashion: They assumed the role of market makers and dealers of last resort—not just for the regulated financial system but also for the shadow banking system. Why did they take such a radical step? In what ways do central banks act as dealers of last resort? And how do their polices affect the stability of the system as a whole? To answer these questions it is necessary to trace the measures implemented by central banks during the global financial crisis and the COVID-19 crisis both in the banking system and the shadow banking system.

Ad Hoc Dealer of Last Resort:
The 2007–2009 Global Financial Crisis

In the period leading up to the global financial crisis, and then once again before the COVID-19 crisis, there was a significant surge in repo transactions. By entering into repo agreements, financial players were able to increase their level of debt, using short-term refinancing to amplify their leverage. During the two major financial crises, however, financial leverage deteriorated (Bank of England 2020).

In the fall of 2007, the market for securitized loans collapsed. The fall was cushioned at first despite sinking prices by fresh banking-sector loans and a surge in repo transactions. The Fed then expanded the range of securities it accepted as collateral, making additional liquidity and safe assets available to the system. At the beginning of 2008, however, there was a significant increase in risk premiums on higher-risk securities. With the near insolvency of Bear Stearns, the entire US repo market came under pressure as haircuts across the board were sharply increased. It was at that point that the Fed stepped in and ramped up its traditional emergency program. Using its function as lender of last resort, the Fed provided the banking system with a vast amount of liquidity. Further, it set up the Term Securities Lending Facility (TSLF), allowing investors to borrow Treasury bonds against other securities through repo transactions (Gorton, Laarits, and Metrick 2018). This move was intended to strengthen the repo market. In addition, it created the Primary Dealer Credit Facility (PDCF) to give primary dealers without central bank accounts access to central bank funds.[9] Eligible collateral was initially limited to investment-grade securities. In September 2008, despite these measures, bankruptcy proceedings became inevitable for Lehman Brothers, which at the time was one of the world's chief market makers in mortgage-backed securities and one of the most important institutions in the shadow banking system. The Lehman Brothers' insolvency triggered panic on repo markets, intensifying the downward trend. Asset values fell, haircuts rose, and margin calls increased. This, in turn, caused securities values to drop. Eventually the money market collapsed and no one wanted to carry out repo transactions any longer, even against government bonds. Trading became impossible for financial dealers. They were no longer able to resell securities or finance their own securities purchases (Mehrling 2011: 119–23; FSB 2017b: 11–12). The impasse brought the financial intermediation system to a standstill. Trading broke down because prices could no longer be negotiated: "[N]o prices means no secured borrowing, because there is no way to evaluate the security offered" (Mehrling et al. 2013: 13).

Liquidity provision by the Fed as lender of last resort was no longer enough to prevent a crisis. As trust vanished among market participants, there was a rush to raise funds, sell securities, and reduce risk exposure. Instead of being channeled into investments, the additional liquidity injected into the banking sector was retained to buffer reserves. Whereas in times of noncrisis, banks try to keep their central bank reserves as low as possible, during and after the financial crisis there was an immense increase in such reserves. The problem remained for the shadow banking system, however, which had no access to that liquidity. The Fed's security structure in place at the time served only the banking system and not the shadow banking system.

When it became clear that the US securities market was no longer functioning, the Fed revolutionized its monetary policy, substantially widening its inventory of intervention strategies: To restore market liquidity, the Fed assumed the role of broker-dealer and market maker: "September 2008 was the moment when the Fed moved from lender of last resort to dealer of last resort" (Mehrling 2011: 122–23). Following the Lehman Brothers bankruptcy, the Fed issued Primary Dealer Credit Facility (PDCF) loans against *all available securities*, regardless of their credit rating, extending collateral eligibility even to unrated securities. In that way it temporarily became possible for primary dealers to exchange non-investment-grade securities for Treasury notes. With the Commercial Paper Facility, the Fed intervened in the commercial paper market by trading directly with investors and giving them access to the Fed's discount window. Money market funds and other primary dealers without Fed accounts were able to purchase short-term US Treasury securities through the existing Term Securities Lending Facility (TSLF), the Term Auction Facility, and the Primary Dealer Credit Facility. TSLF loans were available in exchange for investment-grade securities (those considered medium-quality securities).[10] Similar, although less extensive, programs were also implemented by the ECB and the Bank of England, through central bank specific facilities such as the Indexed Long-Term Repo Facility (ILTR), the bilateral on-demand Discount Window Facility (DWF), and the Contingent Term Repo Facility (CTRF) (Bank of England 2015; Hauser 2014; Wullweber 2020b).

But even those facilities were not enough to stem the decline. Shortly after Lehman Brothers went bankrupt, the first money market fund faltered. Investors withdrew 450 billion US dollars from various money market funds, causing fund managers to drastically reduce their money market activity. In reaction, the Fed set up a number of additional facilities designed specifically for shadow players, and in doing so, in effect created a state security structure for the shadow banking system. The Asset-Backed Commercial Paper Money Market Mutual Fund Liquidity Facility (AMLF), which was launched in September 2008, provided funding that enabled financial institutions to purchase commercial paper from money market funds, thereby helping them to remain solvent. In October 2008, the Fed established the Commercial Paper Funding Facility (CPFF) in order to provide direct support to investors in the commercial paper market by granting them access to the Fed's discount window. It also set up the Money Market Investor Funding Facility (MMIFF) to give money market funds access to the Fed's balance sheets. In March 2009, the Fed introduced the Term Asset-Backed Securities Loan Facility (TALF) so as to be able to intervene directly in the capital market and revitalize private trading in that sector as well (Adrian, Burke, and McAndrews 2009; Adrian, Kimbrough, and Marchioni 2011; Domanski, Moessner, and Nelson 2014: 55–58; Gorton, Laarits, and Metrick 2018). This empowered the Fed to act as dealer of last resort (see Figure 15) and to serve as a counterpart for both borrowers and lenders, first on the money market and later also on the capital market. In the years that followed, the Fed came to purchase 90% of all newly issued securities, in particular mortgage-backed securities (Mehrling 2017).

These monetary policy tools, which gave the shadow banking system access to liquidity and collateral, were created for the specific purpose of stimulating the securitization market while supporting money market funds that are important for the US market. While vastly increasing the scope of its repo operations, the Fed used these instruments to guarantee a certain price corridor for securities, and, in so doing, managed to stabilize the repo market. For the first time in the Fed's history, Federal Reserve facilities were expanded to include the shadow banking system: "The Fed was moving the wholesale money market onto its own balance sheet" (Mehrling 2011: 125). During the financial crisis, market liquidity depended more on the ability to shift securities to the central bank than on financial liquidity: "In effect, by assuming the risk management role of credit derivative issuers such as AIG, the Federal Reserve refashioned itself as market maker of last resort to the shadow banking system, turning private, uninsured money into sovereign money and the credit default swap into a federal function" (Cooper 2015: 398). The Bank of England followed suit and also assumed the role of market maker of last resort, but was the first central bank to lend formal status to the function with a specific reference thereto in

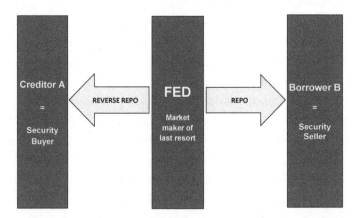

Figure 15 *The Federal Reserve as market maker of last resort.*

its 2015 Sterling Monetary Framework, or Red Book (Bank of England 2015; Birk and Thiemann 2020).

Dealer of Last Resort 2.0: The COVID-19 Crisis

Central bank interventions to curb the financial crisis were undoubtedly unprecedented. But in scope and form the measures taken to stem the COVID-19 crisis were even more radical. Once the financial crisis came to an end, most emergency measures were discontinued. Central banks gradually phased out emergency programs, in particular their lender of last resort facilities. The global financial system, however, remained unstable. Shortly after the outbreak of the pandemic, the global financial system was already on the brink of collapse. A sharp decline was experienced even by the US Treasury bond market—the largest, most important, and most liquid market for securities in the world. As the pandemic took hold, the Fed was quick to reactivate its emergency instruments, once again assuming the role of dealer of last resort (Kaminska 2020). This meant that the Fed actively intervened to influence both supply and demand in the repo market, dramatically increasing the volume of repo transactions and significantly expanding not only the conditions for repo transactions but also its balance sheet operations in general. It provided those financial market participants in possession of money with US Treasuries and those in need of money—securities dealers or hedge funds, for example—with financial resources. As an alternative to the bilateral provision of liquidity, the expansion of balance sheet operations, along with liquidity support through programs such as auctions, was designed to reduce the risk of stigmatizing financial market operators.

The Commercial Paper Funding Facility (CPFF), which had already been created in 2008 during the global financial crisis, was set up again in mid-March 2020 to enhance the liquidity of the commercial paper market and to provide a liquidity backstop for the market by supporting financial players to roll over outstanding commercial paper (Boyarchenko, Crump, and Kovner 2020). As most primary dealers do not hold a reserve account, they are not eligible to access the Fed's discount window. In order to make funds available to these actors as well, the Fed revived a program already used during the financial crisis—the Primary Dealer Credit Facility (PDCF) geared specifically to primary dealers (Martin and McLaughlin 2020). To lend support to the shadow banking system, the Fed also reactivated its repo and reverse repo facilities

(Bernanke and Yellen 2020). It set up two additional programs: the Money Market Mutual Fund Liquidity Facility (MMLF), which is very similar to the Asset-backed Commercial Paper Money Market Mutual Fund Liquidity Facility (AMLF) introduced during the financial crisis, but with a broader range of eligible assets (Cipriani et al. 2020; Politi 2020a); and the Term Asset-Backed Securities Loan Facility (TALF), which was also used during the financial crisis, and is designed to support the capital market by enabling the issuance of asset-backed securities collateralized, among other things, by student loans, auto loans, or credit card loans (Fleming, Sarkar, and Van Tassel 2020). Both of these facilities are tailored to shadow banking institutions, making it possible for the Fed to serve as a counterpart for both money market and capital market borrowers and lenders (Wullweber 2020b). The Fed also announced that it would purchase Treasuries, agency mortgage-backed securities (MBS), and agency commercial MBS to the extent necessary (Fed 2020c). Between 15 and 31 March 2020 alone, the Fed purchased 775 billion US dollars in Treasury bonds and 291 billion dollars in agency MBS (Fleming and Ruela 2020a). These policy measures were a significant contribution to calming financial markets (Cipriani et al. 2020; Boyarchenko, Crump, and Kovner 2020; Fleming and Ruela 2020b).

The lending facilities were set up as emergency instruments for the wider financial system, but they came at a price. Accordingly, they were only taken advantage of by financial institutions that had no alternative. They were created with the intention of supporting financial players that were solvent in principle but, due to adverse market developments, were temporarily unable to raise funds in the short term. The underlying assumption here is that ideally the central bank would assume only the liquidity risk, not the solvency risk (Acharya et al. 2014). This highlights the fundamental difference to classic loan-based banking. The risk of insolvency in loan-based banking can be mitigated by financial liquidity support, with the central bank then acting as lender of last resort. In the shadow banking system, however, a lender of last resort is not enough. When crisis hits, in order to curb downward spirals, the central bank has to restore market liquidity through *promises to buy* by assuming the role of dealer of last resort and acting itself as an intermediary (Mehrling et al. 2013).

The decisive advantage which central banks have over private market makers is that the funds provided are created by the central banks themselves. According to the principles as envisioned by Bagehot (Bagehot 2006 [1873]), the lender of last resort should provide as much money as is needed, but at high interest rates and only to solvent institutions against safe securities. An extension of this idea to include the dealer of last resort implies trading to the extent necessary, but with a wide bid-ask spread against securities deemed safe in noncrisis times (Mehrling 2017: 110). The idea behind opting for a wide bid-ask spread is that it is intended only to support and not replace trading in the financial markets. The expectation here is that rising prices will generate higher profits and that in the medium term financial market participants will be able to liquidate their positions with the central bank.

8.5 State Security Structures for the Shadow Banking System

In combination, the new and diverse facilities created for shadow players and, above all, the dealer of last resort function form a new and elaborately complex security structure. This is noteworthy considering that prior to the financial crisis the shadow banking system was not protected by state security structures. The shadow banking system had no such mechanisms as emergency liquidity assistance, state recapitalization measures (bailouts), or the single resolution funds that were available to the regular commercial banking system since the financial crisis (see chapter 4). So what sets the security framework for the shadow banking system apart from the mechanisms that safeguard the commercial banking system?

Before the financial crisis, the shadow banking system was exclusively based on private protection mechanisms, especially repurchase agreements.[11] Consistent with the laissez-faire mentality prevalent since the 1980s, the system enjoyed international approval and was generally considered very safe. As the Financial Stability Board put it: "Non-bank financing is a valuable alternative to bank financing" (FSB 2019: 4). Market liberal ideology maintains that the state should refrain from intervening directly in the market and only work in the background to support the privately organized circulation of funds on the premise that the market is most efficient when left to its own devices. In line with this way of thinking, central bank policy was basically geared to strengthening the capital market.

The fact that this private security structure was dysfunctional, however, became clear when Lehman Brothers, one of the most important broker-dealers in the shadow banking system, became insolvent, the shadow banking system collapsed, and nearly the entire financial system broke down. When crisis hits, this private system is not capable of restoring stability on its own. The Fed reacted to the meltdown by creating new structures to safeguard the shadow banking system. Through special emergency facilities, shadow players were able to obtain funds and government bonds from the central bank via repo transactions (Mehrling 2011: 122–25; Domanski, Moessner, and Nelson 2014: 55–58). While initially only investment-grade securities were accepted as collateral, the Fed soon began to conclude repo agreements based on any securities available, regardless of their credit rating, and even those without credit ratings (Pozsar 2014: 22).

Most of these facilities were closed after a few years. The only one remaining active was the Overnight Reverse Repurchase Agreement Facility (ON RRP) that gives both the banking system and the shadow banking system access to US Treasuries. In 2013, this facility was converted into a standing arrangement (Fed 2015b). The ON RRP facility allows shadow banks and commercial banks to purchase US Treasury bonds from the Fed through repo transactions.[12] The initial cap of 300 billion US dollars was lifted in 2015 (Frost et al. 2015). With this move, the Fed created a safety mechanism that was specifically tailored to the shadow banking system.

By the end of 2019, the Fed was working on the assumption that the security structures in place for the shadow banking system provided nonbank institutions with adequate protection (Logan 2019). This assessment of the situation, however, turned out to be wrong. What Fed policy makers had overlooked was the fact that a new nexus had formed between the central bank and the shadow banking system—a new hybrid relationship with new set of demands. The problem was that the safety net created for private finance covered only one side of the balance sheet: the need for safe securities in the form of government bonds. The other side, access to central bank money, was still missing. The ON RRP facility lacked a necessary counterpart; namely, an overnight repo facility to provide central bank money. After 2009, this overnight repo facility was closed in order to avoid giving shadow bank operators permanent access to central bank money. In the space between the two major crises, however, it had already become apparent that this approach was not tenable. As events were to demonstrate, even the slightest uncertainty over asset price developments or the liquidity status and solvency of trading partners disrupts the system and can cause it to falter. A smooth-running system relies on secure access to central bank funds. With the ON RRP facility the security framework had an upper limit. The system was supplied with as many securities as were needed to meet demand. In this way prices for collateral in the form of securities could not exceed a certain limit. The security framework, however, did not have a lower limit, which meant that in the event of a sharp fall in collateral value, shadow players would not have enough funds to meet their existing liabilities (Mehrling 2017). The Fed refrained from addressing this concern on the assumption that in such a situation the required funds would be provided by traditional banks, and that interbank competition would automatically keep the repo rate low. As the Fed reasoned, it would have to provide commercial banks only with enough central bank money to meet demands. In 2019, available funds amounted to nearly 2 trillion US dollars. This is two hundred times more than the volume supplied in 2007, when the figure stood at 10 billion dollars. Central bankers assumed it to be enough. As Fed veteran Simon Potter put it: "[R]eserves are no longer scarce" (Potter 2017b).

As incredible as it may sound, however, that was a miscalculation. Just how wrong it was became clear in September 2019, when the repo market experienced a severe liquidity crunch. The so-called *repo crisis* was triggered when the Fed initiated a program of quantitative tightening in an attempt to reduce the size of its balance sheet at least to a moderate extent. To this end it sold a small part of its securities holdings, refrained from renewing a number of repo transactions, and phased out some of its bond holdings—a strategy technically referred to as holding bonds to maturity, without reinvesting the proceeds after they come due. Even though it had become fairly obvious that pre-crisis monetary policy would no longer work, policymakers continued to believe in the ability of markets to stabilize on their own. Dominant opinion still held that a reduction of the money supply would at worst affect the marginal lending facility interest rate, and that arbitrage activities—taking advantage of price differences between the various money markets—would facilitate the smooth transfer of federal funds accessed under this facility to other sectors, including repo markets.

In September 2019, however, contrary to these market-liberal assumptions, repo rates unexpectedly spiked to levels last seen during the global financial crisis. The result was a wave of critical liquidity problems throughout the shadow banking system. The rapid increase in repo rates reflected a very high level of short-term demand for liquidity that the market itself was not willing or able to meet. Despite a slight decline in the money supply, assets on the Fed's balance sheet still totaled 3.8 trillion US dollars, and bank reserves in Fed accounts amounted to nearly 2 trillion dollars. And yet there was not enough liquidity in the shadow banking sector to meet the system's demand (Tran 2019; Pozsar 2019). Ironically, despite ample reserves on the balance sheets of major US financial institutions such as JPMorgan, Citigroup, Bank of America, and Wells Fargo, these private money market players were not willing to counter the liquidity drain by lending out their reserves to the market (Greeley, Smith, and Rennison 2019). In this respect, conditions resembled the run-up to the global financial crisis. Smaller banks, on the other hand, refrained from borrowing at the discount window to avoid the illiquidity stigma associated with the facility (Kaminska 2019). Since neither the Fed nor commercial banks were lending funds, there was ultimately no way for shadow players to acquire the financial liquidity they needed.

On 15 September 2019, overnight repo rates suddenly began to climb and soon reached a peak of 10%, the highest mark recorded since the financial crisis. Even then, instead of adapting to its new nexus with the shadow banking system, the Fed failed to take immediate action. Its reluctance can be explained in part by its pre-crisis approach, which focused on the control of key interest rates rather than on repo rates. But against the background of the new state-market hybridity, and given that the repo market has meanwhile become the driving force of the money market, an upper limit must also be set for the repo rate (Rennison 2019; Wullweber 2020b). To prevent a collapse of the repo market, the Fed eventually did step in and reactivated its repo facility. What is more, it ended its program of QT and once again resumed QE, injecting 75 billion dollars per day into the money market—a measure that quickly managed to restore calm (Fed 2019b). Welcome to the new normal!

Both the Overnight Reverse Repo Facility and the Overnight Repo Facility are crucial to secure a corridor for trading in the shadow banking system. As dealer of last resort, the central bank is responsible for guaranteeing a bid-ask spread for financial products (Mehrling 2017). The Bank of England was the first central bank to formalize this monetary policy instrument. It meanwhile forms part of the official guidelines outlined in the Bank of England's Sterling Monetary Framework: "The market-wide Contingent Term Repo Facility (CTRF) allows the Bank to provide liquidity against the full range of eligible collateral at any time, term and price it chooses" (Bank of England 2015: 6). In

2021, the Fed followed suit with its standing repo facility (SRF) (Afonso et al. 2022a).

From the larger picture that emerges in the overall context of the measures adopted during the last two major crises, it is clear that central banks have taken on a new role in capitalism. They have provided a new security structure that encompasses not only the banking system but also the shadow banking system. The fact that the shadow banking system has become crucial to the functioning of capitalist economies justifies the conclusion that by virtue of their actions, central banks have, in effect, become the guarantors for the survival of modern capitalism. We are living in an era of central bank capitalism.

Can shadow banks then also create money? The answer to this question requires us to backtrack a bit and review a number of basic terms and concepts: Bank money (deposit money) is a promissory note to the borrower. It is "simply an acknowledgment of a private debt, expressed in the money of account, . . . to settle a transaction" (Keynes 1971 [1930]: 5). What makes a bank credit and the corresponding deposit special as compared with a credit between two individuals is the fact that the bank deposit can be traded for central bank money at par and on demand. This was not always the case, but is rather the result of conflicting social developments (Chick 2013). By virtue of this institutionalized security structure, the specific credit becomes quasi-money—that is, a state money-like asset which can therefore serve as a general equivalent for all goods. Accordingly, as long as the state maintains its guarantee of par convertibility, the credit in question represents "a debt owing by the State" (Keynes 1971 [1930]: 5). When banks grant a loan, they create deposits simply by expanding their balance sheets.

What happens, though, when loans are made through the shadow banking system? In most cases when shadow dealers facilitate credit, they do so by transacting repo agreements. Repo credit in the private finance sector works differently from loans in the traditional banking system. The ability to trade at par on demand depends largely on the quality of the underlying collateral. Securities, government bonds in most cases, serve the purpose of collateral. As shadow dealers cannot produce their own collateral, they have to purchase securities that they use to back their trading operations. The purchases are arranged through repo agreements that the dealers transact with financial market participants such as investment banks (see t_1 in Figure 16). They procure the money they need to cover the purchases by borrowing it through repo agreements, which they conclude with third parties such as money market funds (see t_2 in Figure 16). No deposits are created in this process. In this simple example, dealers merely transfer—or intermediate—the deposits from a money market fund, for example, to an investment bank. The securities used as collateral from the investment bank are transferred, in turn, to the money market fund. At the end of the repo term, the trader redeems the collateral from the money market fund for the amount borrowed (plus interest). When shadow dealers act as intermediaries to purchase securities, they make a profit by selling the securities at a bid price that is lower than the ask price.

The picture becomes more complicated, however, when the Fed's standing overnight reverse repo facility (ON RRP) and the Standing Repo Facility (SRF) are considered. These facilities have enabled shadow players to access both government bonds (safe assets) and central bank money (see Figure 17).[13] That is to say, central banks guarantee par convertibility for both sides of the overnight repo trade (which make up the bulk of all repos). This grants financial liquidity and market liquidity to the shadow banking system. Despite the fact that repos do not qualify as bank money, they are remarkably safe as a result of the new monetary policy that has fashioned a state security structure for the shadow

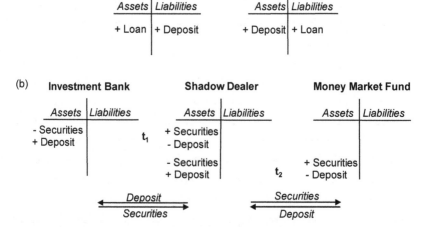

Figure 16 *Stylized comparison between the loan-based credit system and the shadow banking system.*

banking system (Pozsar 2014, 2015; Gabor and Vestergaard 2016). Private loans become a state money-like asset if their convertibility into central bank money at par and on demand is guaranteed by a state-institutionalized security structure (see chapter 4.2). The definition of a state money-like asset—the fact that it can be traded at par on demand with central bank money—is thus also given for repos that use eligible securities.

Shadow money (repos) obviously cannot be used to buy goods at the grocery store. That is still a very special privilege attached to commercial bank deposits. However, shadow money can be used to conduct transactions within the banking and the shadow banking system. There repos can temporarily serve as a substitute for deposits, or at least delay settlement in deposits. This is the case, as Gabor and Vestergaard (2016) argue, if a bank's trading partner, e.g., a pension fund, prefers a repo instead of a demand deposit when selling a bond to the bank (to avoid an uninsured exposure to the bank, for example). This means that when purchasing securities, a bank can either pay with deposits or conclude a repo transaction based on their counterparty's preference. Repos can even substitute for central bank money, or at least delay its settlement. If, for instance, Bank A needs to transfer deposits to Bank B to settle its balance, but does not have enough central bank reserves to cover the amount, the two banks could instead transact a repo agreement. In that case, Bank A would borrow central bank money from Bank B without transferring central bank reserves. For Bank A, the advantage of a repo would be that it would not have to borrow central bank money on the (more expensive) money market. And for Bank B the repo transaction instead of reserves would be an opportunity to use

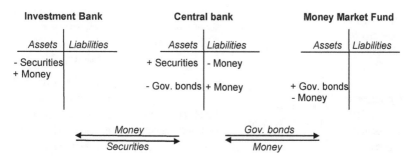

Figure 17 *The central bank as dealer of last resort.*

the underlying security to make a profit. Accordingly, at least in the financial realm, the boundary is blurred between central bank money (reserves), bank money (deposits) and shadow money (repos) (see Table 4).

Unlike deposits created by commercial banks, however, a repo cannot be used to discharge an outstanding debt, but only to temporarily defer its settlement.[14] Repos are a promise to trade at par on demand. In times of crisis, depending how grave the situation becomes, this promise can prove to be a costly one in terms of margin calls, increases in haircuts, and repo rates. Repos become increasingly vulnerable when assets are caught in a downward spiral, a situation that can eventually lead to liquidity shortages and ultimately cause the collapse of the entire financial system. The instability of the system as a whole is compounded by the fact that repos are intertwined with money and capital markets, including derivative markets. In this way, a crisis in one market segment can directly become a crisis in the other segments. What is more,

Table 4 *Security structures for bank deposit and repos. Wullweber 2021, modified.*

	Par convertibility secured by the state	Par convertibility secured by market mechanisms	Backstop
Bank deposits	Deposit insurance provided by the state	–	Minimum capital requirements + marginal lending facility of the central bank (discount window) + lender of last resort
Repos before the financial crisis 2007–09	–	Mark-to-market, margin calls, short maturity	Haircuts, various types of collateral and private hedges such as credit default swaps (CDS)
Repos since the creation of the new security structure	Shadow money "insurance" provided through ON RRP and SRF	Mark-to-market, margin calls, short maturity	Haircuts, various types of collateral and private hedges such as credit default swaps (CDS); + market maker of last resort

Source: Wullweber 2021, modified

leveraging and rehypothecation (the resale of securities) lead to additional balance sheet expansion. By acting as dealer of last resort, the central bank can prevent a collapse. In this role, it can guarantee a price floor for collateral underlying repo transactions and at the same time a price ceiling for the provision of liquidity.

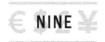

NINE

Central Bank Capitalism
and the Elasticity Provision
of Last Resort

THE QUESTION NOW IS HOW to interpret and evaluate the new importance that central banks have taken on in the sense of the historical era referred to earlier as
central bank capitalism. What problems does the new state-market configuration entail, and what challenges, and perhaps even dangers, arise from this new
form of interdependence? Does central bank capitalism mark the end of the
neoliberal era that began with the termination of the Bretton Woods system,
and gained impetus with Ronald Reagan's deregulatory policies and Margaret
Thatcher's Big Bang period of financial services deregulation in the 1980s? Has
the prevailing layered structure of central banking been renegotiated? Is this
new era of central bank capitalism a return to strong government control of
the financial system? At first glance this would seem to be the case in view of
the massive and comprehensive measures taken by central banks in the wake
of the two great crises of the early twenty-first century. Indeed, it is the central
banks and their day-to-day interventions that keep the financial system going,
and ultimately also the productive economy. It is also the central banks that
can slow down the economy and even push it into recession when key interest
rates are too high. Through central bank policies, the state meanwhile inter-
venes in financial trading to a far greater and more direct extent than during
the thirty years prior to the 2007–9 financial crisis. At the same time, however,

the shadow banking system continues to grow in importance. Shadow banking players have emerged from the last two crises not weaker but stronger.

9.1 Laissez-Faire with a Safety Net

At the beginning of the global financial crisis the initial reaction was to try and stop the downturn with measures guided by traditional market liberal logic. Central bankers lowered key interest rates and began serving as lender of last resort. When these two instruments failed to stabilize the system, they implemented a program of quantitative easing. The idea was that with central bank support, the financial system would regain stability on its own. Key interest rate policy can be understood as a Foucauldian security power mechanism par excellence. The aim of this type of monetary policy is to regulate not the financial players but the circulation of money: "[K]eep inflation within a tight range through control of a short-term interest rate, and everything else will take care of itself" (Borio 2015: 191). Lowering key interest rates tends to increase the volume of bank loans, and consequently the amount of money in circulation, while raising the policy rate tends to reduce credit activities. Instead of a governance modality that relies on sovereign and discipline power and "a binary division between the permitted and the prohibited, [security power] establishes an average considered as optimal on the one hand, and, on the other, a bandwidth of the acceptable that must not be exceeded" (Foucault 2009: 6). Lender of last resort facilities and quantitative easing are similarly mechanisms based on market liberal security power. All these instruments merely involve the provision of liquidity or incentives and not the introduction of new financial regulations, the assumption being that the market is able to regulate itself, and that any imbalance is merely a matter of short-term abnormal payment difficulties that pose no challenge to the functioning of the overall financial market.

At the end of 2008, when the Lehman Brothers bankruptcy triggered panic on financial markets, it became clear that despite massive provision of liquidity, financial players would not be able to stem the crisis on their own. Market liberal security power had ceased to be an effective mode of financial market governance. Central bankers were briefly at a loss, but once they realized—first at the Fed and the Bank of England—that their conventional monetary policy had failed, they were surprisingly quick to change their strategy to one of direct intervention in market processes. It was ultimately the central banks as market makers of last resort that stabilized the money market, and, at the same time, guaranteed supply and demand on capital markets. Their measures focused particularly on mortgage-backed securities but eventually extended to practically all forms of collateral.

Does this, then, constitute a return to the model of a *strong state* that exercises greater control through financial market intervention? The fact that in the years since the financial crisis central banks have increasingly acted as a "central point of . . . circulation" (Foucault 2009: 15) would seem to point in this direction. Acting as sovereign power, central banks offer financial players a bid-ask spread for certain financial products; in other words, a buyer and a seller price. In this way, they provide a safe corridor in which financial trade can take place (Mehrling 2011, 2022; see Figure 18). Intervention on the part of the state in the form of the central bank has been so massive that at first glance it does appear to suggest a return to the rationality of sovereign power. Moreover, the aim behind the measures has been to more effectively transform unpredictable uncertainty into calculable risk. It has not been the intention to organize uncertainty but rather to regulate risk (Foucault 2009: 20–23).

There is no question that in the years since the global financial crisis it has

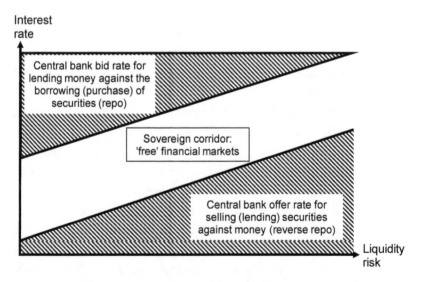

Figure 18 *Secured trade corridor for the shadow banking system. Author illustration based on Treynor 1987 and Mehrling 2022.*

been the central banks, through their day-to-day interventions in the financial system, which have stabilized and sustained that very system, even if in doing so they sometimes added new instabilities. The state has come to intervene in financial trading far more intensively and directly than ever before. Related to the layered structure of central banking, the assumption that central banks should refrain from interfering in market processes necessarily had to be adjusted. The question remains, however, whether this does, in fact, constitute a departure from the logic of (market liberal) security power. On closer examination, it becomes clear that the new unconventional forms of intervention can be understood in the sense of classical sovereign power only to a limited degree, because this would imply the creation of new legal regulations, a financial transaction tax (the so-called "Tobin tax"),[1] or the punishment of financial players. This, however, was the case only to a limited degree. Instead, it is more of a silent, albeit radical, change that is taking place, because it is still a matter of "making possible, guaranteeing, and ensuring circulations" (Foucault 2009: 29). Nevertheless, it is a different form of laissez-faire circulation than before the global financial crisis.

Accordingly, central bank crisis interventions do not constitute a return to the rationality of sovereign power, but rather a modification of security power as the mode of governance, even though the modification is admittedly a significant one. It is not the case that market liberal security logic has been replaced by stronger sovereign power. Central banks still prefer to act in the background. Sovereign power in this sense merely draws the parameters for the logic of market liberalism. Within the parameters set by the state, however, market forces are supposed to be allowed to continue developing *freely*. No fixed price is established for financial products, only the framework. The intention is for prices to continue to develop independently but "within acceptable limits" (Foucault 2009: 66). Neither is it therefore a question of a return to disciplinary power. That would mean that robust legal requirements would dictate how financial trading should take place: "By definition, discipline regulates everything. . . . Not only does it not allow things to run their course, its principle is that things, the smallest things, must not be abandoned to themselves" (Foucault 2009: 45).[2] Market liberal security logic, however, still remains present and dominant. What we are witnessing is the *adaptation of market liberal logic to crisis mode*. Faith in efficient self-regulation has not been rejected. The "thesis of the just price" (Foucault 2009: 343) determined by market forces still holds. It was merely suspended *at the fringes* of the price corridor until the purported end of the crisis. Market liberal rationality has now gained a much stronger degree of sovereign support than it had before the financial crisis of 2007–9. Liquidity circulation has once again been bolstered and secured. In the "general economy of power" (Foucault 2009: 378), there has been a significant shift in the rationality of governance, but only so that market liberal logic can continue to be safeguarded.

Even the massive state subsidy programs implemented during the pandemic have not weakened or even suspended market liberal logic. On the contrary, they have actually strengthened it. There is an astonishing degree of elasticity in the relationship between state and market that is characteristic of capitalism and rife with possibilities for reacting to crisis (Mirowski 2014; Scherrer 2014; Konings 2018). The massive support lent to the economy and the financial system in times of crisis serves not to overturn market liberal logic but rather to uphold it. The measures of support establish a framework for neoliberal laissez-faire policy. And not only that: Considering that the financial system would collapse without central bank intervention, it is precisely this intervention that keeps the laissez-faire system functioning on an artificial basis. What this neoliberal safety net amounts to in effect is *laissez-faire on life support*.

9.2 The Shifting State-Market Relationship

Financial system governance has undergone a fundamental transformation since the global financial crisis. The stabilization of the financial system today is largely based on the stabilization of the shadow banking system, and, consequently, on the guarantee of a liquid market for collateral. This, in turn, requires a well-functioning repo market. While in order to continue funding liquidity in a crisis, a bank-based credit system needs a lender of last resort, the capital-market-based credit system relies on a dealer of last resort to guarantee market liquidity.

The repo market currently requires day-to-day intervention on the part of central banks, and the demand for secured repo transactions is on the rise (ECB 2017, 2019; FSB 2022). At the same time, demand continues to be high for the Fed's overnight reverse repo facility (ON RRP). Since August 2021, the Fed has been conducting more than one trillion US dollars in repo transactions every working day—at times even reaching a peak of more than two trillion

US dollars per day—"to support the effective implementation of policy and the smooth functioning of short-term US dollar funding markets" (Federal Reserve Bank of New York 2021, 2023). In addition, the regular banking system has begun to experience an increase in cash outflow. Money market funds have been buying Treasury securities via repos from the Fed and selling them to institutional investors, who have been buying them with cash they normally would have deposited at banks. In this way, the ON RRP "turns from a largely passive tool that provided an interest rate floor to the deposits that large banks have been pushing away, into an active tool that 'sucks' the deposits away that banks decided to retain" (Pozsar 2021: 1). Obviously, the global financial system remains inherently unstable and continues to be a constant trouble spot. Indeed, it has become a permanent *emergency case*. The system fails to provide sufficient liquidity as a public good because it functions in a perpetually reinforcing procyclical fashion. Either there is too much liquidity, in which case the money supply keeps expanding, or there is not enough, and funds become even less available due to the tendency to hoard in times of scarcity. The only reason why it has not become blatantly obvious that the financial system has been operating in crisis mode ever since the 2008 financial meltdown is the fact that it is constantly being stabilized through a multitude of interventions on the part of the most important central banks, above all the Fed.

Because of inherent structural problems and inconsistencies, financial markets regularly fail to meet their claim to guarantee liquidity. And what is more, as demonstrated in the foregoing chapters, they cannot manage to do so without the support of the central banks and ultimately the state. The state has always established the political and legal framework in which the "free market" can develop, often against the will of its own people (Scherrer 1999; Pistor 2020; Scherrer, Saggioro Garcia, and Wullweber 2023). The guarantee of liquidity is therefore not an issue that would arise in a context detached from the state.

As shown above, significant shifts have occurred in certain areas because of the fact that liquidity generation is taking place now, more than ever before, in the shadow banking system. The development appears to be a paradox: The shadow banking system, which is largely outside the regulated financial system, has come to play an increasingly important role in the generation of liquidity. At the same time, central banks have been escalating their intervention and expanding their range of measures in order to secure this creation of liquidity in the nonbank sector. The paradox is resolved, however, if the state is not re-garded as separate from the financial system. The state-market dichotomy leads to an analytical dead end, because the constellation in central bank capitalism is characterized by more state intervention and more market activity. The gov-ernance of liquidity is based on a deeply entrenched interaction between state and private actors. This close entanglement, which has become even closer since the financial crises, reduces ad absurdum the frequently invoked dichotomy between market and state (Knafo 2013; Wullweber 2020b; Coombs and Thie-mann 2022).

Before the financial crisis, central banks largely operated quietly and behind the scenes. Today, however, central bank policy decisions, including whether to raise key interest rates, to continue quantitative easing, or to implement cli-mate protection measures, have become the focus of political contention. It is ultimately the central banks, above all the C6 (perhaps soon to be joined by the People's Bank of China), and primarily the Fed, which, because of their special position in and provision of the security structure, determine the liquidity of the financial system through their monetary policy. The massive intervention programs implemented by central banks during the 2007–9 financial crisis and the COVID-19 pandemic were not just exceptions to the rule; in other words, reversible measures taken merely to help restore financial markets and the world's economies back to a *natural* state of equilibrium. Apart from the fact that there has never been such an equilibrium, a return to central bank policies of the past is no longer possible. The global economy and the world financial system have become far too unstable.

In the long run, it remains to be seen how this new form of monetary policy will affect the financial system as a whole. Some scholars see the development in a positive light, at least in part (Pozsar 2014, 2015). They argue that the course being followed by central banks allows them to impose minimum capital re-quirements not only on traditional banks but also on broker-dealers, creating new possibilities for state control. They point out further that new options are opening up for central bank monetary policy, since in repo transactions central banks can determine what securities to accept as collateral from which counterparties. In this sense, the Financial Stability Board hopes that the regu-latory reforms will transform the shadow banking sector into a resilient system (FSB 2017b). On the other hand, the new security structure facilitates access to central bank balance sheets. And more market participants have gained access to central bank accounts. It is not unlikely that the new development will lead to new credit and liquidity cycles, which will inevitably generate greater instability. As Minsky famously noted: "All capitalisms are unstable, but some capitalisms are more unstable than others" (Minsky 1982b: 36).

9.3 Superheroes and the Transformation of the Financial System

The massive scale of intervention on the part of central banks has sharply expanded their balance sheets. At the end of 2020, the combined balance sheets of the twenty-two most important central banks amounted to an equivalent of over 41 trillion US dollars (FSB 2021b: 7). Since 2022, all QE programs have been stopped, and instead balance sheets have been reduced through quantitative tightening, which involves the selling of assets. The first attempt on the part of the Fed to shrink its balance sheet led to the repo crisis in 2019. In March 2023, after the collapse of Silicon Valley Bank, the Fed had to interrupt its QT efforts and launch another QE program to prevent the spread of further bank failures in the United States. The Bank of England also had to temporarily suspend its QT program to calm the crisis in the gilt market in September 2022 (Stubbington 2022). As these developments suggest, it remains to be seen whether central banks will be able to shrink their balance sheets significantly and how the balance sheet tapering will affect the stability of the financial system (Tett 2017; Leonard, Martin, and Potter 2017). It is not unlikely that central banks will continue to maintain an ample reserve regime for the foreseeable future. In order to protect the cohesion of the euro area, the ECB has already developed an instrument to mitigate the destabilizing effects of QT. The Transmission Protection Instrument (TPI) allows the ECB to buy bonds of individual countries (ECB 2022).[3] Hence, if the spreads between the government bonds of individual eurozone countries widen too much, this instrument can be used to provide targeted support for individual government bonds. Even if TPI does not amount to sovereign financing, as it is often criticized (Buiter 2023), the political dimension of this monetary policy is much more evident than with other unconventional monetary policies.

The immense expansion of central bank balance sheets is not per se a problem to financial stability. Many central bank monetary policies today are implemented through the creation or destruction of money. When central banks purchase government bonds, or other assets, from banks, they create central bank money for that purpose and credit it to the banks deposit (reserve) account at the central bank. The money is therefore not taken from somewhere else. When the central bank sells the assets back to the bank or other eligible counterparts, it destroys the money again. The supply of money should therefore not be understood in terms of a set of fixed assets such as gold but rather as a supply of credit that increases or decreases as needed. In other words, it changes in an elastic and dynamic manner. It is important to understand this elasticity of the monetary and financial system. There is no natural or objective limit to the amount of money or credit that can be issued. Optimal elasticity depends on the social, environmental, and politico-economic context. It has become clear that since the end of Bretton Woods in the early 1970s, private financial actors alone are not capable of generating a stable financial system. In good times, stability is overestimated and the profit motive leads to gigantic financial bubbles. When these bubbles burst, panic among private investors leads to rapid downward spirals that can bring down the entire financial system, including the productive economy.

The once-prevailing "reason of least government as the principle organizing raison d'Etat" (Foucault 2008: 28) has inevitably given way to the realization that because of the lack of strong and effective legal regulations, it has become necessary for central banks to lend the financial system massive support. It is not so much a question of the concrete amount of support that they provide but of the *theoretically* unlimited amount of promises to pay and promises to purchase—that is to say, the volume of money that they *can* provide and the amount of trading transactions they can make in order to stabilize the financial system. The mere awareness that in case of doubt central banks would also intervene in the market-based credit system—the shadow banking system—has been sufficient to stabilize and reactivate trading in securities, as clearly demonstrated during the financial crisis of 2007–9: "Simply knowing that the Fed was there as a backstop made others willing to deal privately inside the Fed's bid-ask spread" (Mehrling 2011: 125). This kind of assurance works the same way for other central banks, just as it did in 2012, for example, when former ECB president Mario Draghi famously promised to do whatever it would take to save the euro. The effect was immediate. Panic was calmed and spreads between eurozone government bonds narrowed, lessening the gravity of the euro crisis.

Central bank interventions can also alter the modalities of the financial system. When central banks intervene in the financial markets by buying up securities, for example, their intervention changes the value of the collateral because of the mark-to-market process: "[M]onetary policy sets the universal price of leverage" (Borio 2015: 195). By concluding large numbers of repo transactions with primary dealers, central banks increase the amount of liquidity available to those dealers. The expanded liquidity supply also allows intermediaries to redeem more expensive credits and, on the whole, to conduct more repo transactions with other financial players. This, in turn, increases the demand for collateral assets, driving up the price of those assets. In this manner, central bank policy significantly stimulates both the traditional banking system as well as the shadow banking system. It affects the entire financial system, inducing, among other things, new liquidity spirals and asset price bubbles. In this sense, central bank monetary policy geared to *stabilizing* the system also has a *destabilizing* effect.

The central role that the repo market and the shadow banking system play in the overall financial system has radically redefined the link that exists between state institutions and the financial market, bringing it to an entirely new level. As issuer of the collateral-eligible securities most in demand, the state itself plays a significant role in supporting, protecting, and strengthening the shadow banking system. Rather pointedly, Gabor and Vestergaard (2016: 29) speak of the state as a de facto "shadow central bank," and, as Gabor (2016a: 969) has argued, "the state has become a collateral factory for shadow banking." The analogy is justified considering that government bonds are the prime source of collateral for the shadow banking system. Shadow banking entities would not be able to function without these securities. For the shadow banking system, government bonds serve a role that parallels that of central bank money for the traditional banking system. Nevertheless, ministries of finance so far do not print more bonds to meet rising demands. They do not issue government bonds flexibly. For the most part, they act in line with budgetary criteria based on the macroeconomic situation of their respective countries as well as on political considerations of a domestic nature. The distinction between monetary and fiscal policy, however, is growing increasingly blurred.

Measures to safeguard the repo market are therefore significant in a double respect: On the one hand, they secure the market-based financial system, which is dependent on safe assets that can serve as collateral with little risk of any considerable value loss. On the other, they stabilize the monetary policy transmission channel itself: "[R]epo markets have become more and more important in the monetary policy transmission process" (Bundesbank 2013: 57). Central banks have therefore become active in the repo market in order to implement their monetary policy (FSB 2017b: 5; Logan 2017). In other words, in addition to implementing traditional interest rate policy, central banks also operate in the shadow banking system so as to stabilize key interest rates for both the banking system and the shadow banking system (Fed 2015b; Frost et al. 2015). For them to exercise control in this sector with their interventions, they have to act as dealers and market makers even in times of relative stability. It was a first in the history of central banking when the Fed and other central banks established the permanent facilities for overnight repos, giving nonbanks indirect access to central bank money. This course of action also highlights the importance of market makers in today's world. In line with their role as dealers and market makers, Western central banks have adopted common market practices such as mark-to-market calculations, haircuts, and margin calls. Central banks such as the Fed, the ECB, and the Bank of England have made it a daily practice to revalue securities that are used as collateral to back repo transactions (Bank of England 2015).[4] Such market-based practices, however, are not neutral in terms of impact. The ECB's reliance on private credit ratings, for example, worsened the euro crisis during its first few years, and contributed to the widening of spreads on euro area government bonds (Orphanides 2017). As a result, by 2010, traders stopped accepting Portuguese, Greek, and Irish government bonds as collateral. At the start of 2012, the crisis began to spread beyond the peripheral countries, affecting the interest rate premium for Italian government bonds, the second-largest market for collateral in the euro zone. Only then, when the entire European repo market began to falter as a consequence, did the ECB intervene: "[T]he ECB's 'whatever it takes' committed to put a floor on sovereign bond prices, and prevent the safe asset universe in Eurozone from shrinking to German bunds. Whatever it takes saved shadow euro money" (Gabor and Vestergaard 2016: 29). Paradoxically, central bank intervention is now required to control the liquidity spirals brought about, or at least intensified, not only by the states as a result of their austerity policies but also by the central banks themselves through their market-based financial practices. For an overview of a selection of key central bank instruments, see Table 5.

Table 5 *Selected central bank monetary policy tools.*

Monetary Policy Instruments	Description of Approach
Key interest rate change	adjusts the cost of central bank money for banks
Lender of last resort function	makes massive central bank money available to systemically important banks
Since the financial crisis 2007–9	
Extended lender of last resort function	makes funding liquidity available also to systemically important financial players such as investment banks
Quantitative easing	greatly expands the central bank money supply
Fed's Primary Dealer Credit Facility (PDCF); Money Market Investor Funding Facility (MMIFF)	provides financial liquidity and market liquidity for primary dealers and money market funds
Fed's Term Securities Lending Facility (TSLF)	provides safe assets and market liquidity for the shadow banking system
Overnight Reverse Repo Facility (ON RRP)	grants banks and shadow banks access to US Treasuries
Overnight Repo Facilities	grants shadow banks access to funding liquidity
Dealer of last resort function	allows central banks to assume the role of market maker in the shadow banking system, thereby guaranteeing market liquidity and funding liquidity
Fed's Central bank liquidity swaps (swap lines)	provide US dollars from the Fed to eligible foreign central banks
Since the Covid-19 financial crisis 2020	
Fed's Standing repo facility (SRF)	provides the shadow banking system (and banking system) with permanent access to funding liquidity
Foreign and International Monetary Authorities (FIMA) Repo Facility	enables central banks to conduct repos with the Fed to access US dollars by using their US government bonds
Fed's Primary Market Corporate Credit Facility	extends credit to the productive economy and local governments
Since 2022 (inflation)	
Quantitative tightening	reduces central bank money supply
Fed's Bank Term Funding Program	provides funding liquidity for banks at favorable terms
ECB's Transmission Protection Instrument	counteracts fragmentation in the eurozone bond market through the targeted purchase of government bonds

9.4 Mind the Gap!

Ever since the *neoliberal turn* of the 1970s, there has been a steady increase in the amount of assets and wealth that remains concentrated in the hands of a small group of people (Piketty 2014; Konings 2018; Pistor 2020). In the United States, the richest 1% own 33% of all wealth, and the richest 10% more than 70%. Half of the US population owns only 2% of the total wealth (Fed 2023f). By contrast, real wages and salaries—purchasing power adjusted for inflation—have seen a continual decline (St. Louis Fed 2022b; US Bureau of Labor Statistics 2023), while household expenditures keep rising (St. Louis Fed 2023e). This means that on the whole, and in relation to wages and salaries, private households are going deeper and deeper into debt (Adkins, Cooper, and Konings 2019).

The situation for financial players, on the other hand, is altogether different: Despite the vast scale of the two crises, and the massive levels of state intervention and safety-net programs, a large number of private financial players have emerged from the crises stronger than before (Durden 2020; FSB 2020b): In the banking sector, the market concentration led by companies such as Wells Fargo, JPMorgan, Bank of America, and Citigroup continues to gain in strength (Franklin et al. 2023). Especially the big banks, asset managers, and hedge funds benefit from current policies (Haldane 2014; Fichtner, Heemskerk, and Garcia-Bernardo 2017): "Quantitative easing . . . has bailed out bonus-happy banks and made the rich richer" (Marshall 2015). At the end of 2021, private financial players in the euro area together with twenty-one of the world's most important non-euro area jurisdictions held a total of more than 422 trillion dollars in financial assets. This is a share of around 87% of total global financial assets—a record high in a sharply rising trend (FSB 2022: 3–7). By now, the financial assets of nonbanks, or shadow banks, significantly exceed those of commercial banks. The nonbank sector continues to account for the strongest growth rates in financial assets. The widening gap between rich and poor has actually contributed to the rise of the shadow banking system. A small segment of society owns an increasing proportion of global assets and is in urgent need of profitable opportunities for investment (Boyer 2000; Helgadóttir 2016; Gabor 2016a; see also Pozsar 2011; Piketty 2014).

Ninety-five percent of the world population, however, has no share in this increasing amount of wealth. And the new and unconventional monetary policies are actually intensifying the redistribution of wealth from the bottom up, widening the social inequality gap even further (Young 2018; McKinsey Global Institute 2021; Sharma 2021; *Financial Times* 2022).[5] Final conclusions are still pending on the specifics of how monetary policy affects wealth disparity, but it remains relatively beyond dispute that monetary policy does have a bearing on the distribution of income and wealth (Carney 2016; Schnabel 2021b).

Central bank independence, which, as pointed out earlier, gained global acceptance during the 1990s, also found its legitimization in the fact that issues of distribution in society continued to be decided by democratically elected governments. Monetary policy, on the other hand, was purported to be largely neutral in terms of effect and, by nature, ultimately apolitical. This has proven to be a surprisingly resilient myth (van 't Klooster and Fontan 2020). From experience gained during the two major crises of the twenty-first century and in light of the massive measures implemented by central banks to restabilize the economic and financial system, it has meanwhile become clearer than ever that monetary policy is anything but apolitical. Monetary policy—the policy of central banks—should therefore become more strongly democratized.

TEN

Outlook

Navigating in Turbulent Times

AS A GROUP OF SOVEREIGN STATES, each with its own separate fiscal policy and government bonds but united by a common currency, the euro area has to deal with very unique challenges. To prevent the euro area from becoming a *German Bund area* (Gabor and Vestergaard 2016: 25), it would actually have been necessary to launch a eurobond, a debt instrument issued by every euro area member with joint liability shared by all members. This option, however, was rejected especially by Northern European members, with the result that the European Commission and the ECB have come to rely on the repo market. To collateralize its repo transactions, the ECB accepts nearly all EU country government bonds on equal terms, a strategy that has considerably decreased the interest rate spreads among those bonds. In this respect, the ECB has crossed the line separating fiscal and monetary policy since the 1980s, a separation that was intended to prevent central banks from monetizing national debt. State financing, however, was not the intention of the ECB strategy. The aim was rather to secure the euro area and to narrow the interest rate spreads of the various euro country government bonds. The frequently heard argument that bond purchase programs call into question central bank independence and blur monetary and fiscal policy consequently overlooks the deeper issue and the core problem at stake—the fact that an entirely new state-market constellation has developed, a *new normal* in which the shadow banking system has taken on the central role in the global financial system.

According to market liberal thinking, the free interplay of financial market participants or market forces must also reckon with the possibility of failure. But because the shadow banking system has such a pivotal role in today's world, its failure would inevitably lead to the collapse of the entire system. Such a disaster would have immeasurable consequences for the productive economy and society as a whole. Instead of drawing the logical conclusion and implementing effective measures to regulate the entire financial system including shadow banks, decision makers persist in holding on to the idea that financial market players and market forces should be allowed to develop as freely as possible. This means, however, that in times of crisis central banks must come to their rescue.

There is another paradox inherent in market liberalism in relation to the shadow banking system. Its policies embrace structural reforms designed to lower government spending and government debt. These policies, however, stand in diametric opposition to what shadow players need, namely collateral in the form of government bonds. In other words, while market liberal fiscal policy is based on the idea of a debt limit or debt ceiling designed to reduce government spending and therefore the supply of government bonds, market liberal monetary policy seeks to strengthen a shadow banking system that cannot function without continuously increasing the supply of government bonds, although both financial securitization[1] as well as central bank repo practices can provide a buffer (Gabor/ Ban 2016). In this way, market liberal policies turn against themselves, ultimately requiring strong state intervention via the central bank in order to ensure that the two versions of this logic can exist side by side without causing the financial system or the economy to collapse: "The political economy of shadow money is nothing short of radical" (Gabor and Vestergaard 2016: 32). Even before the COVID-19 crisis, a new kind of amalgamation had evolved between state and market: "We are heading for fiscal and monetary policy co-ordination that is of a form that we haven't seen before in our lifetimes" (Tett 2019; Borio 2021; ECB 2021b). Ultimately, however, the decisive role that central banks play in the governance of the financial system results from the lack of political willingness to build a robust, legally sanctioned, highly regulated financial structure, and to pursue an active fiscal policy that strengthens the economy and benefits society (Arnold 2021). Monetary policy alone cannot stimulate the economy. It must go hand in hand with fiscal policy (Pettifor 2019; Schnabel 2021c). The Bank of England has taken an important step in this direction. For the first time in its history, namely, when the coronavirus pandemic threatened to destabilize the British economy, the BOE directly financed government spending to combat the damaging consequences (Giles and Georgiadis 2020).

Despite these very fundamental problems with which the economy and society are struggling, market liberal logic continues with tenacious persistence to be the dominant paradigm. It has become even clearer now than it was before the global financial crisis, however, that the state is vital to the stability of the financial system and the economy as a whole. The new normal is marked by political governance of a permanent state of crisis—one that makes it indispensable for central banks to intervene on a day-to-day basis: "The years ahead will be a period of experimentation in central banking" (Borio 2015: 191).

Central banks are currently the only actors willing to stabilize the system and capable of doing so. But in their efforts in this connection, they have come under immense political pressure. The very measures that were necessary to restore and maintain stability have been challenged by many market liberal advocates as allegedly unlawful state financing. Their criticism has mainly but not solely targeted the ECB. So here we face another paradoxical situation: The only institution whose measures have been effective in stabilizing the euro area and, at the same time, the only European institution to take immediate action in response to the COVID-19 crisis, has become the object of attack by the governments of many countries precisely because of its intervention. In the summer of 2020, the ECB even faced a German Constitutional Court verdict classifying parts of its earlier euro area measures of support as ultra vires, that is, beyond the scope of its delegated powers (Sandbu 2020; Politi, Smith, and Arnold 2020).

Central bank capitalism raises pressing questions about the accountability and political legitimacy of central banks (Best 2016, 2019; Coombs 2023). The prevailing political construct of central bank neutrality, which has existed across the world since the 1990s, has enabled politicians to delegate ostensibly apolitical central bank technocrats with complicated and unpopular political decisions pertaining to monetary policy. Even though central banks are an integral part of the state, the claim that they are neutral has accordingly made it possible for political actors to outsource their political responsibility. With the exception of the two years during the COVID-19 crisis, instead of actively intervening with strong fiscal policy, governments have been pursuing a strict course of austerity.[2] The idea behind reduced spending is to maintain a rigidly balanced federal budget in the style of Germany's notorious *black zero* policy. For many years, a third of the world's government bonds carried negative interest rates. In this way, issuing government bonds—incurring new debt—led to additional revenues for the state (ECB 2020a). These governments could have used the time to make necessary investments, especially, but not only, to promote socioecological transformation. Among other things, to name just a few examples, they could have expanded public transport and rail networks on a massive scale; advanced the development of sustainable energy production to become less dependent on coal, oil, and gas; renovated energy systems in public and private buildings; and improved bicycle transport infrastructures. But they failed to take advantage of this opportunity (Sandbu 2022b). On the contrary, they allowed existing infrastructures to deteriorate. Schools were not renovated, far too few teachers were hired, and protective measures to mitigate the growing climate crisis were for the most part neglected. This kind of neglect is a costly lack of foresight. Today's investments create tomorrow's innovations and also provide the necessary protection against increasing—and ultimately much more expensive—climate catastrophes. It is hard to believe, but many politicians still insist on even more rigorous strategies of belt-tightening. Precisely because of austerity efforts, however, we have become increasingly ill-prepared to deal with the simultaneous crises that face us. Compounded by financial and economic crises, large and small, increasing climate change is threatening to destroy the very basis of society. Every year we are witnessing a higher incidence of climate change–related disasters: forest fires, floods, heat shocks, crop failures, power outages, but also global supply difficulties owing to receding waterway levels such as in the Panama Canal, among other things.

Although central banks have managed to keep the overall system going despite these deficits, which are mainly due to inadequate government fiscal and financial policies, there has been an increasing amount of criticism over unconventional monetary policy, even from within the central banks themselves (McPhilemy and Moschella 2019; Tett 2019; Volcker et al. 2019; Hannoun et al. 2019; BIS 2019b). The fact that central banks have only a limited amount of leeway to reach their objectives, however, is often overlooked by critics. With all the vulnerabilities facing the global financial system, as long as governments refrain from steering their economies in a sustainable direction, central banks will be forced to take steps to stabilize markets in order to prevent the collapse of the entire system (Schnabel 2021d). And although during periods of low inflation it had become increasingly clear that instead of boosting investments in the productive economy as intended, quantitative easing measures were actually driving asset prices even higher, central banks remained trapped in the market liberal logic. Conversely, they decided to scale back quantitative easing programs at the very point when inflation demanded a more appropriate fiscal response on the part of governments. The tapering of QE has only made financing more difficult (see Duguid, Smith, and Stubbington 2022).

The decoupling of financial markets from developments in the productive economy is becoming more and more evident. While the economy was down after the near global lockdown in March and April of 2020, which turned out to be the worst global recession since the Great Depression of the 1930s, stock market prices began to soar again already in April. Even the COVID-19 pandemic with all its problems for the economy did not affect surging asset prices. On the contrary prices kept climbing to new highs (McKinsey Global Institute 2021; *Financial Times* 2022). Although central bank interventions did succeed in stabilizing the financial markets, the present state of stability remains extremely precarious. The alternative—not to give the financial system access to funds—is a dead-end strategy as long as there is a lack of any real fiscal policy capable not only of stabilizing but also of strongly boosting the economy, and as long as no effective legislative framework exists to regulate financial markets. Without appropriate policy responses and robust regulations, it is only a matter of time until the next financial and economic crisis occurs. And the impact of another crisis on today's already weakened economy would be even graver than the last.

Another trait that governments of market liberal states have in common today is that they invariably ignore or deny their own responsibility in the shaping of their economies. Not least for this reason, more and more central banks have come to demand stronger government commitment to fiscal policy objectives (Politi 2020b; Arnold and Khan 2019; Furman and Summers 2020; Schnabel 2021c). In reaction, governments have shifted the blame for political indecision to their central banks. Central bank capitalism almost invariably leads to a permanent state of technocratic exceptionalism (Best 2018). And the trend in this direction could escalate if governments maintain legal restrictions on borrowing, continue to impose debt ceilings, and remain on a course of reduced spending. In fact, extending programs of austerity would have dramatic consequences for virtually all economies and societies. The main, but not the only, reason is that even in a postpandemic world and without Russia's war, we will still have to contend with accelerating climate change, the greatest human challenge of our time. In order to have any chance of tackling the climate crisis, all available resources must be made available. Every dollar that is saved today and not invested in renewable energies, climate protection measures, and the development of strategies for a sustainable future will cause significantly more climate damage and multiply costs in the years to come. People also need to be involved, and vulnerable groups in particular need to be supported. None of this comes for free. With good reason, many economists have therefore called for a departure from austerity policies (Blanchard, Leandro, and Zettelmeyer 2020a; Gabor 2021; Mazzucato 2021; Rogoff 2021). Among other economists, Joseph Stiglitz, Paul Rubin, and Oliver Blanchard argue against fixed limits for fiscal deficits not only on the grounds that they are always arbitrary (there is no rational basis for the debt ceilings set down in agreements such as the Maastricht Treaty), but also because they are too inflexible to meet the challenges of our time (Blanchard, Leandro, and Zettelmeyer 2020b; Orszag, Rubin, and Stiglitz 2021). Even institutions such as the Organization for Economic Cooperation and Development (OECD), the World Bank, and the International Monetary Fund are now urging governments to adopt active, investment-oriented fiscal and economic policies geared to sustainability (IMF 2021; World Bank 2022a). Provided that governments take the lead, central banks can and certainly should support such climate-related investment policies (BIS 2020b; Banque de France 2020; Pereira da Silva 2021).

As demonstrated, the massive scale on which central banks have been intervening in the financial system cannot be construed as a return to the strong state or a new form of Keynesianism. Despite the severity of the crises, there have yet to be any far-reaching changes in government economic and financial policies. As I have argued throughout the book, what we are witnessing instead is a form of governance that is being pursued within the scope of the still-prevailing market liberal economic order. That form of governance implies "a sort of 'laisser-faire', a certain 'freedom of movement (laisser-passer)', a sort of '[laisser]-aller', in the sense of 'letting things take their course'" (Foucault 2009: 41), and that is where the problem lies. The relevant authorities are not calling into question the operational logics of the financial system, the prevailing sedimented layers of central banking, or even of the shadow banking system. On the contrary, instead of rethinking these logics, and taking steps toward transformation by introducing mechanisms such as a tax on financial transactions, by establishing effective coordination between governments and central banks, or by creating a scheme to curb the pace of trading on the financial assets market, they are leaving the system the way it is. Despite the radical nature of their measures, central banks have kept a low profile with their intervention. Their avoidance of publicity has obscured the paradoxes inherent in the fact that their novel programs and facilities have moved the shadow banking system to the core of the market liberal financial system. At the same time, this very situation is creating a new set of contradictions. A revolution is taking place in the financial system for which no one accepts responsibility— neither shadow bankers nor the central banks themselves. The central banks have implemented their revolutionary instruments more or less behind closed doors. We therefore currently find ourselves in the midst of a *revolution without revolutionaries* (Gabor 2021). A discursive separation is taking place. One side articulates the need for the makers of monetary policy to intervene in the financial system with radically new instruments geared to containing the global financial crisis, the COVID-19 crisis, and the next crises to come. The other concentrates on the *natural* laws ascribed to the markets (laissez-faire reasoning, free competition, profit orientation and generation, etc.), which remain unchallenged and inviolable as common goods. This is precisely the logic described by Foucault as the political rationality at the heart of the market (neo) liberal project (Foucault 2008).

During the past fifty years, the realm of finance and the global financial system have undergone an enormous process of transformation. We are no longer living in the age of "boring banking" (Krugman 2009), or boring central banking. The financial system and the global economy have become so closely intertwined that sector dislocations can easily spread and expand into crises of systemic proportions. At present we can only guess what challenges such developments will entail not only for politics and policy as well as society and the economy but also for research and science. Recent events clearly reveal the shortcomings of neoclassical theory, in particular with regard to its assumptions about efficient equilibrium (the balance between supply and demand). The fact that this aspect has received comparatively little attention in academic circles is therefore all the more surprising (Bofinger 2020; Kelton 2020).

And yet, the vastness of the crises confronting the world since the beginning of the twenty-first century underlines how crucial it has become to demonstrate impatience in developing the kind of commitment that it takes to transcend narrow perspectives and compartmentalized thinking in areas related to politics and economics and the academic disciplines dedicated to their study (Boy, Burgess, and Leander 2011). Those crises have shown how problematic it can be when broad political and economic knowledge exists only on the periphery of academic fields. A multidisciplinary approach to analysis increases the chances of identifying problems of political and economic import early enough so as to allow for the development of a wide range of strategies toward their solution (Wullweber and Scherrer 2011; Mehrling 2022a). Ultimately it is also a question of democracy—a question of academic monoculture versus intellectual diversity. Only if based on a pluralistic approach can scientific research succeed in enabling and strengthening processes of democratic decision-making (Wullweber 2019d).

Instead of overtaxing the competencies of central banks in their role to meet the demands of a deregulated financial system based on market liberal logic, what needs to be done is to restore the conditions that allow them to resume the function for which they were created; in other words, to serve as a guardian and provider of elasticity of credit and liquidity for the productive economy. Profit maximization is the sole concern of financial players themselves. Nothing else can be expected of them in a profit-oriented market economy. The responsibility for taking action lies with the sovereign states and international regulatory bodies (Mazzucato 2014). They are the ones who must make the rules (Pistor 2020). It is up to them to design a clear framework of enforceable regulations and restrictions that effectively delineates the scope within which financial players can operate while at the same time reducing the pace of trading in financial assets (Systemic Risk Council 2020). Recent work therefore calls for the creation of a new Bretton Woods system (Gallagher and Kozul-Wright 2021). Some scholars go a step further and propose that such a system be founded on green principles specifically designed to support the requirements of worldwide socioecological transformation. The core of such a green Bretton Woods system would be a green world central bank that could create its own currency to finance the process of sustainable transformation necessary to overcome the climate crisis (Aguila, Haufe, and Wullweber 2022).

This would serve to prevent—or at least mitigate—both the irrational surging of asset prices that has nothing to do with the productive economy, as well as the panic sales that are prompted by waves of market hysteria (BIS 2021). Finance should once again become a monotonous undertaking (although it would be naive to assume that a less volatile market would automatically be risk free). Besides crafting appropriate regulatory conditions, policy makers must rethink the central bank mandate, which is primarily to maintain stability and keep inflation down to a narrow margin of 2%. This 2% target regularly leads central banks to tighten interest rates too much when inflation is higher, stifling the economy and sending it into recession. More leeway would be helpful here. In addition, the shaping of monetary policy must become a more democratic process (van 't Klooster 2021). Central banks are definitely heading in the right direction in some respects, for example, by taking sustainable factors into consideration in their monetary policy decisions (Banque de France 2020, 2021; BIS 2020b; Schnabel 2020b; Aguila and Wullweber under review). Nevertheless, because those decisions have far-reaching implications for the economy and society as a whole, the public and democratically elected parliaments should be allowed to participate in the decision-making process. Monetary policy must become more inclusive. It must go hand in hand with fiscal policy on a foundation of strong democratic principles. Achieving this kind of transformation would allow us to concentrate all our attention and energy on developing, financing, and implementing social, ecological, and sustainable solutions to climate change and the many other pressing challenges of our time.

Notes

Preface

1. Strictly speaking, government debt has only been rising in nominal terms. However, the much more important debt-to-GDP ratio is falling because inflation has been rising faster than interest rates, and inflation leads to higher government revenues through taxes. Nevertheless, there has been a cut in spending in most countries.

2. Energy prices are also the main reason why inflation in the United States has fallen much faster and more sharply than in the euro area. Greater dependence in the eurozone on Russian gas that also affected electricity prices, especially in Germany, meant that expensive alternatives had to be used after the decision to impose sanctions on Russia over its war of aggression against Ukraine (Koester et al. 2022; Giles, Arnold, and Smith 2023). Also, while companies are quick to pass on increased input costs, they are far more reluctant to make downward price adjustments to reflect decreased costs, which, according to ECB board member Isabel Schnabel, leads to persistent inflation (Schnabel 2023).

Chapter 1: Introduction

1. In July 2020, despite massive opposition on the part of a number of Northern European Member States, agreement was reached to establish a European Union economic recovery fund. As a result, for the first time in the history of Europe's single currency union, the members of the euro area became jointly indebted (Saraceno, Semmler, and Young 2020).

2. Initially Lagarde had stressed that it was not the task of the ECB to harmonize the differences in the interest rates on euro area government bonds. In reaction to her re-

marks, rates began to drift apart even more noticeably. In a complete about-face, Lagarde resorted to Twitter with this statement to put a stop to the trend. She had to learn quickly and the hard way what it means to live in the age of central bank capitalism.

3. Whether the US Inflation Reduction Act is an exception is a matter of dispute, but overall the additional fiscal stimulus seems to be modest (Tooze 2023b).

4. The United Nations Environment Programme (UNEP) estimates that by 2030 in developing countries alone the annual costs of climate change adaptation and mitigation will amount to between 140 and 300 billion US dollars (UNEP 2021).

5. In this book, market liberalism (or neoliberalism) refers to a strong belief in self-regulating, efficient markets and self-adjusting equilibria. It is a rationality that is guided by the "question concerning the extent to which competitive, optimizing market relations and behaviour can serve as a principle not only for limiting governmental intervention, but also for rationalizing government itself" (Burchell 1993: 270). Accordingly, the role of government in economic policy is to provide the political, legal, and institutional framework in which market forces can develop freely. Under no circumstances, however, is government supposed to intervene directly in market activity (Dean 1991; Rose 1996).

6. An exception to this rule occurred, for example, in Hong Kong, where so-called helicopter money was transferred directly from the central bank to the accounts of private citizens (Jones 2020). Although this extremely unconventional exercise of monetary policy does manage to strengthen the purchasing power of the public in general, it is unspecific by nature. It does not serve to bolster struggling sectors of the economy or to assist socially disadvantaged populations. Further examples of this nature include some of the instruments that central banks employed during the COVID-19 economic crisis (Milstein and Wessel 2021).

7. The term *COVID-19 crisis* as used here and throughout this book refers to the financial and economic crisis that followed the outbreak of the COVID-19 pandemic.

8. Although crossing this red line is considered taboo in market liberalism, it does tend to happen regularly (Bateman and van 't Klooster 2023).

Chapter 2: The "Boring" World of Central Banking

1. In the financial sector, assets that have received an AAA rating are normally considered *safe* (Ricks 2016: 46–47). For financial players, *safety* implies low probability of investment losses from credit default, interest rate fluctuations, market volatility, or counterparty insolvency (Potter 2018).

2. This differs from the creation of money by private banks, a topic which will be dealt with in chapter 4.

3. In theory, the same applies to potential losses. In practice, however, central banks keep losses on their balance sheets. They are therefore called *unrealized losses*.

4. The world's oldest central bank is the Bank of Sweden, the *Sveriges Riksbank*, which was founded in 1656.

5. When it comes to price stability, the point of reference differs depending on the prevailing monetary regime. It can be based, for example, on the gold standard, a certain exchange rate with another currency, a currency basket, or an inflation target.

6. The difference between the ECB's inflation target of *below but close to 2%* until 2021 and the new target of *2%* that was announced in July 2021 may seem negligible at first glance. However, the medium-term 2% inflation target gives the ECB significantly more flexibility to react or not to react to short-term changes in inflation (Schnabel 2021a).

7. Before then, price stability was formally on equal footing with the maximization of employment. De facto, however, price stability took precedence over employment.

8. The term *discount window* refers to a special teller window that existed at the Bank of England and also at the Federal Reserve where banks had access to short-term financing.

9. Assets with short-term to ultra short-term (overnight) maturities are traded on money markets (see Stigum and Crescenzi 2007).

10. During the global financial crisis, the interest rate of the Fed's discount window was lower than on the money market. Nevertheless, many banks preferred to procure funds via the money market (Domanski, Moessner, and Nelson 2014: 48–50).

11. The eurozone, also called the euro area, is the group of EU countries that use the euro as their official currency.

12. In addition to directly changing the conditions for borrowing money from a central bank, changes in key interest rates can also impact the economy through other channels. Changes, for example, can also occur in share prices, income from government bonds, income from corporate bonds, the value of the currency, and the conditions under which banks grant loans to companies (Stigum and Crescenzi 2007: 393–95).

13. When hyperinflation occurs, however, legal tender can lose its importance as a means of payment.

14. Theoretically, a central bank can monetize any kind of assets, including stocks or commodities, for example. Government bonds have the advantage that they are normally available in sufficient quantities and easy to liquidate (Stigum and Crescenzi 2007: 347).

15. The limit on money creation is determined through political processes. A high level of money creation activity in any one country generally leads to a decrease in the value of that country's currency relative to other currencies.

Chapter 3: A Political Theory of Money

1. Chartalism, a term coined at the beginning of the last century by Georg Friedrich Knapp, is derived from the Latin word *charta*, the document that forms the legal foundation of a system of government (Knapp 1924).

2. It is interesting to note that many neo-Marxist analyses also share this view (Fine and Lapavitsas 2000; Lapavitsas 2003), but whether it reflects the position of Marx himself is a matter of controversy (Lapavitsas 2005; Ingham 2006; Knafo 2007).

3. This particular example was the official price of an ounce of gold under the Bretton Woods system that was established in 1944 and lasted until 1971.

4. In the state theory of money (chartalism), the criterion that transforms an object into money is especially its ability to function as the legally authorized means of payment for taxes that come due on a regular basis.

5. "But it comes in doubly when, in addition, it claims the right to determine and declare *what thing* corresponds to the name, and to vary its declaration from time to time" (Keynes 1971 [1930]: 4).

6. In the case of a weak state, or a state that is not trusted to keep the currency stable, parallel currencies can develop, or a foreign currency may gain preference over the domestic currency of the state, a process that has come to be known as dollarization (Priewe and Herr 2005).

7. Within a particular community, cryptoassets may well be referred to as a form of privately generated money. Here, they serve as a general equivalent for various traded goods. De facto, however, most cryptoassets today are primarily assets that are used for speculation or hedging or to transfer remittances without a bank account. Unless they are integrated into the state security structure, cryptoassets are highly volatile and vulnerable to crises.

8. When Ingham asserts that the state not only determines the form of money but also the substantive value of money (Ingham 2004: 84), he at least expresses himself misleadingly. As Beggs (2017: 5–6) explains, an interpretation of "substantive value" goes back to Weber, who uses the term to denote its exchange value (against other currencies). Despite the prominent role that states, or their central banks, play in today's world, they are still not in a position to specify the value of their currency. On this point, see also Schumpeter's criticism of Knapp (1986 [1954]: 1056–57). Ingham does not refer to Weber's definition in this connection, but rather to Mirowski's (1991) interpretation of value as a *working fiction*.

9. Historical studies also demonstrate that forms of money preceded forms of government, that the money form can exist independently of the state, and that the enforcement of a national currency was very often accompanied by political struggles (Zelizer 1995; Ingham 2004; Desan 2014).

10. See Zelizer's exploration (1995) of the conflicts that took place in nineteenth-century America over the introduction of the greenback, the unofficial name of the US dollar bill.

11. Laclau also uses the term "empty signifier" (Laclau 1996b; Wullweber 2015b).

12. On the relationship between value and price, see Beckert and Aspers 2011.

13. Value as used here refers to market value and not to any other connotations of the term based on moral or aesthetic criteria, for example.

14. On a central bank balance sheet, currency in circulation is accordingly shown as a liability (see the next chapter).

15. Or, to quote Ingham (2004: 74, emphasis in the original): "Money is *assignable* trust."

16. It may seem confusing at first, but this is also the case with gold, cryptoassets, or other assets that are accepted as a form of money. When gold is minted, put into circulation, and used to pay for a purchase, it is only accepted as payment because it comes with the promise that the purchaser can use it to buy other goods. So it is a promise to pay that increases the amount of promises to pay and thus credit. Of course, gold cannot be created by balance sheet expansion in the same way as, say, deposits, and it is not destroyed when paid back.

17. This relationship can also exist in other forms—for example, between the central bank and the state, the central bank and commercial banks, or through claims that a commercial bank grants against itself through proprietary trading.

Chapter 4: Security Structures and Socioeconomic Layers

1. While funding liquidity involves the possibility of obtaining money (central bank money or bank deposits), market liquidity refers to whether a given asset can be traded close to par on demand (Mehrling 2011).

2. As used in this book the terms deposits and deposit money refer to bank deposits. More broadly speaking, deposits can exist in various forms, for example as deposit-like accounts, such as money market mutual fund accounts (Pozsar 2014).

3. In many respects the need for liquidity is closely related to the need for security. Despite the overlap, a distinction is made here because secure assets are not necessarily highly liquid. They only promise to retain their value for a certain period of time (e.g., repos with a longer term) (Golec and Perotti 2017).

4. The euro is a global exception in this respect. Now that the individual central banks in the euro area share a common currency and no longer have national currencies, only the ECB can create that common currency, namely the euro. At the height of the euro crisis in 2011, for example, it was impossible to withdraw large amounts of cash in countries such as Greece or Cyprus because the ECB had restricted access to the euro by those countries. It suddenly became clear that even central bank money can become illiquid when the central bank tightens the screws. The euro is a foreign currency for the central banks of the euro area, since they cannot create it themselves.

5. There are various ways to create, or at least to a large extent to secure, par value, some of which involve highly complex institutional arrangements. In addition to the central bank, the main institutions involved in this process are commercial banks, securities dealers (dealer banks), and money market funds (Pozsar 2014).

6. In addition to the central bank, many finance ministries can also issue legal tender, although in the form of coins, not reserves. US coins, for example, are produced by the US Mint, which is part of the US Department of the Treasury.

7. However, this privilege, now taken for granted and ingrained in everyday consciousness, was for a long time anything but self-evident (see Dwyer 1996 for the period of wildcat banking in the United States).

8. This fact cannot be attributed to a high velocity of money circulation, because in that case the same money would have to be in different places at the same time: "[B]ankers increase not the velocity but the quantity of money" (Schumpeter 1986 [1954]: 304).

9. Deposit protection is regulated differently from state to state, based partly on security arrangements shared among banks, savings banks, and cooperative banking associations and partly on state security systems.

10. In the company's balance sheet, the loans are shown as *bank balances* inversely to the entry on the bank balance sheet.

11. This refers to Keynes's explanation that "the bank may create a claim against itself in favor of a borrower, in return for his promise of subsequent reimbursement" (Keynes 1971 [1930]: 21).

12. After fifteen years of quantitative easing policies, which have immensely increased the volume of reserves held by commercial banks, the minimum reserve requirement has lost its importance as a monetary instrument.

13. The Latin word *fiat* literally means *let it be done*.

14. Ultimately, however, the distinction between money and fiat money is based on the misconception that money is coupled to certain fundamental values, such as gold.

15. Taken together, the two make up what is also called the primary market. Securities that have already been issued are resold on the secondary market through stock exchanges or in trading that takes place over-the-counter.

16. Whereas companies in Anglo-Saxon countries are financed primarily through stock markets, in continental Europe the most common form of financing continues to be through bank loans.

17. The Eurodollar market emerged in the 1950s and includes US dollar–denominated bank deposits held in banks outside the United States. Eurodollars are US dollars created outside the US regulatory system by European banks and backed by their deposits in US banks. The Fed and swap agreements between central banks act as an indirect backstop to this flexible, private, offshore liquidity system (Mehrling 2015).

18. An object does not constitute an asset per se. The creation of an asset presupposes a process of valorization and commodification. To become an asset, the object must first be regarded as a commodity with an ascribed value (Wullweber 2004).

19. A limit order, in contrast to a market order, specifies the price a buyer is willing to pay for a particular security.

20. In order to downplay the importance of the state, the metaphor of money as water was later invoked. Money would find the optimal path all by itself to where it would be most wanted (Desan 2014).

21. Despite repeated attempts to challenge the status of the US dollar as global reserve currency, particularly by the euro, the dollar has managed to prevail without difficulty (Cohen 2015; Mehrling 2023).

22. Swap lines not only safeguard the international monetary system but also the supremacy of the US dollar, and at the same time can be used to redirect global credit flows and direct capital to the United States (Pape 2022). As is so often the case, politics and finance are closely intertwined (Strange 1971, 1998).

Chapter 5: Sources of Instability in the Financial System

1. The average time for a human to react is around 200 milliseconds (MacKenzie et al. 2012: 286).

2. Ponzi finance results when expenses exceed income to an extent that requires indebted individuals to take out ever new loans. The phenomenon was named after Charles Ponzi, an Italian who developed a fraudulent investment and finance scheme in the United States during the 1920s.

3. Fisher (1933: 341–42) subdivided this phase even further. His concept describes nine steps.

4. During the early part of twentieth century, the instrument today known as a mutual fund was still called an investment trust. After the 1929 stock market crash

destroyed the funds that scores of people had invested in investment trusts to finance their retirement, the term was replaced by the name mutual fund for its resemblance to the more confidence-inspiring Mutual Savings Banks and Mutual Insurance Companies, institutions that were state supported and cooperatively organized (Shiller 2000: 35–36).

5. Until early 2011, information was sent through fiber optic cables. After a new line was laid through the Allegheny Mountains in Pennsylvania, it took only 6.65 milliseconds for a communication to arrive (for more detail, see MacKenzie et al. 2012).

6. The E-Mini S&P is a very popular stock market index futures contract. Its value is measured at fifty times the value of the Standard & Poor's 500 stock index.

Chapter 6: The Shadow Banking System and Free Market Capitalism

1. The vast majority of repos are short-term contracts, often maturing in just one day, which is why they are called overnight repos.

2. Commercial bank loans, however, still clearly remain the dominant source of funding. Mention is also made in this connection to the exceptional circumstances of 2021. The year was different in many respects because of the emergency lending measures implemented by central banks to support the private banking sector (FSB 2021b).

3. In the United States, instead of being subject to legal ownership, the collateral securing the repo is granted exemption from the automatic stay (safe harbor status) of bankruptcy law (Sissoko 2010).

4. Prior to the global financial crisis, the haircut on many government bonds stood at zero percent (CGFS 2010: 1–3). According to current market practice, the less creditworthy party has to pay the haircut. Over the course of the repo transaction, a fluctuating market can change the creditworthiness of the parties (Baklanova et al. 2017: 2–3).

5. Unlike loans, repos are exempt from the regulatory provision known as an *automatic stay* that exists in the United States, for example, as a mechanism to prevent creditors from collecting on debts in bankruptcy proceedings. This means that repo transactions can continue to be settled even after insolvency proceedings have been initiated.

6. It is possible for one and the same market participant, a large investment bank for example, to act in each capacity and conduct each of the three operations (as creditor, market maker, and borrower), but by means of different transactions and in different divisions.

7. There are exceptions, however. For some time now, LCH Clearnet, an intermediary and clearinghouse, has had access to central bank money because it is regulated like a bank in France (Gabor and Vestergaard 2016: 17). Subdivisions of commercial banks can also act as intermediaries.

8. According to Pozsar (2011), increasing demand for safe assets has fostered the practice of securitization because the existing amount of government bonds did not sufficiently cover the need for collateral.

9. Consequently, excessive financial liquidity is also a problem. When too much money circulates, riskier securities are also accepted as collateral and market liquidity

significantly increases for exotic financial products. This, in turn, means that more and more financial players become heavily leveraged.

10. The increased use of nongovernment securities as collateral has also received political support. In the early 2000s, the Fed began to expand the range of collateral it accepted for repo transactions. Against the background of fiscal consolidation policy and the consequent restrictions on the issuance of government bonds, there was a shortage of securities as collateral (Gabor 2016a: 981–82).

11. This also includes regular auctions and a central bank system based on primary dealers. Gabor (2016a) has shown that the changeover based on the model of the US market was very controversial among the European states. While France played a leading role in this regard, Germany and the United Kingdom were initially skeptical.

12. The European repo market, in contrast to the US market, is largely concentrated in a few large banks and focuses mainly on short-term transactions (Gabor 2016b). Repos are transacted both within as well as outside the shadow banking system.

13. Central banks in many countries, including in the United States, Canada, France, the United Kingdom, Italy, Japan, and China, conduct trading operations through so-called primary dealers instead of acting on the money market directly. Primary dealers are market players that are financially strong and have privileged access to the government bond market in return for the commitment to submit a minimum bid at government bond auctions (primary dealers at the Fed include BNP Paribas, Barclays, Citigroup, Credit Suisse, Deutsche Bank, Goldman Sachs, JPMorgan, and Morgan Stanley).

14. The demand for safe securities in the form of government bonds is so high that even the high level of debt in the United States is insufficient to meet demand (see Golec and Perotti 2017).

15. Countries such as Germany and the Netherlands have accused the ECB of undermining fiscal discipline in low-rated countries such as Greece, Italy, and Portugal by taking this approach (Weidmann 2013a). The ECB has sought to deflect this accusation by arguing that its repo monetary policy is based on common market valuation practices.

Chapter 7: A Never-Ending Crisis

1. This does not mean, however, that the banking sector or other parts of the financial system are not vulnerable to crises. Banks also play an important role in the shadow banking system (see later in chapter). Nevertheless, the shadow banking system is the main driver of past and current crisis dynamics.

2. A *bad bank* is a special-purpose vehicle set up by a country's state authorities or its central bank.

3. The unemployment rate in the United States rose to 10 million by the end of 2009, 5.5 million more than at the start of the crisis. It would take until March 2017 for US unemployment to return to pre-crisis levels (St. Louis Fed 2023b).

4. In November 2008, the Fed established Maiden Lane II LLC and Maiden Lane III to purchase mortgage-backed securities from AIG subsidiaries in support of AIG's restructuring (Fed 2010b).

5. Indices are not passive and neutral reflections of financial market developments, however. They are created by index providers that cater to their own interests. What is more, they can have a performative effect and intensify liquidity spirals (Wullweber 2016; Petry, Fichtner, and Heemskerk 2019).

Chapter 8: Masters of Stability

1. Bagehot's recommendations were directed at the Bank of England. At the time, the BoE had already assumed the role of a central bank by prioritizing financial stability over profit maximization, although it was still a privately owned joint-stock company and not yet a real central bank.

2. In mid-2012, it was confirmed that Maiden Lane LLC had fully repaid its New York Fed loans, including interest (Federal Reserve Bank of New York 2012).

3. The more effective solution, instead of just constantly battling the symptoms of crisis, would involve fundamental changes in the structuring of the financial system. This would require deeper and more radical transformation in the layered structure of finance (see chapter 4).

4. Some central banks, such as the Fed, are prohibited from purchasing private securities. The Fed, for example, only has the authority to buy US government Treasuries, foreign currencies, and securities issued by federal agencies such as Ginnie Mae or government-sponsored enterprises such as Fannie Mae and Freddie Mac. Not affected by this rule are repo agreements—and therewith also the collateral used to back repos.

5. In general, balance sheet operations can be conducted bilaterally or as auctions (tenders) with several players involved.

6. The assets side (debits) of the central bank balance sheet also includes components such as gold reserves and foreign currency reserves.

7. The Bank of Japan was the first central bank to initiate quantitative easing monetary policy. It introduced QE measures in 2001 when the Japanese economy was in deep recession and struggling with persistent deflation.

8. Article 18.1 of the Protocol on the Statute of the European System of Central Banks and of the European Central Bank only uses the word *adequate* to specify what kind of collateral is required for credit issued by central banks to credit institutions and other market participants (ECB 2004: 7).

9. Although nonbank financial market operators are still not permitted to hold Fed accounts, they can trade more or less directly with the Fed through clearinghouses (Pozsar 2019).

10. The volume of TSLF loans totaled 230 billion US dollars while credit granted through the Primary Dealer Credit Facility amounted to 150 billion US dollars (Domanski, Moessner, and Nelson 2014: 55–57).

11. In large part, however, government bonds were (and still are) used as collateral to back repos. At least indirectly, therefore, the government did play a role in securing transactions.

12. Eligible counterparties include money market funds, government-sponsored enterprises, primary dealers, and banks (Afonso et al. 2022b).

13. During noncrisis periods, the SRF is available only to primary dealers and cer-

tain banks. Eligible securities include US Treasuries, agency debt, and agency mortgage-backed securities (Afonso et al. 2022a).

14. The delay and deferral of payment and settlements through loans or other financial instruments, however, is an important feature of the financial system and the profit-oriented market economy as a whole (Ingham 2004: 139–42).

Chapter 9: Central Bank Capitalism and the Elasticity Provision of Last Resort

1. This tax was named after James Tobin, an American economist who proposed a similar tax in 1972.

2. However, certain statutory regulations such as the Dodd-Frank Act in the United States or the Financial Services (Banking Reform) Act in the United Kingdom work in the sense of sovereign power, as does the banking union in Europe (the Single Supervisory Mechanism).

3. With its QE program, the ECB has purchased a basket of government bonds from different eurozone countries, thereby driving down the spreads, or interest rate differences, between these government bonds.

4. As the Bank of England argues: "[T]he Bank revalues its collateral daily to ensure it remains sufficient to cover the amount that has been lent" (Bank of England 2015: 8). This market-based approach is all the more surprising in light of the fact that the Bank of England itself states that it can create liquidity at any time according to need. Central banks are not exposed to any formal liquidity risk (in their own currency). Consequently, they have no risk of insolvency.

5. See also https://inequality.org/facts/wealth-inequality/.

Chapter 10: Outlook

1. This refers to the financial practice of securitizing various debt instruments such as mortgage-backed securities, and thus making them tradable.

2. It merits mention that some developing countries are seeing a renewed interest in state-led industrial and infrastructure planning (Schindler, Alami, and Jepson 2023).

References

Ablan, Jennifer, Brendan Greeley, and Richard Henderson. 2020. "Federal Reserve Taps BlackRock to Manage Bond Purchases." *Financial Times*, 25 March. https://www.ft.com/content/f9c7e4de-6e25-11ea-89df-41bea055720b.

Acharya, Viral V., Rahul S. Chauhan, Raghuram Rajan, and Sascha Steffen. 2022. *Liquidity Dependence: Why Shrinking Central Bank Balance Sheets Is an Uphill Task*. https://www.kansascityfed.org/Jackson%20Hole/documents/9040/JH_Paper_Acharya.pdf.

Acharya, Viral V., Michael J. Fleming, Warren B. Hrung, and Asani Sarkar. 2014. *Dealer Financial Conditions and Lender-of-Last-Resort Facilities*. Federal Reserve Bank of New York Staff Report No. 673, May. https://www.newyorkfed.org/medialibrary/media/research/staff_reports/sr673.pdf.

Adkins, Lisa, Melinda Cooper, and Martijn Konings. 2019. "Class in the Twenty-First Century: Asset Inflation and the New Logic of Inequality." *Environment and Planning A: Economy and Space* 53(3): 548–72.

Adler, Jerry. 2012. "Raging Bulls: How Wall Street Got Addicted to Light-Speed Trading." *Wired.com*, 9 March. http://www.wired.com/2012/08/ff_wallstreet_trading.

Adrian, Tobias, Christopher R. Burke, and James J. McAndrews. 2009. "The Federal Reserve's Primary Dealer Credit Facility." *Current Issues in Economics and Finance* 15(4): 1–12.

Adrian, Tobias, Michael Fleming, Or Shachar, and Erik Vogt. 2017. *Market Liquidity after the Financial Crisis*. Federal Reserve Bank of New York Staff Report No. 796. https://www.newyorkfed.org/medialibrary/media/research/staff_reports/sr796.pdf?la=en.

Adrian, Tobias, Karin Kimbrough, and Dina Marchioni. 2011. "The Federal Reserve's Commercial Paper Funding Facility." *FRBNY Economic Policy Review*, May, 25–39.

Afonso, Gara, Lorie Logan, Antoine Martin, William Riordan, and Patricia Zobel. 2022a. "The Fed's Latest Tool: A Standing Repo Facility." Liberty Street Economics, 13 January. https://libertystreeteconomics.newyorkfed.org/2022/01/the-feds-latest-tool-a-standing-repo-facility/.

Afonso, Gara, Lorie Logan, Antoine Martin, William Riordan, and Patricia Zobel. 2022b. "How the Fed's Overnight Reverse Repo Facility Works." Liberty Street Economics, 11 January. https://libertystreeteconomics.newyorkfed.org/2022/01/how-the-feds-overnight-reverse-repo-facility-works/.

Aglietta, Michel. 2000. "Shareholder Value and Corporate Governance: Some Tricky Questions." *Economy and Society* 29(1): 146–59.

Aguila, Nicolás, Paula Haufe, and Joscha Wullweber. 2022. "The Ecor as Global Money: Towards a Green Bretton Woods System to Finance Sustainable and Just Transformation." SSRN. https://ssrn.com/abstract=4152448.

Aguila, Nicolás, and Joscha Wullweber. 2024. "Legitimising Green Monetary Policies: Market Liberalism, Layered Central Banking, and the ECB's Ongoing Discursive Shift from Environmental Risks to Price Stability." *Journal of European Public Policy*. DOI: 10.1080/13501763.2024.2317969.

Aitken, Rob. 2003. "The Democratic Method of Obtaining Capital: Culture, Governmentality and Ethics of Mass Investment." *Consumption, Markets and Culture* 6(4): 293–317.

Aitken, Rob. 2011. "Financializing Security: Political Prediction Markets and the Commodification of Uncertainty." *Security Dialogue* 42(2): 123–41.

Akerlof, George A., and Robert J. Shiller. 2009. *Animal Spirits: How Human Psychology Drives the Economy, and Why It Matters for Global Capitalism*. Princeton, NJ: Princeton University Press.

Aldasoro, Iñaki, Torsten Ehlers, and Eren Egemen. 2019. "Global Banks, Dollar Funding, and Regulation." SSRN Paper. http://dx.doi.org/10.2139/ssrn.3368973.

Aldasoro, Iñaki, Wenqian Huang, and Esti Kemp. 2020. "Cross-border Links between Banks and Non-bank Financial Institutions." *BIS Quarterly Review*, September. https://www.bis.org/publ/qtrpdf/r_qt2009e.pdf.

Allen, Franklin, Elena Carletti, Itay Goldstein, and Agnese Leonello. 2015. "Moral Hazard and Government Guarantees in the Banking Industry." *Journal of Financial Regulation* 1(1): 30–50.

Allenbach-Ammann, János. 2023. "ECB-Lagarde Says Corporate Profits Contributed to Inflation." Euractiv, 6 June. https://www.euractiv.com/section/economy-jobs/news/ecb-lagarde-says-corporate-profits-contributed-to-inflation/.

Allon, Fiona. 2015. "Money, Debt, and the Business of 'Free Stuff.'" *South Atlantic Quarterly* 114(2): 283–305.

Amato, Massimo, and Luca Fantacci. 2012. *The End of Finance*. Cambridge: Polity.

Amoore, Louise. 2011. "Data Derivatives on the Emergence of a Security Risk: Calculus for Our Times." *Theory, Culture & Society* 28(6): 24–43.

Angel, James J. 2011. *Impact of Special Relativity on Securities Regulation: The Future of*

Computer Trading in Financial Markets. Foresight Driver Review, DR 15. https:// www.gov.uk/government/uploads/system/uploads/attachment_data/file/289020/11 -1242-dr15-impact-of-special-relativity-on-securities-regulation.pdf.

Aradau, Claudia, Luis Lobo-Guerrero, and Rens Van Munster. 2008. "Security, Technologies of Risk, and the Political." *Security Dialogue* 39(2/3): 147–54.

Arnold, Martin. 2021. "Lagarde Warns against Early Tightening of Stimulus Efforts." *Financial Times*, 13 January. https://www.ft.com/content/3984312c-5278-42ef-94f1-597c 6f0a40cb.

Arnold, Martin, and Barney Jopson. 2023. "Inflation in Spain Falls More than Expected to 2.9%." *Financial Times*, 30 May. https://www.ft.com/content/91aacfda-34 ec-4ee5-befb-78bca4e5326e.

Arnold, Martin, and Mehreen Khan. 2019. "Lagarde Calls on European Governments to Launch Fiscal Stimulus." *Financial Times*, 4 September. https://www.ft.com/con tent/off70e24-cef8-11e9-99a4-b5ded7a7fe3f.

Bagehot, Walter. 2006 [1873]. *Lombard Street*. New York: Cosima Classics.

Bailey, Andrew, Jonathan Bridges, Richard Harrison, Josh Jones, and Aakash Mankodi. 2020. *The Central Bank Balance Sheet as a Policy Tool: Past, Present and Future*. Paper prepared for the Jackson Hole Economic Policy Symposium, 27–28 August. https:/ /www.bankofengland.co.uk/-/media/boe/files/speech/2020/the-central-bank-bal ance-sheet-as-a-policy-tool-past-present-and-future-speech-by-andrew-bailey.pdf.

Bair, Sheil. 2020. "Force Global Banks to Suspend Bonuses and Payouts." *Financial Times*, 22 March. https://www.ft.com/content/ed87b5d6-6a8e-11ea-a6ac-912254if204.

Bajaj, Vikas, and Mark Landler. 2007. "Mortgage Losses Echo in Europe and on Wall Street." *New York Times*, 10 August. http://www.nytimes.com/2007/08/10/business /10markets.html?pagewanted=all.

Baker, Andrew. 2006. *The Group of Seven: Finance Ministries, Central Banks and Global Financial Governance*. London: Routledge.

Baker, Andrew. 2010. "Restraining Regulatory Capture? Anglo-America, Crisis Politics and Trajectories of Change in Global Financial Governance." *International Affairs* 86(3): 647–63.

Baker, Andrew. 2015. "Varieties of Economic Crisis, Varieties of Ideational Change: How and Why Financial Regulation and Macroeconomic Policy Differ." *New Political Economy* 20(3): 342–66.

Baker, Andrew. 2017. "Political Economy and the Paradoxes of Macroprudential Regulation." *SPERI Paper* 40: 1–27.

Baklanova, Viktoria, Cecilia Caglio, Marco Cipriani, and Adam Copeland. 2017. *The Use of Collateral in Bilateral Repurchase and Securities Lending Agreements*. Federal Reserve Bank of New York Staff Report No. 758. https://www.newyorkfed.org/me dialibrary/media/research/staff_reports/sr758.pdf?sc_lang=en&hash=48A2F9C47E 03D48CF308C7893B86042.

Bank of England. 2015. *The Bank of England's Sterling Monetary Framework*. https:// www.bankofengland.co.uk/-/media/boe/files/freedom-of-information/2016/ster ling%20monetary%20framework%20june%202015.pdf.

Bank of England. 2020. *Proprietary Trading Review*. https://www.bankofengland.co.uk

/-/media/boe/files/prudential-regulation/report/proprietary-trading-review-2020. pdf.

Banque de France. 2020. "'Green Swans': Central Banks in the Age of Climate-Related Risks." *Bulletin de la Banque de France* 229/8: 1–15.

Banque de France. 2021. "Biodiversity Loss and Financial Stability: A New Frontier for Central Banks and Financial Supervisors?" *Bulletin de la Banque de France* 237/7: 1–12.

Bartels, Bernhard, Barry Eichengreen, and Beatrice Weder di Mauro. 2016. "No Smoking Gun: Private Shareholders, Governance Rules, and Central Bank Financial Behaviour." *VoxEU & CEPR*, 14 November. https://voxeu.org/article/private-sharehol ders-governance-rules-and-central-bank-financial-behaviour.

Bateman, Will, and Jens van 't Klooster. 2023. "The Dysfunctional Taboo: Monetary Financing at the Bank of England, the Federal Reserve, and the European Central Bank." *Review of International Political Economy*. DOI: 10.1080/09692290.2023.22 05656.

Beattie, Alan. 2008. "Good Question, Ma'am." *Financial Times*, 14 November. http:// www.ft.com/cms/s/0/5b306600-b26d-11dd-bbc9-0000779fd18c.html#axzz2MaM x6Ftt.

Beckert, Jens, and Patrik Aspers, eds. 2011. *The Worth of Goods: Valuation and Pricing in the Economy*. Oxford: Oxford University Press.

Beggs, Michael. 2017. "The State as a Creature of Money." *New Political Economy* 22(5): 463–77.

Bell, Stephanie. 2001. "The Role of the State and the Hierarchy of Money." *Cambridge Journal of Economics* 25(2): 149–63.

Bernanke, Ben S. 2004. "The Great Moderation." Remarks at the meetings of the Eastern Economic Association, Washington, DC, 20 February. http://www. federalreserve.gov/Boarddocs/Speeches/2004/20040220.

Bernanke, Ben S. 2008. "Liquidity Provision by the Federal Reserve." Remarks at the Federal Reserve Bank of Atlanta Financial Markets Conference, Sea Island, Georgia, 13 May. https://fraser.stlouisfed.org/scribd/?item_id=8994&filepath=/docs/ historical/bernanke/bernanke_20080513.pdf.

Bernanke, Ben S. 2010. "Aiding the Economy: What the Fed Did and Why." *Washington Post*, 5 November. https://www.federalreserve.gov/newsevents/other/o_bernan ke20101105a.htm.

Bernanke, Ben S. 2017. *Monetary Policy in a New Era*. Paper presented at the Rethinking Macroeconomic Policy, Washington, DC, 12–13 October. https://piie.com/sys tem/files/documents/bernanke20171012paper.pdf.

Bernanke, Ben S., and Janet Yellen. 2020. "The Federal Reserve Must Reduce Long-Term Damage from Coronavirus." *Financial Times*, 18 March. https://www.ft.com /content/01f267a2-686c-11ea-a3c9-1fe6fedcca75.

Besley, Tim, and Peter Hennessy. 2009. "Letter to Her Majesty the Queen." http://www .ft.com/cms/3e3b6ca8-7a08-11de-b86f-00144feabdco.pdf.

Best, Jacqueline. 2016. "Rethinking Central Bank Accountability in Uncertain Times." *Ethics & International Affairs* 30(2): 215–32.

Best, Jacqueline. 2018. "Technocratic Exceptionalism: Monetary Policy and the Fear of Democracy." *International Political Sociology* 12(4): 328–45.

Best, Jacqueline. 2019. "The Inflation Game: Targets, Practices and the Social Production of Monetary Credibility." *New Political Economy* 24(5): 623–40.

Beunza, Daniel, and David Stark. 2012. "Tools of the Trade: The Socio-technology of Arbitrage in a Wall Street Trading Room." *Industrial and Corporate Change* 13(2): 369–400.

Bhagwati, Jagdish N. 1998. "The Capital Myth." *Foreign Affairs* 77(3): 7–12.

Bholat, David, and Karla Martinez Gutierrez. 2019. "The Ownership of Central Banks." Bank Underground, Bank of England, 18 October. https://bankunderground .co.uk/2019/10/18/the-ownership-of-central-banks/.

Bieler, Andreas, and Adam D. Morton. 2008. "The Deficits of Discourse in IPE: Turning Base Metal into Gold?" *International Studies Quarterly* 52(1): 103–28.

Birk, Marius, and Matthias Thiemann. 2020. "Open for Business: Entrepreneurial Central Banks and the Cultivation of Market Liquidity." *New Political Economy* 25(2): 267–83.

BIS. 2007. *Triennial Central Bank Survey: Foreign Exchange and Derivatives Market Activity in 2007*. Basel: BIS.

BIS. 2014. "Re-thinking the Lender of Last Resort." BIS Papers No. 79. http://www.bis .org/publ/bppdf/bispap79.pdf.

BIS. 2017. "Repo Market Functioning." Committee on the Global Financial System, CGFS Papers No. 59. https://www.bis.org/publ/cgfs59.pdf.

BIS. 2018. "Structural Changes in Banking after the Crisis." Committee on the Global Financial System, CGFS Papers No. 60. https://www.bis.org/publ/cgfs60.pdf.

BIS. 2019a. "Establishing Viable Capital Markets." Committee on the Global Financial System, CGFS Papers No. 60. https://www.bis.org/publ/cgfs62.htm.

BIS. 2019b. "Unconventional Monetary Policy Tools." Committee on the Global Financial System, CGFS Papers No. 63. https://www.bis.org/publ/cgfs63.htm.

BIS. 2020a. "Markets Rise despite Subdued Economic Recovery." *BIS Quarterly Review*, September. https://www.bis.org/publ/qtrpdf/r_qt2009a.pdf.

BIS. 2020b. "The Green Swan: Central Banking and Financial Stability in the Age of Climate Change." https://www.bis.org/publ/othp31.htm.

BIS. 2021. "International Banking and Financial Market Developments." *BIS Quarterly Review*, December. https://www.bis.org/publ/r_qt0008.pdf.

Blanchard, Olivier, Álvaro Leandro, and Jeromin Zettelmeyer. 2020a. "Revisiting the EU Fiscal Framework in the Era of Low Interest Rates." Working Paper, March. https://wwwde.uni.lu/fdef/news/revisiting_the_eu_fiscal_framework_in_an_era_of_low_interest_rates.

Blanchard, Olivier, Álvaro Leandro, and Jeromin Zettelmeyer. 2020b. *"Redesigning EU Fiscal Rules: From Rules to Standards." Working Paper*, Peterson Institute for International Economics, Washington, DC.

Blickle, Kristian, Matteo Crosignani, Fernando Duarte, Thomas Eisenbach, Fulvia Fringuellotti, and Anna Kovner. 2020. "How Has COVID-19 Affected Banking System Vulnerability?" Liberty Street Economics, Fed of New York, 16 November.

https://libertystreeteconomics.newyorkfed.org/2020/11/how-has-covid-19-affected
-banking-system-vulnerability.html.

Bloom, Nicholas, Philip Bunn, Paul Mizen, Pawel Smietanka, and Gregory Thwaites.
2020. "The Impact of Covid-19 on Productivity." Bank of England Staff, Working
Paper No. 900, December. www.bankofengland.co.uk/working-paper/staff-work
ing-papers.

Bloomberg. 2023. "US Banks Have $620 Billion of Unrealized Losses on Their Books."
31 March. https://www.bloomberg.com/graphics/2023-svb-exposed-risks-banks/.

Blyth, Mark. 2013. *Austerity: The History of a Dangerous Idea.* Oxford: Oxford University Press.

Bofinger, Peter. 2020. "Modeling the Financial System with a Corn Economy—
'Misleading and Disastrous.'" https://www.ineteconomics.org/perspectives/blog/
modeling-the-financial-system-with-a-corn-economy-misleading-and-disastrous.

Bonner, William, and Addison Wiggin. 2003. *Financial Reckoning Day: Surviving the
Soft Depression of the 21st Century.* Chichester: John Wiley & Sons.

Borio, Claudio. 2009. "Implementing the Macroprudential Approach to Financial
Regulation and Supervision." *Banque de France Financial Stability Review* 13(1): 31–
41.

Borio, Claudio. 2012. *Central Banking Post-crisis: What Compass for Uncharted Waters?*
BIS Working Paper No. 353. London: Anthem Press. http://www.bis.org/publ/
work353.pdf.

Borio, Claudio. 2015. "Central Banking Post-crisis." In *Central Banking at a Crossroads*,
edited by Charles Goodhart, Daniela Gabor, Ismail Ertürk, and Jakob Vestergaard,
191–216. London: Anthem Press.

Borio, Claudio. 2021. "Monetary and Fiscal Policies at a Crossroads: New Normal or
New Path?" Panel remarks, Latvijas Banka Economic Conference. https://www.bis
.org/speeches/sp210920.pdf.

Borio, Claudio, and Piti Disyatat. 2009. "Unconventional Monetary Policies: An Ap-
praisal." BIS Working Papers No. 292, November. https://www.bis.org/publ/
work292.pdf.

Boy, Nina. 2017. "Finance-Security: Where to Go?" *Finance and Society* 3(2): 208–15.

Boy, Nina, Peter J. Burgess, and Anna Leander. 2011. "The Global Governance of Security and Finance: Introduction to the Special Issue." *Security Dialogue* 42(2): 115–
22.

Boy, Nina, and Daniela Gabor. 2019. "Collateral Times." *Economy and Society* 48(3):
295–314.

Boyarchenko, Nina, Richard Crump, and Anna Kovner. 2020a. "The Commercial
Paper Funding Facility." Liberty Street Economics, Fed of New York, 15 May. https:
//libertystreeteconomics.newyorkfed.org/2020/05/the-commercial-paper-funding
-facility.html.

Boyarchenko, Nina, Richard Crump, Anna Kovner, and Peter Van Tassel. 2020b. "The
Primary and Secondary Market Corporate Credit Facilities." Liberty Street Economics, Fed of New York, 26 May. https://libertystreeteconomics.newyorkfed.org/
2020/05/the-primary-and-secondary-market-corporate-credit-facilities.html.

Boyer, Robert. 2000. "Is a Finance-Led Growth Regime a Viable Alternative to Fordism? A Preliminary Analysis." *Economy and Society* 29(1): 111–45.

Boyer, Robert. 2013a. "The Present Crisis: A Trump for a Renewed Political Economy." *Review of Political Economy* 25(1): 1–38.

Boyer, Robert. 2013b. "The Global Financial Crisis in Historical Perspective: An Economic Analysis Combining Minsky, Hayek, Fisher, Keynes and the Regulation Approach." *Accounting, Economics and Law* 3(3): 93–139.

Boyer-Xambeau, Marie-Therese, Ghislain Deleplace, and Lucien Gillard. 1994. *Private Money and Public Currencies: The 16th-Century Challenge.* New York: M.E. Sharpe.

Brantlinger, Patrick. 1996. *Fictions of State: Culture and Credit in Britain.* Ithaca, NY: Cornell University Press.

Braun, Benjamin. 2018. "Central Banking and the Infrastructural Power of Finance: The Case of ECB Support for Repo and Securitization Markets." *Socio-Economic Review.* doi: 10.1093/ser/mwy008.

Braun, Benjamin, and Marina Hübner. 2018. "Fiscal Fault, Financial Fix? Capital Markets Union and the Quest for Macroeconomic Stabilization in the Euro Area." *Competition and Change* 22(2): 117–38.

Brunnermeier, Markus K., and Lasse H. Pedersen. 2009. "Market Liquidity and Funding Liquidity." *Review of Financial Studies* 22(6): 2201–38.

Bryan, Dick, and Michael Rafferty. 2007. "Financial Derivatives and the Theory of Money." *Economy and Society* 36(1): 134–58.

Bryan, Dick, and Michael Rafferty. 2016. "Decomposing Money: Ontological Options and Spreads." *Journal of Cultural Economy* 9(1): 27–42.

Bryan, Dick, Michael Rafferty, and Duncan Wigan. 2016. "Politics, Time and Space in the Era of Shadow Banking." *Review of International Political Economy* 23(6): 941–66.

Buiter, Willem H. 2023. "Will Europe's New TPI Be an ATM?" *Project Syndicate,* 22 July. https://www.project-syndicate.org/commentary/ecb-tpi-anti-fragmentation-tool-fewer-conditions-than-omt-by-willem-h-buiter-2022-07?barrier=accesspaylog.

Bundesbank. 2013. *The Financial System in Transition: The New Importance of Repo Markets.* Monthly Report, December. https://www.bundesbank.de/Redaktion/EN/Downloads/Publications/Monthly_Report_Articles/2013/2013_12_repo_markets.pdf?__blob=publicationFile.

Bundesbank. 2017. "Zu den gesamtwirtschaftlichen Auswirkungen der quantitativen Lockerung im Euro-Raum." *Monatsbericht* 68(6): 29–54.

Bundesbank. 2019. *Money and Monetary Policy.* Frankfurt am Main: Deutsche Bundesbank.

Burchell, Graham. 1993. "Liberal Government and Techniques of the Self." *Economy and Society* 22(3): 267–82.

Campbell, David. 2005. "The Biopolitics of Security: Oil, Empire, and the Sports Utility Vehicle." *American Quarterly* 57(3): 943–72.

Carney, Mark. 2015. "Building Real Markets for the Good of the People." Speech by Governor of the Bank of England. https://www.bankofengland.co.uk/speech/2015/building-real-markets-for-the-good-of-the-people.

Carney, Mark. 2016. "The Spectre of Monetarism." Speech by Governor of the Bank of England. https://www.bankofengland.co.uk/-/media/boe/files/speech/2016/the -spectre-of-monetarism.pdf.

Carruthers, Bruce G., and Sarah Babb. 1996. "The Color of Money and the Nature of Value." *American Journal of Sociology* 101(6): 1556–91.

Carruthers, Bruce G., and Jeong-Chul Kim. 2011. "The Sociology of Finance." *Annual Review of Sociology* 37: 239–59.

Carruthers, Bruce G., and Arthur L. Stinchcombe. 1999. "The Social Structure of Liquidity: Flexibility, Markets, and States." *Theory and Society* 28(3): 353–82.

Castle, Stephen. 2014. "That Debt from 1720? Britain's Payment Is Coming." *New York Times*, 27 December. https://www.nytimes.com/2014/12/28/world/that-debt-from -1720-britains-payment-is-coming.html?_r=1.

Cerny, Philip G. 2010. *Rethinking World Politics: A Theory of Transnational Neopluralism*. Oxford: Oxford University Press.

CGFS. 2010. "The Role of Margin Requirements and Haircuts in Procyclicality." Committee on the Global Financial System Paper No. 36. http://www.bis.org/publ /cgfs36.pdf.

Chick, Victoria. 2013. "The Current Banking Crisis in the UK: An Evolutionary View." In *Financial Crises and the Nature of Capitalist Money*, edited by Jocelyn Pixley and G. C. Harcourt, 148–61. Basingstoke, Hampshire: Palgrave Macmillan.

Cihák, Martin, and Ratna Sahay. 2020. "Finance and Inequality." IMF Discussion Note, SDN 20/1. https://www.imf.org/en/Publications/Staff-Discussion-Notes/ Issues/2020/01/16/Finance-and-Inequality-45129.

Cipriani, Marco, Gabriele La Spada, Reed Orchinik, and Aaron Plesset. 2020. "The Money Market Mutual Fund Liquidity Facility." Liberty Street Economics, Fed of New York. https://libertystreeteconomics.newyorkfed.org/2020/05/the-money -market-mutual-fund-liquidity-facility.html.

Clarida, Richard, Jordi Gali, and Mark Gertler. 1999. "The Science of Monetary Policy: A New Keynesian Perspective." *Journal of Economic Literature* 37(7): 1661–707.

Cohen, Benjamin J. 1996. "Phoenix Risen: The Resurrection of Global Finance." *World Politics* 48(2): 268–96.

Cohen, Benjamin J. 1998. *The Geography of Money*. Ithaca, NY: Cornell University Press.

Cohen, Benjamin J. 2015. *Currency Power: Understanding Monetary Rivalry*. Princeton, NJ: Princeton University Press.

Cohen, Benjamin J. 2019. *Currency Statecraft: Monetary Rivalry and Geopolitical Ambition*. Princeton, NJ: Princeton University Press.

Cohen, Benjamin J., and Tabitha M. Benney. 2014. "What Does the International Currency System Really Look Like?" *Review of International Political Economy* 21(5): 1017–41.

Commodity Futures Trading Commission / Securities and Exchange Commission. 2010. *Findings Regarding the Market Events of May 6, 2010: Report of the Staffs of the CFTC and SEC to the Joint Advisory Committee on Emerging Regulatory Issues*. 30 September. https://www.sec.gov/news/studies/2010/marketevents-report.pdf.

Commodity Futures Trading Commission / Securities and Exchange Commission.

2019. *Automated Trading in Futures Markets*. https://www.cftc.gov/sites/default/files/2019-04/ATS_2yr_Update_Final_2018_ada.pdf.

Conti-Brown, Peter. 2016. *The Power and Independence of the Federal Reserve*. Princeton, NJ: Princeton University Press.

Cookson, Clive. 2013. "Time Is Money When It Comes to Microwaves." *Financial Times*, 10 May. http://www.ft.com/cms/s/2/2bf37898-b775-11e2-841e-00144feabdco.html.

Coombs, Nathan. 2023. "The Democratic Dangers of Central Bank Planning." *Accounting, Economics, and Law*. DOI: 10.1515/ael-2022–0063.

Coombs, Nathan, and Matthias Thiemann. 2022. "Recentering Central Banks: Theorizing State-Economy Boundaries as Central Bank Effects." *Economy and Society*. DOI: 10.1080/03085147.2022.2118450.

Cooper, Melinda. 2015. "Shadow Money and the Shadow Workforce: Rethinking Labor and Liquidity." *South Atlantic Quarterly* 114(2): 395–423.

Creswell, Julie. 2007. "Shaky Markets Prompt Rumors of Who's in Trouble." *New York Times*, 10 August.

Crouch, Colin. 2009. "Privatised Keynesianism: An Unacknowledged Policy Regime." *British Journal of Politics and International Relations* 11(3): 382–99.

Cœuré, Benoît. 2016. "Sovereign Debt in the Euro Area: Too Safe or Too Risky?" Keynote address by member of the Executive Board of the ECB at Harvard University. https://www.ecb.europa.eu/press/key/date/2016/html/sp161103.en.html.

de Goede, Marieke. 2001. "Discourses of Scientific Finance and the Failure of Long-Term Capital Management." *New Political Economy* 6(2): 149–70.

de Goede, Marieke. 2010. "Financial Security." In *The Routledge Handbook of the New Security Studies*, edited by J. Peter Burgess, 100–109. London: Routledge.

de Goede, Marieke. 2017. "Chains of Securitization." *Finance and Society* 3(2): 197–207.

Dean, Mitchell. 1991. *The Constitution of Poverty: Toward a Genealogy of Liberal Governance*. London: Routledge.

Der Derian, James. 2001. *Virtuous War: Mapping the Military-Industrial-Media-Entertainment Network*. Boulder, CO: Westview Press.

Desan, Christine A. 2014. *Making Money: Coin, Currency, and the Coming of Capitalism*. Oxford: Oxford University Press.

Dillon, Michael. 2007. "Governing Terror: The State of Emergency of Biopolitical Emergence." *International Political Sociology* 1: 7–28.

Dillon, Michael. 2010. "Biopolitics of Security." In *The Routledge Handbook of the New Security Studies*, edited by J. Peter Burgess, 61–71. London: Routledge.

Domanski, Dietrich, Richhild Moessner, and William Nelson. 2014. "Central Banks as Lender of Last Resort: Experiences during the 2007–2010 Crisis and Lessons for the Future." BIS Paper No. 79, 43–75. https://www.federalreserve.gov/econresdata/feds/2014/files/2014110pap.pdf.

Dow, Sheila C. 2015. "The Relationship between Central Banks and Governments." In *Central Banking at a Crossroads*, edited by Charles Goodhart, Daniela Gabor, Ismail Ertürk, and Jakob Vestergaard, 229–43. London: Anthem Press.

Duguid, Kate, and Colby Smith. 2022. "US Economy Shrinks for Second Consecutive

Quarter." *Financial Times*, 28 July. https://www.ft.com/content/8e4caa59-5799-43 ob-9896-e494369900dc.

Duguid, Kate, Colby Smith, and Tommy Stubbington. 2022. "Fed Begins Quantitative Tightening on Unprecedented Scale." *Financial Times*, 14 June. https://www.ft .com/content/2496105a-d211-4abe-ab5d-46a91876428f.

Durden, Tyler. 2020. "Inequality Has Never Been Bigger: Financial Assets Hit a Record 620% of GDP." *Zerohedge*, 8 July. https://www.zerohedge.com/markets/ inequality-has-never-been-bigger-financial-assets-hit-record-620-gdp.

Dwyer, Gerald P. 1996. "Wildcat Banking, Banking Panics, and Free Banking in the United States." *Federal Reserve Bank of Atlanta Economic Review* 81: 1–20.

ECB. 2004. *Protocol on the Statute of the European System of Central Banks and the European Central Bank*. https://www.ecb.europa.eu/ecb/pdf/orga/escbstatutes_en.pdf.

ECB. 2015a. "The Role of the Central Bank Balance Sheet in Monetary Policy." *Economic Bulletin*, no. 4. https://www.ecb.europa.eu/pub/pdf/other/art01_eb201504.en.pdf.

ECB. 2015b. *Guideline (EU) 2015/510 of the European Central Bank of 19 December 2014 on the Implementation of the Eurosystem Monetary Policy Framework (ECB/2014/60)*. http://data.europa.eu/eli/guideline/2015/510/oj.

ECB. 2015c. *The Financial Risk Management of the Eurosystem's Monetary Policy Operations*. https://www.ecb.europa.eu/pub/pdf/other/financial_risk_management_of_ eurosystem_monetary_policy_operations_201507.en.pdf.

ECB. 2017. *Financial integration in Europe*. https://www.ecb.europa.eu/pub/pdf/other/ ecb.financialintegrationineurope201705.en.pdf.

ECB. 2019. *Financial Stability Review*, November. https://www.ecb.europa.eu/pub/pdf /fsr/ecb.fsr201911-facado251f.en.pdf.

ECB. 2020a. *Financial Stability Review*, November. https://www.ecb.europa.eu/pub/ pdf/fsr/ecb.fsr202011-b7be9ae1f1.en.pdf.

ECB. 2020b. "Pandemic Emergency Purchase Programme (PEPP): ECB Announces €750 Billion Pandemic Emergency Purchase." https://www.ecb.europa.eu/mopo/ implement/pepp/html/index.en.html.

ECB. 2020c. "Monetary Policy Decisions." Press release, 4 June. https://www.ecb. europa.eu/press/pr/date/2020/html/ecb.mp200604-a307d3429c.en.html.

ECB. 2021a. "Monetary Policy Accounts." https://www.ecb.europa.eu/press/accounts/ 2021/html/ecb.mg210114-14ef04b8bd.en.html.

ECB. 2021b. "Strategy Review: Monetary-Fiscal Policy Interactions in the Euro Area." https://www.ecb.europa.eu/pub/research/occasional-papers/html/index.en.html.

ECB. 2022. "The Transmission Protection Instrument." Press release, 21 July. https:// www.ecb.europa.eu/press/pr/date/2022/html/ecb.pr220721-973e6e7273.en.html.

Editorial Board *New York Times*. 2022. "Russia Is Making Heaps of Money from Oil, But There Is a Way to Stop That." *New York Times*, 29 July. https://www.nytimes. com/2022/07/29/opinion/russia-oil-sanctions-biden.html.

Ehrhart, Karl-Martin, Ingmar Schlecht, and Runxi Wang. 2022. "Price Cap Versus Tariffs: The Case of the EU-Russia Gas Market." ZBW—Leibniz Information Centre for Economics, Kiel, Hamburg. https://www.econstor.eu/handle/10419/261 834.

Eich, Stefan. 2022. *The Currency of Politics: The Political Theory of Money from Aristotle to Keynes*. Princeton, NJ: Princeton University Press.

Eichengreen, Barry J. 2008. *Globalizing Capital: A History of the International Monetary System*, 2nd ed. Princeton, NJ: Princeton University Press.

Engelen, Ewald. 2018. "How Shadow Banking Became Non-bank Finance: The Conjectural Power of Economic Ideas." In *Shadow Banking: Scope, Origins and Theories*, edited by Anastasia Nesvetailova, 40–54. London: Routledge.

Epstein, Gerald A. 2005. *Financialization and the World Economy*. Cheltenham: Edward Elgar.

Ertürk, Ismail, Julie Froud, Adam Leaver, Sukhedev Johal, and Karel Williams, eds. 2008a. *Financialization at Work: Key Texts and Commentary*. London: Routledge.

Ertürk, Ismail, Julie Froud, Adam Leaver, Sukhedev Johal, and Karel Williams. 2008b. "Financialization, Coupon Pool and Conjuncture." In *Financialization at Work: Key Texts and Commentary*, edited by Ismail Ertürk, Julie Froud, Adam Leaver, Sukhedev Johal, and Karel Williams, 1–44. London: Routledge.

ESRB. 2019. *Can ETFs Contribute to Systemic Risk?* Report of the Advisory Scientific Committee No. 9, European Systemic Risk Board. https://www.esrb.europa.eu/pub/pdf/asc/esrb.asc190617_9_canetfscontributesystemicrisk~983ea11870.en.pdf.

European Parliament; European Council. 2002. "Directive 2002/47/EC of 6 June 2002 on Financial Collateral Arrangements." https://www.legislation.gov.uk/eudr/2002/47/introduction.

Featherstone, Kevin. 2011. "The Greek Sovereign Debt Crisis and EMU: A Failing State in a Skewed Regime." *Journal of Common Market Studies* 49(2): 193–217.

Fed. 2010a. "Bear Stearns, JPMorgan Chase, and Maiden Lane LLC." https://www.federalreserve.gov/regreform/reform-bearstearns.htm.

Fed. 2010b. "American International Group (AIG), Maiden Lane II and III." https://www.federalreserve.gov/regreform/reform-aig.htm.

Fed. 2013. "Federal Reserve and Other Central Banks Convert Temporary Bilateral Liquidity Swap Arrangements to Standing Arrangements." Press release, 31 October 31. https://www.federalreserve.gov/newsevents/pressreleases/monetary20131031a.htm.

Fed. 2015a. *Domestic Open Market Operations during 2014*. http://www.newyorkfed.org/markets/omo/omo2014.pdf.

Fed. 2015b. "Statement Regarding Overnight Reverse Repurchase Agreements." 16 December. https://www.newyorkfed.org/markets/opolicy/operating_policy_151216.html.

Fed. 2019a. *Financial Stability Report, November*. Washington, DC: Board of Governors of the Federal Reserve System.

Fed. 2019b. "Statement Regarding Repurchase Operations." 20 September. https://www.newyorkfed.org/markets/opolicy/operating_policy_190920.

Fed. 2020a. "Federal Reserve Will Establish a Facility to Facilitate Lending to Small Businesses." 6 April. https://www.federalreserve.gov/newsevents/pressreleases/monetary20200406a.htm.

Fed. 2020b. "Federal Reserve Announces Establishment of a Temporary FIMA Repo Facility." 31 March. https://www.federalreserve.gov/newsevents/pressreleases/monetary20200331a.htm.

Fed. 2020c. "Federal Reserve Issues FOMC Statement." 23 March. https://www.federalreserve.gov/newsevents/pressreleases/monetary20200323a.htm.

Fed. 2021. "Federal Reserve Announces the Extension of Its Temporary U.S. Dollar Liquidity Swap Lines with Nine Central Banks through December 31, 2021." https://www.weforum.org/reports/globalrisks-report-2023/.

Fed. 2022. "Foreign and International Monetary Authorities (FIMA) Repo Facility." https://www.federalreserve.gov/monetarypolicy/fima-repo-facility.htm.

Fed. 2023a. "Distribution of Household Wealth in the U.S. since 1989." https://www.federalreserve.gov/releases/z1/dataviz/dfa/distribute/chart/#range:1989.3,2021.2; quarter:127;series:Net%20worth;demographic:networth;population:all;units:levels.

Fed. 2023b. "Corporate Debt." https://www.federalreserve.gov/releases/z1/dataviz/z1/nonfinancial_debt/chart/#series:corporate.

Fed. 2023c. "Federal Reserve Board Announces It Will Make Available Additional Funding to Eligible Depository Institutions to Help Assure Banks Have the Ability to Meet the Needs of All Their Depositors." Press release, 12 March. https://www.federalreserve.gov/newsevents/pressreleases/monetary20230312a.htm.

Fed. 2023d. "Bank Term Funding Program." https://www.federalreserve.gov/financial-stability/bank-term-funding-program.htm.

Fed. 2023e. "Bank Term Funding Program, Frequently Asked Questions." https://www.federalreserve.gov/financial-stability/files/bank-term-funding-program-faqs.pdf.

Fed. 2023f. "Distribution of Household Wealth in the U.S. since 1989." https://www.federalreserve.gov/releases/z1/dataviz/dfa/distribute/chart/#range:1989.3,2021.2; quarter:127;series:Net%20worth;demographic:networth;population:all;units:levels.

Federal Reserve Bank of Atlanta. 2020. "A Moral and Economic Imperative to End Racism." https://www.frbatlanta.org/about/feature/2020/06/12/bostic-a-moral-and-economic-imperative-to-end-racism.

Federal Reserve Bank of New York. 2012. "New York Fed Announces Full Repayment of Its Loans to Maiden Lane LLC and Maiden Lane III LLC." Press release, 14 June. http://www.newyorkfed.org/newsevents/news/markets/2012/an120614.html.

Federal Reserve Bank of New York. 2021. "Repurchase Agreement Operational Details." https://www.newyorkfed.org/markets/domestic-market-operations/monetary-policy-implementation/repo-reverse-repo-agreements/repurchase-agreement-operational-details.

Federal Reserve Bank of New York. 2023. "Reverse Repo Operations." https://www.newyorkfed.org/markets/desk-operations/reverse-repo.

Fichtner, Jan, Eelke Heemskerk, and Javier Garcia-Bernardo. 2017. "Hidden Power of the Big Three? Passive Index Funds, Re-concentration of Corporate Ownership, and New Financial Risk." *Business and Politics* 19(2): 298–326.

Financial Crisis Inquiry Commission. 2011. *The Financial Crisis Inquiry Report.* Washington, DC: U.S. Government Printing Office.

Financial Services Authority. 2009. *The Turner Review: A Regulatory Response to the Global Banking Crisis,* March. http://www.actuaries.org/CTTEES_TFRISKCRISIS/Documents/turner_review.pdf.

Financial Times. 2020. "The Fed Must Act to Keep Markets Functioning." 18 March. https://www.ft.com/content/3608d546-691e-11ea-800d-da70cff6e4d3.

Financial Times. 2022. "Global Wealth: Asset Inflation Decouples Rich from GDP." 23 January. https://www.ft.com/content/4d942f89-386d-4d21-a037-41e0964a5631.

Fine, Ben, and Costas Lapavitsas. 2000. "Markets and Money in Social Theory: What Role for Economics." *Economy and Society* 29(3): 357–82.

Fisher, Irving. 1932. *Booms and Depressions*. New York: Adelphi.

Fisher, Irving. 1933. "The Debt Deflation Theory of Great Depressions." *Econometrica* 1(4): 337–57.

Fleming, Michael, and Francisco Ruela. 2020a. "Treasury Market Liquidity during the COVID-19 Crisis." Liberty Street Economics, Fed of New York, 17 April. https://libertystreeteconomics.newyorkfed.org/2020/04/treasury-market-liquidity-during-the-covid-19-crisis.html.

Fleming, Michael, and Francisco Ruela. 2020b. "Treasury Market Liquidity and the Federal Reserve during the COVID-19 Pandemic." Liberty Street Economics, Fed of New York, 29 May. https://libertystreeteconomics.newyorkfed.org/2020/05/treasury-market-liquidity-and-the-federal-reserve-during-the-covid-19-pandemic.html.

Fleming, Michael, Asani Sarkar, and Peter Van Tassel. 2020. "The COVID-19 Pandemic and the Fed's Response." Liberty Street Economics, Fed of New York, 15 April. https://libertystreeteconomics.newyorkfed.org/2020/04/the-covid-19-pandemic-and-the-feds-response.html.

Fletscher, Laurence. 2020. "Markets Draw Comfort from 'Maximum' Central Bank Stimulus." *Financial Times*, 27 March. https://www.ft.com/content/25b67610-096f-4bd0-ac1d-d4dd8941d05f.

Foucault, Michel. 1980. *Power/ Knowledge: Selected Interviews and Other Writings*. New York: Pantheon.

Foucault, Michel. 2008. *The Birth of Biopolitics*. Basingstoke, Hampshire: Palgrave Macmillan.

Foucault, Michel. 2009. *Security, Territory, Population*. New York: Palgrave.

Franklin, Joshua, et al. 2023. "JPMorgan: The Bank That Never Lets a Crisis Go to Waste." *Financial Times*, 5 May. https://www.ft.com/content/af7e2188-097c-48d1-bde0-bdee30021931.

Frost, Josh, Lorie Logan, Antoine Martin, Patrick McCabe, Fabio Natalucci, and Julie Remache. 2015. *Overnight RRP Operations as a Monetary Policy Tool: Some Design Considerations*. Finance and Economics Discussion Series 2015–010. Washington, DC: Board of Governors of the Federal Reserve System.

Froud, Julie, Sukhdev Johal, Adam Leaver, and Karel Williams. 2006. *Financialization and Strategy: Narrative and Numbers*. London: Routledge.

FSB. 2013. *Strengthening Oversight and Regulation of Shadow Banking: An Integrated Overview of Policy Recommendations*. 18 November. http://www.financialstabilityboard.org/publications/r_130829b.pdf.

FSB. 2015. *Transforming Shadow Banking into Resilient Market-Based Finance: An Overview of Progress*. http://www.fsb.org/wp-content/uploads/shadow_banking_overview_of_progress_2015.pdf.

FSB. 2017a. *Global Shadow Banking Monitoring Report 2016*. http://www.fsb.org/wp-content/uploads/global-shadow-banking-monitoring-report-2016.pdf.

FSB. 2017b. *Transforming Shadow Banking into Resilient Market-Based Finance: Re-*

hypothecation and Collateral Re-use. http://www.fsb.org/wp-content/uploads/Re-hypothecation-and-collateral-re-use.pdf.

FSB. 2019. *Global Monitoring Report on Non-bank Financial Intermediation 2018.* https://www.fsb.org/2019/02/global-monitoring-report-on-non-bank-financial-intermediation-2018/.

FSB. 2020a. *Global Monitoring Report on Non-bank Financial Intermediation 2019.* https://www.fsb.org/2020/01/global-monitoring-report-on-non-bank-financial-intermediation-2019/.

FSB. 2020b. *Global Monitoring Report on Non-bank Financial Intermediation 2020.* 16 December. https://www.fsb.org/wp-content/uploads/P161220.pdf.

FSB. 2020c. *COVID-19 Pandemic: Financial Stability Implications and Policy Measures Taken.* 15 April. https://www.fsb.org/wp-content/uploads/P150420.pdf.

FSB. 2021a. *Global Monitoring Report on Non-bank Financial Intermediation 2020,* 16 December. https://www.fsb.org/wp-content/uploads/P161221.pdf.

FSB. 2021b. *Global Monitoring Report on Non-bank Financial Intermediation 2021.* https://www.fsb.org/wp-content/uploads/P161221.pdf.

FSB. 2022. *Global Monitoring Report on Non-bank Financial Intermediation 2022.* https://www.fsb.org/wp-content/uploads/P201222.pdf.

Furman, Jason, and Lawrence Summers. 2020. *A Reconsideration of Fiscal Policy in the Era of Low Interest Rates.* 30 November. https://www.brookings.edu/wp-content/uploads/2020/11/furman-summers-fiscal-reconsideration-discussion-draft.pdf.

Gabor, Daniela. 2016a. "The (Impossible) Repo Trinity: The Political Economy of Repo Markets." *Review of International Political Economy* 23(6): 967–1000.

Gabor, Daniela. 2016b. "A Step Too Far? The European Financial Transactions Tax on Shadow Banking." *Journal of European Public Policy* 23(6): 925–45.

Gabor, Daniela. 2020. "Why You Shouldn't Fall for the Panic about Britain's Public Debt." *The Guardian,* 29 October. https://www.theguardian.com/commentisfree/2020/oct/29/panic-britain-public-debt-government-borrowing-pandemic.

Gabor, Daniela. 2021. *Revolution without Revolutionaries: Interrogating the Return of Monetary Financing.* Berlin: Finanzwende, Heinrich-Böll-Foundation.

Gabor, Daniela. 2023. "(Shadow) Money without a Central Bank: Towards a Theory of Monetary Time." SocArXiv ajx8f, Center for Open Science. https://ideas.repec.org/p/osf/socarx/ajx8f.html.

Gabor, Daniela, and Cornel Ban. 2016. "Banking on Bonds: The New Links between States and Markets." *Journal of Common Market Studies* 54(3): 617–35.

Gabor, Daniela, and Jakob Vestergaard. 2016. "Towards a Theory of Shadow Money." Working Paper, Institute for New Economic Thinking. https://www.ineteconomics.org/perspectives/blog/towards-a-theory-of-shadow-money.

Gallagher, Kevin P., and Richard Kozul-Wright. 2021. *The Case for a New Bretton Woods.* London: Polity.

Galí, Jordi, and Luca Gambetti. 2009. "On the Sources of the Great Moderation." *American Economic Journal* 1(1): 26–57.

Ganssmann, Heiner. 2004. "Geoffrey Ingham: The Nature of Money." *Economic Sociology* 6(1): 29–32.

Ganssmann, Heiner. 2012. *Doing Money: Elementary Monetary Theory from a Sociological Standpoint*. New York: Routledge.

Georgiadis, Philip, Tommy Stubbington, Joe Rennison, Eva Szalay, and Steve Johnson. 2020. "How Coronavirus Tore through Global Markets in the First Quarter." *Financial Times*, 1 April. https://www.ft.com/content/5f631cce-f75a-41d3-8f62-cff2fe8 3e90a.

Germain, Randall D. 1997. *The International Organization of Credit: States and Global Finance in the World-Economy*. Cambridge: Cambridge University Press.

Germain, Randall D. 2010. *Global Politics and Financial Governance*. Basingstoke, Hampshire: Palgrave Macmillan.

Germann, Julian. 2014. "State-Led or Capital-Driven? The Fall of Bretton Woods and the German Currency Float Reconsidered." *New Political Economy* 19(5): 769–89.

Giannini, Curzio. 2011. *The Age of Central Banks*. Cheltenham: Edward Elgar.

Giles, Chris, Martin Arnold, and Colby Smith. 2023. "Europe Grapples with Higher Inflation than the US." *Financial Times*, 4 September. https://www.ft.com/content /db281424-1fd6-440d-8368-dc88f8a8332b.

Giles, Chris, and Philip Georgiadis. 2020. "Bank of England to Directly Finance UK Government's Extra Spending." *Financial Times*, 9 April. https://www.ft.com/con tent/664c575b-0f54-44e5-ab78-2fd30ef213cb.

Golec, Pascal, and Enrico Perotti. 2017. "Safe Assets: A Review." ECB Working Paper No. 2035. https://www.ecb.europa.eu/pub/pdf/scpwps/ecbwp2035.en.pdf.

Golub, Stephen, Ayse Kaya, and Michael Reay. 2015. "What Were They Thinking? The Federal Reserve in the Run-up to the 2008 Financial Crisis." *Review of International Political Economy* 22(4): 657–92.

Goodhart, Charles. 1989. "The Conduct of Monetary Policy." *Economic Journal* 99(396): 293–346.

Goodhart, Charles. 1991. *The Evolution of Central Banks, 3rd ed.* Cambridge, MA: MIT Press.

Goodhart, Charles. 1998. "The Two Concepts of Money: Implications for the Analysis of Optimal Currency Areas." *European Journal of Political Economy* 14(3): 407–32.

Goodhart, Charles. 2011. "The Changing Role of Central Banks." *Financial History Review* 18(2): 135–54.

Goodhart, Charles, and Rosa Lastra. 2023. "The Changing and Growing Roles of Independent Central Banks Now Do Require a Reconsideration of Their Mandate." *Accounting, Economics, and Law*. DOI: 10.1515/ael-2022–0097.

Gopinath, Gita. 2023. "Three Uncomfortable Truths for Monetary Policy." Remarks by IMF First Deputy Managing Director for the European Central Bank Forum on Central Banking 2023, 26 June. https://www.imf.org/en/News/Articles/2023/06/26 /fdmd-speech-sintra-3-uncomfortable-truths.

Gopinath, Gita, Emine Boz, Camila Casas, Federico J. Díez, Pierre-Olivier Gourinchas, and Mikkel Plagborg-Møller. 2020. "Dominant Currency Paradigm." *American Economic Review* 110(3): 677–719.

Gorton, Gary B. 2017. "The History and Economics of Safe Assets." NBER Working Paper Series 22210. *Annual Review of Economics* 9: 547–86.

Gorton, Gary, Toomas Laarits, and Andrew Metrick. 2018. "The Run on Repo and the Fed's Response." NBER Working Paper No. 24866. https://www.nber.org/papers/w24866.

Gorton, Gary, and Andrew Metrick. 2012. "Securitized Banking and the Run on Repo." *Journal of Financial Economics* 104(3): 425–51.

Gramsci, Antonio. 1971. *Selections from the Prison Notebooks*. London: Lawrance & Wishart.

Greeley, Brendan, Colby Smith, and Joe Rennison. 2019. "Fed Official Cites Banks' Taste for Reserves in Repo Glitch." *Financial Times*, 7 October. https://www.ft.com/content/95a03bfa-e874-11e9-a240-3b065ef5fc55.

Green, Jeremy, and Scott Lavery. 2015. "The Regressive Recovery: Distribution, Inequality and State Power in Britain's Post-crisis Political Economy." *New Political Economy* 20(6): 894–923.

Greenspan, Alan. 2008. "Testimony on Sources of Financial Crisis: Former Federal Reserve Chairman Is Set to Testify Today before the House Committee of Government Oversight and Reform." http://blogs.wsj.com/economics/2008/10/23/greenspan-testimony-on-sources-of-financial-crisis/.

Greenspan, Alan, Arthur Levitt, Lawrence H. Summers, and William J. Rainer. 1999. *Over-the-Counter Derivatives Markets and the Commodity Exchange Act*. Report of the President's Working Group on Financial Markets, November. Washington DC. http://www.treasury.gov/resource-center/fin-mkts/documents/otcact.pdf.

Gross, Anna. 2020. "Coronavirus Sell-off Weighs Heavily on Bond and Equity Issuance." *Financial Times*, 17 March. https://www.ft.com/content/d6af8806-67a1-11ea-800d-da70cff6e4d3.

Haldane, Andrew G. 2014. "The Age of Asset Management?" Speech, Bank of England. https://www.bis.org/review/r140507d.pdf.

Hall, Rodney Bruce. 2008. *Central Banking as Global Governance: Constructing Financial Credibility*. Cambridge: Cambridge University Press.

Hannoun, Hervé, Otmar Issing, Klaus Liebscher, Helmut Schlesinger, and Jürgen Stark. 2019. "Memorandum." *FAZ*, 4 October. https://www.faz.net/-gqe-9rvee.

Hardie, Iain, David Howarth, Sylvia Maxfield, and Amy Verdun. 2013. "Banks and the False Dichotomy in the Comparative Political Economy of Finance." *World Politics* 65(4): 691–728.

Harvey, David. 1982. *The Limits to Capital*. London: Verso.

Harvey, David. 2011. *The Enigma of Capital and the Crises of Capitalism*. London: Profile Books.

Hauser, Andrew. 2014. "Lender of Last Resort Operations during the Financial Crisis: Seven Practical Lessons from the United Kingdom." BIS Paper No. 79, 81–92.

Helgadóttir, Oddný. 2016. "Banking Upside Down: The Implicit Politics of Shadow Banking Expertise." *Review of International Political Economy* 23(6): 915–40.

Helleiner, Eric. 1994. *States and the Reemergence of Global Finance: From Bretton Woods to the 1990s*. Ithaca, NY: Cornell University Press.

Helleiner, Eric. 2011. "Understanding the 2007–2008 Global Financial Crisis: Lessons for Scholars of International Political Economy." *Annual Review of Political Science* 14(1): 67–87.

Helleiner, Eric, and Stefano Pagliari. 2011. "The End of an Era in International Financial Regulation? A Postcrisis Research Agenda." *International Organization* 65(1): 169–200.

Henderson, Richard, and Joe Rennison. 2020. "Investor Appetite Returns for Junk Bonds." *Financial Times*, 3 April. https://www.ft.com/content/b6d8c592-85c3-45c9-bc47-89eb3ce2cf0f.

Henderson, Richard, and Robin Wigglesworth. 2020. "Asset Managers Rocked by Record Bond Fund Outflows." *Financial Times*, 20 March. https://www.ft.com/content/30e8928e-6a33-11ea-800d-da70cff6e4d3.

Hockett, Robert, and Aaron James. 2020. *Money from Nothing*. Brooklyn, NY: Melville House.

Howarth, David, Aletta J. Norval, and Yannis Stavrakakis, eds. 2000. *Discourse Theory and Political Analysis: Identities, Hegemonies and Social Change*. Manchester: Manchester University Press.

Humphrey, Thomas M. 2010. "Lender of Last Resort: What It Is, Whence It Came, and Why the Fed Isn't It." *Cato* 30(2): 333–64.

Husserl, Edmund. 1978. "The Origin of Geometry." In *Edmund Husserl's "Origin of Geometry": An Introduction*, edited by Jacques Derrida, 157–80. New York: Nicolas Hays.

Ihrig, Jane, Zeynep Senyuz, and Gretchen C. Weinbach. 2020. *Implementing Monetary Policy in an "Ample-Reserves" Regime*. FEDS Notes. Washington, DC: Board of Governors of the Federal Reserve System. https://www.federalreserve.gov/econres/notes/feds-notes/implementing-monetary-policy-in-an-ample-reserves-regime-the-basics-note-1-of-3-20200701.html.

Ihrig, Jane, Gretchen C. Weinbach, and Scott A. Wolla. 2021. *Teaching the Linkage between Banks and the Fed: R.I.P. Money Multiplier*. Federal Reserve Bank of St. Louis, Econ Primer, September 2021. https://files.stlouisfed.org/files/htdocs/publications/page1-econ/2021/09/17/teaching-the-linkage-between-banks-and-the-fed-r-i-p-money-multiplier_SE.pdf.

IMF. 2008. *Global Financial Stability Report: Financial Stress and Deleveraging Macro-Financial Implications and Policy*. Washington, DC: IMF Publications Services.

IMF. 2015. *Global Financial Stability Report: Vulnerabilities, Legacies, and Policy Challenges: Risks Rotating to Emerging Markets*. Washington, DC: IMF Publications Services.

IMF. 2019a. *Global Financial Stability Report, April*. Washington, DC: International Monetary Fund.

IMF. 2019b. *Global Financial Stability Report, October*. Washington, DC: International Monetary Fund.

IMF. 2020a. *Global Financial Stability Report*. Washington, DC: International Monetary Fund.

IMF. 2020b. "The Great Lockdown: Worst Economic Downturn since the Great Depression." Press release, 23 March. https://www.imf.org/en/News/Articles/2020/03/23/pr2098-imf-managing-director-statement-following-a-g20-ministerial-call-on-the-coronavirus-emergency.

IMF. 2021. "IMF Strategy to Help Members Address Climate Change Related Policy

Challenges." 30 July. https://www.imf.org/en/Publications/Policy-Papers/Issues/2021/07/30/IMF-Strategy-to-Help-Members-Address-Climate-Change-Related-Policy-Challenges-Priorities-463093.

IMF. 2022. "Gloomy and More Uncertain." July. https://www.imf.org/-/media/Files/Publications/WEO/2022/Update/July/English/text-en.ashx.

Ingham, Geoffrey. 2004. *The Nature of Money*. Cambridge: Polity.

Ingham, Geoffrey. 2006. "Further Reflections on the Ontology of Money: Responses to Lapavitsas and Dodd." *Economy and Society* 35(2): 259–78.

Ingham, Geoffrey. 2011. *Capitalism*. Cambridge: Polity.

IOSCO Technical Committee. 2008. *Report on the Subprime Crisis Report—Final Report*. May 2008. http://www.iosco.org/library/pubdocs/pdf/IOSCOPD273.pdf.

Jakab, Zoltan, and Michael Kumhof. 2015. "Banks Are Not Intermediaries of Loanable Funds—and Why This Matters." Working Paper No. 529. https://www.bankofengland.co.uk/working-paper/2015/banks-are-not-intermediaries-of-loanable-funds-and-why-this-matters.

Jenkins, Patrick. 2023. "Credit Suisse's Demise: A New Twist on the 'Swiss Finish.'" *Financial Times*, 27 March. https://www.ft.com/content/6b9909f1-0a1f-4c4e-b11a-cc4a13991b9d.

Jessop, Bob. 2001. "What Follows Fordism? On the Periodization of Capitalism and Its Regulation." In *Phases of Capitalist Development: Booms, Crises and Globalizations*, edited by Robert Albritton, Makoto Itoh, Richard Westra, and Alan Zuefe, 283–300. London: Macmillan.

Johnson, Neil, et al. 2012. "Financial Black Swans Driven by Ultra Fast Machine Ecology." SSRN Paper. https://papers.ssrn.com/sol3/papers.cfm?abstract_id=2003874.

Jones, Claire. 2015. "Legal Opinion Paves Way for ECB Bond-Buying Programme." *Financial Times*, 14 January. http://www.ft.com/intl/cms/s/0/45850d86-9bca-11e4-b6cc-00144feabdco.html?siteedition=intl#axzz3OsBVtoLD.

Jones, Claire. 2020. "Helicopter Money Is Here." *Financial Times*, 20 February. https://ftalphaville.ft.com/2020/02/26/1582705518000/Helicopter-money-is-here/.

Jones, Erik. 2023. "Managing the Risks of Quantitative Tightening in the Euro Area." *Funcas SEFO* 12(1): 23–31.

Kaltenbrunner, Annina, and Photis Lysandrou. 2017. "The US Dollar's Continuing Hegemony as an International Currency: A Double-Matrix Analysis." *Development and Change* 48(4): 663–91.

Kaminska, Izabella. 2008. "Three Maids a Milking." *Financial Times*, 4 December. https://next.ft.com/content/777a853d-0322-31c8-bd22-6f794bb2c301.

Kaminska, Izabella. 2019. "A Story about a Liquidity Regime Shift." *Financial Times*, 17 September. https://ftalphaville.ft.com/2019/09/17/1568721798000/A-story-about-a-liquidity-regime-shift/.

Kaminska, Izabella. 2020. "When Central Banks Take Over Securities Markets." *Financial Times*, 25 March. https://ftalphaville.ft.com/2020/03/25/1585143723000/When-central-banks-take-over-securities-markets/.

Kelton, Stephanie. 2020. *The Deficit Myth: Modern Monetary Theory and the Birth of the People's Economy*. New York: Public Affairs.

Kessler, Oliver. 2008. *Die internationale politische Ökonomie des Risikos: Eine Analyse am Beispiel der Diskussion um die Reformierung der Finanzmärkte.* Wiesbaden: VS Verlag.

Keynes, John Maynard. 1971 [1930]. *A Treatise on Money.* London: Macmillan.

Keynes, John Maynard. 2018 [1936]. *The General Theory of Employment, Interest and Money.* Basingstoke, Hampshire: Palgrave Macmillan.

Kindleberger, Charles P., and Robert Z. Aliber. 2005. *Manias, Panics and Crashes: A History of Financial Crisis,* 5th ed. Basingstoke, Hampshire: Palgrave Macmillan.

Kindleberger, Charles P., and Robert Z. Aliber. 2015. *Manias, Panics, and Crashes: A History of Financial Crisis,* 7th ed. Basingstoke, Hampshire: Palgrave Macmillan.

Knafo, Samuel. 2007. "Political Marxism and Value Theory." *Historical Materialism* 15(2): 75–104.

Knafo, Samuel. 2013. *The Making of Modern Finance: The Gold Standard and the Rise of Liberal Financial Governance.* London: Routledge.

Knapp, Georg Friedrich. 1924. *The State Theory of Money.* London: Macmillan.

Koester, Gerrit, et al. 2022. "Inflation Developments in the Euro Area and the United States." *ECB Economic Bulletin,* no. 8.

Konings, Martijn. 2015. "State of Speculation: Contingency, Measure, and the Politics of Plastic Value." *South Atlantic Quarterly* 114(2): 251–82.

Konings, Martijn. 2016. "The Spirit of Austerity." *Journal of Cultural Economy* 9(1): 86–100.

Konings, Martijn. 2018. *Capital and Time: For a New Critique of Neoliberal Reason.* Stanford, CA: Stanford University Press.

Kovner, Anna, and Antoine Martin. 2020. "Expanding the Toolkit: Facilities Established to Respond to the COVID-19 Pandemic." Liberty Street Economics, Fed of New York, 22 September. https://libertystreeteconomics.newyorkfed.org/2020/09/expanding-the-toolkit-facilities-established-to-respond-to-the-covid-19-pandemic.html.

Krippner, Greta R. 2007. "The Making of US Monetary Policy: Central Bank Transparency and the Neoliberal Dilemma." *Theory and Society* 36(6): 477–513.

Krippner, Greta R. 2011. *Capitalizing on Crisis: The Political Origins of the Rise of Finance.* Cambridge, MA: Harvard University Press.

Krugman, Paul. 2009. "Making Banking Boring." *New York Times,* 9 April. http://www.nytimes.com/2009/04/10/opinion/10krugman.html?_r=0.

Laclau, Ernesto, ed. 1990. *New Reflections on the Revolution of Our Time.* London: Verso.

Laclau, Ernesto, ed. 1996a. *Emancipation(s).* London: Verso.

Laclau, Ernesto. 1996b. "Why Do Empty Signifiers Matter to Politics?" In *Emancipation(s),* edited by Ernesto Laclau, 34–46. London: Verso.

Laclau, Ernesto. 1996c. "Universalism, Particularism and the Question of Identity." In *Emancipation(s),* edited by Ernesto Laclau, 20–35. London: Verso.

Laclau, Ernesto. 2000. "Constructing Universality." In *Contingency, Hegemony, Universality,* edited by Judith Butler, Ernesto Laclau, and Slavoj Žižek, 281–307. London: Verso.

Laclau, Ernesto. 2004. "Glimpsing the Future." In *Laclau: A Critical Reader*, edited by Simon Critchley and Oliver Marchart, 279–328. London: Routledge.

Laclau, Ernesto. 2005. *On Populist Reason*. London: Verso.

Laeven, Luc, and Fabián Valencia. 2012. "Systemic Banking Crises Database: An Update." IMF Working Paper WP/12/163. https://www.imf.org/external/pubs/ft/wp/2012/wp12163.pdf.

Langley, Paul. 2007. "The Uncertain Subjects of Anglo-American Financialization." *Cultural Critique* 65: 66–91.

Langley, Paul. 2013. "Toxic Assets, Turbulence and Biopolitical Security: Governing the Crisis of Global Financial Circulation." *Security Dialogue* 44(2): 111–26.

Langley, Paul. 2015. *Liquidity Lost: The Governance of the Global Financial Crisis*. Oxford: Oxford University Press.

Langley, Paul. 2017. "Finance/Security/Life." *Finance and Society* 3(2): 173–79.

Lapavitsas, Costas. 2003. *Social Foundations of Markets, Money and Credit*. London: Routledge.

Lapavitsas, Costas. 2005. "The Social Relations of Money as Universal Equivalent: A Response to Ingham." *Economy and Society* 34(3): 389–403.

Lee, Helene, and Asani Sarkar. 2018. "Is Stigma Attached to the European Central Bank's Marginal Lending Facility?" Liberty Street Economics, Fed of New York. http://libertystreeteconomics.newyorkfed.org/2018/04/is-stigma-attached-to-the-european-central-banks-marginal-lending-facility.html.

Lemke, Thomas. 2001. "'The Birth of Bio-politics': Michel Foucault's Lecture at the Collège de France on Neo-liberal Governmentality." *Economy and Society* 30(2): 190–207.

Leonard, Deborah, Antoine Martin, and Simon Potter. 2017. "How the Fed Changes the Size of Its Balance Sheet." Liberty Street Economics, Fed of New York. http://libertystreeteconomics.newyorkfed.org/2017/07/how-the-fed-changes-the-size-of-its-balance-sheet.html.

Leyshon, Andrew, and Nigel Thrift. 2007. "The Capitalization of Almost Everything: The Future of Economy and Finance." *Theory, Culture & Society* 24 (7/8): 97–115.

Lobo-Guerrero, Luis. 2011. *Insuring Security: Biopolitics, Security and Risk*. New York: Routledge.

Logan, Lorie K. 2017. "Implementing Monetary Policy: Perspective from the Open Market Trading Desk." Speech by the Senior Vice President of the FED, 18 May. https://www.newyorkfed.org/newsevents/speeches/2017/log170518.

Logan, Lorie K. 2018. "Operational Perspectives on Monetary Policy Implementation: Panel Remarks on 'The Future of the Central Bank Balance Sheet.'" Speech by the Senior Vice President of the FED, 4 May. https://www.newyorkfed.org/newsevents/speeches/2018/log180504.

Logan, Lorie K. 2019. "Observations on Implementing Monetary Policy in an Ample-Reserves Regime." Speech by the Senior Vice President of the FED, 17 April. https://www.newyorkfed.org/newsevents/speeches/2019/log190417.

Mabbett, Deborah, and Waltraud Schelkle. 2019. "Independent or Lonely? Central Banking in Crisis." *Review of International Political Economy* 26(3): 436–60.

MacKenzie, Donald. 2006. *An Engine, Not a Camera: How Financial Models Shape Markets*. Cambridge, MA: MIT Press.

MacKenzie, Donald. 2009. *Material Markets: How Economic Agents Are Constructed*. Oxford: Oxford University Press.

MacKenzie, Donald. 2012. "Knowledge Production in Financial Markets: Credit Default Swaps, the ABX and the Subprime Crisis." *Economy and Society* 41(3): 335–59.

MacKenzie, Donald. 2014. "A Sociology of Algorithms: High-Frequency Trading and the Shaping of Markets." Paper for the SCOOPs Seminar MaxPo. http://www.maxpo.eu/Downloads/Paper_DonaldMacKenzie.pdf.

MacKenzie, Donald. 2021. *Trading at the Speed of Light: How Ultrafast Algorithms Are Transforming Financial Markets*. Princeton, NJ: Princeton University Press.

MacKenzie, Donald, Daniel Beunza, Yuval Millo, and Juan P. Pardo-Guerra. 2012. "Drilling through the Allegheny Mountains: Liquidity, Materiality and High-Frequency Trading." *Journal of Cultural Economy* 5(3): 279–96.

MacKenzie, Donald, and Yuval Millo. 2003. "Constructing a Market, Performing Theory: The Historical Sociology of a Financial Derivatives Exchange." *American Journal of Sociology* 109(1): 107–45.

Mackenzie, Kate. 2023. "The Gigantic Austerity Drive Underway." *Phenomenal World*, 20 April. https://www.phenomenalworld.org/analysis/the-gigantic-austerity-drive-underway/.

Mankiw, Gregory N. 2017. *Makroeconomics*, 9th ed. New York: Worth.

Marshall, Paul. 2015. "Central Banks Have Made the Rich Richer." *Financial Times*, 22 September. http://www.ft.com/intl/cms/s/0/4c53586a-6114-11e5-9846-de406ccb37f2.html#axzz3nIvOpcOa.

Martin, Antoine, and Susan McLaughlin. 2020. "The Primary Dealer Credit Facility." Liberty Street Economics, Fed of New York, 19 May. https://libertystreeteconomics.newyorkfed.org/2020/05/the-primary-dealer-credit-facility.html.

Martin, Randy. 2002. *Financialization of Daily Life*. Philadelphia: Temple University Press.

Martin, Randy. 2007. *An Empire of Indifference: American War and the Financial Logic of Risk Management*. Durham, NC: Duke University Press.

Marx, Karl. 1976a. *Capital: A Critique of Political Economy, Volume 1*. London: Penguin.

Marx, Karl. 1976b. "The Commodity: Chapter One, Volume One, of the First Edition of *Capital*." In *Value: Studies by Karl Marx*, edited by Albert Dragstedt, 7–40. London: New Park.

Masters, Brooke, Stephen Gandel, James Fontanella-Khan, James Politi, and Colby Smith. 2023. "The Difference between First Republic and Other Recent Bank Failures." *Financial Times*, 1 May. https://www.ft.com/content/3044e4c8-d26a-4f75-b33f-376b9865aa22.

Mazzucato, Mariana. 2014. *The Entrepreneurial State: Debunking Public vs. Private Sector Myths*. London: Anthem.

Mazzucato, Mariana. 2021. *Mission Economy: A Moonshot Guide to Changing Capitalism*. London: Allen Lane-Penguin.

McDowell, Daniel. 2012. "The US as 'Sovereign International Last-Resort Lender': The Fed's Currency Swap Programme during the Great Panic of 2007–09." *New Political Economy* 17(2): 157–78.

McKinsey Global Institute. 2021. "The Rise and Rise of the Global Balance Sheet: How Productively Are We Using Our Wealth?" 15 November. https://www.mckinsey.com/industries/financial-services/our-insights/the-rise-and-rise-of-the-global-balance-sheet-how-productively-are-we-using-our-wealth.

McLeay, Michael, Amar Radia, and Thomas Ryland. 2014a. "Money Creation in the Modern Economy." *Bank of England Quarterly Bulletin* 54(1): 14–27.

McLeay, Michael, Amar Radia, and Thomas Ryland. 2014b. "Money in the Modern Economy." *Bank of England Quarterly Bulletin* 54(1): 4–13.

McNamara, Kathleen R. 1998. *The Currency of Ideas*. Ithaca, NY: Cornell University Press.

McNamara, Kathleen R. 2002. "Rational Fictions: Central Bank Independence and the Social Logic of Delegation." *West European Politics* 25(1): 47–76.

McPhilemy, Samuel, and Manuela Moschella. 2019. "Central Banks under Stress: Reputation, Accountability and Regulatory Coherence." *Public Administration* 97(3): 489–98.

Mehrling, Perry. 2011. *The New Lombard Street: How the Fed Became the Dealer of Last Resort*. Princeton, NJ: Princeton University Press.

Mehrling, Perry. 2013. "The Inherent Hierarchy of Money." In *Social Fairness and Economics*, edited by Lance Taylor, Armon Rezai, and Thomas Michl, 394–404. New York: Routledge.

Mehrling, Perry. 2015. "Elasticity and Discipline in the Global Swap Network." *International Journal of Political Economy* 44(4): 311–24.

Mehrling, Perry. 2017. "Why Central Banking Should Be Re-imagined." *BIS Paper* No. 79, 108–18.

Mehrling, Perry. 2022a. *Money and Empire: Charles P. Kindleberger and the Dollar System*. Cambridge: Cambridge University Press.

Mehrling, Perry. 2022b. "Where's my swap line? A Money View of International Lender of Last Resort." *Jahrbuch für Wirtschaftsgeschichte* 63(2): 1–16.

Mehrling, Perry. 2023a. "Exorbitant Privilege? On the Rise (and Rise) of the Global Dollar System." Working Paper No. 198, Institute for New Economic Thinking. https://www.ineteconomics.org/research/research-papers/exorbitant-privilege-on-the-rise-and-rise-of-the-global-dollar-system.

Mehrling, Perry. 2023b. "The Minsky-Kindleberger Connection and the Making of Manias, Panics, and Crashes." *Oeconomia* 13(4): 1029–1053.

Mehrling, Perry, Zoltan Pozsar, James Sweeney, and Dan Neilson. 2013. "Bagehot Was a Shadow Banker: Shadow Banking, Central Banking, and the Future of Global Finance." SSRN Working Paper. https://ssrn.com/abstract=2232016.

Menger, Carl. 1892. "On the Origins of Money." *Economic Journal* 2(6): 239–55.

Menger, Carl. 1970. *Schriften über Geld und Währungspolitik*. Tübingen: Mohr.

Meyer, Gregory. 2019. "Automation Is the Future of Futures Markets." *Financial Times*, 24 April. https://www.ft.com/content/4d589796-6211-11e9-a27a-fdd51850994c.

Michell, Jo. 2016. "Do Shadow Banks Create Money? 'Financialisation' and the Monetary Circuit." UWE Economics Working Paper Series. eprints.uwe.ac.uk/28552/1/1602.pdf.

Milstein, Eric, and David Wessel. 2021. "What Did the Fed Do in Response to the COVID-19 Crisis?" Brookings Institution, 17 December. https://www.brookings.edu/articles/fed-response-to-covid19/.

Minsky, Hyman P. 1982a. *Can "It" Happen Again? Essays on Instability and Finance.* Armonk, NY: Sharpe.

Minsky, Hyman P. 1982b. "The Financial Instability Hypothesis: Capitalist Processes and the Behaviour of the Economy." In *Financial Crisis: Theory, History, Policy,* edited by Charles Kindleberger and Jean-Pierre Laffargue, 13–47. Cambridge: Cambridge University Press.

Minsky, Hyman P. 2008. *John Maynard Keynes.* New York: McGraw-Hill.

Mirowski, Philip. 1986. "Mathematical Formalism and Economic Explanation." In *The Reconstruction of Economic Theory,* edited by Philip Mirowski, 179–240. Boston: Kluwer.

Mirowski, Philip. 1991. "Postmodernism and the Social Theory of Value." *Journal of Post Keynesian Economics* 13(4): 565–82.

Mirowski, Philip. 2014. *Never Let a Serious Crisis Go to Waste: How Neoliberalism Survived the Financial Meltdown.* London: Verso.

Mises, Ludwig von. 1981 [1912]. *The Theory of Money and Credit.* Indianapolis: Liberty Fund.

Mitchell Innes, Alfred. 1913. "What Is Money?" *Banking Law Journal* 30(May): 377–408.

Moe, Thorvald G. 2014. "Shadow Banking: Policy Challenges for Central Banks." Working Paper No. 802, Levy Economics Institute of Bard College, Annandale-on-Hudson, NY. https://www.levyinstitute.org/pubs/wp_802.pdf.

Moreira, Alan, and Alexi Savov. 2017. "The Macroeconomics of Shadow Banking." *Journal of Finance* 72(6): 2381–432.

Moschella, Manuela, and Eleni Tsingou. 2013. "Regulating Finance after the Crisis: Unveiling the Different Dynamics of the Regulatory Process." *Regulation & Governance* 7(4): 407–16.

Münchau, Wolfgang. 2020. "Italy Is in More Danger than the Eurozone Will Acknowledge." *Financial Times,* 19 April. https://www.ft.com/content/8e03cf2e-80bd-11ea-8fdb-7ec06edeef84.

Murau, Steffen. 2017a. "Shadow Money and the Public Money Supply: The Impact of the 2007–2009 Financial Crisis on the Monetary System." *Review of International Political Economy* 24(5): 802–38.

Murau, Steffen. 2017b. *"The Political Economy of Private Credit Money Accommodation."* PhD thesis, City University of London.

Murau, Steffen, Fabian Pape, and Tobias Pforr. 2021. *The Hierarchy of the Offshore US-Dollar System: On Swap Lines, the FIMA Repo Facility and Special Drawing Rights.* https://www.bu.edu/gdp/files/2021/02/Steffen-Murau-GEGI-Study-2-Feb-2021.pdf.

Murau, Steffen, Fabian Pape, and Tobias Pforr. 2023. "International Monetary Hierarchy through Emergency US-Dollar Liquidity: A Key Currency Approach." *Competition and Change* 27 (3/4): 495–515.

Murau, Steffen, and Tobias Pforr. 2020. "What Is Money in a Critical Macro-Finance Framework?" *Finance and Society* 6(1): 56–66.

Nesvetailova, Anastasia. 2010. *Financial Alchemy in Crisis: The Great Liquidity Illusion.* London: Pluto.

Nesvetailova, Anastasia. 2015. "A Crisis of the Overcrowded Future: Shadow Banking and the Political Economy of Financial Innovation." *New Political Economy* 20(3): 431–53.

Neuhoff, Karsten. 2022. *Defining Gas Price Limits and Gas Saving Targets for a Large-Scale Gas Supply Interruption.* Berlin: German Institute for Economic Research.

Nitzan, Jonathan, and Shimshon Bichler. 2009. *Capital as Power: A Study of Order and Creorder.* London: Routledge.

Noona, Laura, and Brooke Masters. 2023. "How Rising Interest Rates Are Exposing Bank Weaknesses." *Financial Times*, 30 March. https://www.ft.com/content/fb4fd417-01db-4c99-bf45-c341d1d14f36.

Oakley, David. 2015. "Central Banks Rule in the Age of the Flash Crash." *Financial Times*, 10 May. https://www.ft.com/content/379975b0-f569-11e4-bc6d-00144feab7de.

Orphanides, Athanasios. 2017. "ECB Monetary Policy and Euro Area Governance." MIT Sloan School Working Paper 5258–17. https://papers.ssrn.com/sol3/Delivery.cfm/SSRN_ID3076184_code285952.pdf?abstractid=3076184&mirid=1.

Orszag, Peter R., Robert E. Rubin, and Joseph E. Stiglitz. 2021. *Fiscal Resiliency in a Deeply Uncertain World.* Policy Brief PIIE. https://www.piie.com/sites/default/files/documents/pb21-2.pdf.

Panitch, Leo, and Sam Gindin. 2014. "Political Economy and Political Power: The American State and Finance in the Neoliberal Era." *Government and Opposition* 49(3): 369–99.

Pape, Fabian. 2022. "Governing Global Liquidity: Federal Reserve Swap Lines and the International Dimension of US Monetary Policy." *New Political Economy* 27(3): 455–72.

Paudyn, Bartholomew. 2013. *Credit Rating Agencies and the Sovereign Debt.* Basingstoke, Hampshire: Palgrave Macmillan.

Pauly, Louis W. 1997. *Who Elected the Bankers? Surveillance and Control in the World Economy.* Ithaca, NY: Cornell University Press.

Pereira da Silva, Luiz A. 2021. "Green Swan 2—Climate Change and Covid-19: Reflections on Efficiency Versus Resilience." Speech based on Remarks at the OECD Chief Economist Talk Series. https://www.bis.org/speeches/sp200514.pdf.

Petry, Johannes, Jan Fichtner, and Eelke Heemskerk. 2019. "Steering Capital: The Growing Private Authority of Index Providers in the Age of Passive Asset Management." *Review of International Political Economy.* 10.1080/09692290.2019.1699147.

Pettifor, Ann. 2006. *The Coming First World Debt Crisis.* Houndmills, Basingstoke: Palgrave Macmillan.

Pettifor, Ann. 2019. *The Case for the Green New Deal*. London: Verso.

Piketty, Thomas. 2014. *Capital in the Twenty-First Century*. Cambridge, MA: Harvard University Press.

Piketty, Thomas, and Emmanuel Saez. 2003. "Income Inequality in the United States, 1913–1998." *Quarterly Journal of Economics* 118(1): 1–39.

Pistor, Katharina. 2020. *The Code of Capital: How the Law Creates Wealth and Inequality*. Princeton, NJ: Princeton University Press.

Pitluck, Aaron Z. 2011. "Distributed Execution in Illiquid Times: An Alternative Explanation of Trading in Stock Markets." *Economy and Society* 40(1): 26–55.

Plender, John. 2022. "Lessons from the Gilts Crisis." *Financial Times*, 21 December. https://www.ft.com/content/2a2e7a9b-d984-45c1-8ada-0d0a6e57911b.

Polanyi, Karl. 1957. *The Great Transformation: The Political and Economic Origins of Our Time*. Boston: Beacon Press.

Politi, James. 2020a. "Federal Reserve Sets Up Facility to Make Loans to Banks." *Financial Times*, 19 March. https://www.ft.com/content/0e6029be-6995-11ea-800d-da70cff6e4d3.

Politi, James. 2020b. "Fed's Powell is Chief Cheerleader for Fiscal Stimulus." *Financial Times*, 11 October. https://www.ft.com/content/91322629-0668-49b5-aba0-13bd72b436e8.

Politi, James, Colby Smith, and Martin Arnold. 2020. "Fed to Tolerate Higher Inflation in Policy Shift." *Financial Times*, 27 August. https://www.ft.com/content/e1e59faa-5005-4e1c-9d54-b1a8d4de9586.

Popper, Nathaniel. 2012. "Knight Capital Says Trading Glitch Cost It \$440 Million." *New York Times*, 2 August. http://dealbook.nytimes.com/2012/08/02/knight-capital-says-trading-mishap-cost-it-440-million/.

Potter, Simon. 2017a. "Implementing Monetary Policy with the Balance Sheet." Speech at the ECB. https://www.newyorkfed.org/newsevents/speeches/2017/pot171106.

Potter, Simon. 2017b. "Money Markets at a Crossroads: Policy Implementation at a Time of Structural Change." Remarks at the Master of Applied Economics' Distinguished Speaker Series, UCLA, 5 April. https://www.newyorkfed.org/newsevents/speeches/2017/pot170405.

Potter, Simon. 2018. "The Supply of Money-Like Assets." Remarks for American Economic Association, Federal Reserve Bank of New York. https://www.newyorkfed.org/newsevents/speeches/2018/pot180106.

Powell, Jerome H. 2020. "New Economic Challenges and the Fed's Monetary Policy Review." 27 August. https://www.federalreserve.gov/newsevents/speech/powell20200827a.htm.

Pozsar, Zoltan. 2011. "Institutional Cash Pools and the Triffin Dilemma of the U.S. Banking System." IMF Working Paper WP 11/190.

Pozsar, Zoltan. 2014. "Shadow Banking: The Money View." U.S. Treasury, Office of Financial Research, Working Paper 14-4, 1–71.

Pozsar, Zoltan. 2015. "A Macro View of Shadow Banking." Shadow Banking Colloquium (INET) Working Paper. https://papers.ssrn.com/sol3/Delivery.cfm/SSRN_ID2558945_code1930453.pdf?abstractid=2558945&mirid=1.

Pozsar, Zoltan. 2019. "Collateral Supply and o/n Rates, Global Money Notes #22." Credit Suisse Economic Research. https://research-doc.credit-suisse.com.

Pozsar, Zoltan. 2021. "Global Money Dispatch." Credit Suisse, 18 June. https://plus.credit-suisse.com/rpc4/ravDocView?docid=V7rztG2AN-Ux8.

Pozsar, Zoltan. 2022. "Bretton Woods III." Credit Suisse Economics, 7 March. https://plus2.credit-suisse.com.

Pozsar, Zoltan, and Manmohan Singh. 2011. "The Nonbank-Bank Nexus and the Shadow Banking System." IMF Working Paper WP/11/289. https://papers.ssrn.com/sol3/Delivery.cfm/wp11289.pdf.

Priewe, Jan, and Hansjörg Herr. 2005. *The Macroeconomics of Development and Poverty Reduction*. Baden-Baden: Nomos.

Quaglia, Lucia. 2023. "Explaining the Response of the ECB to the COVID-19 Related Economic Crisis: Inter-crisis and Intra-crisis Learning." *Journal of European Public Policy* 30(4): 635–54.

Rennison, Joe. 2019. "Repo Glitches Expose Flaws in Fed's Approach." *Financial Times*, 5 October. https://www.ft.com/content/d2cd761a-e64d-11e9-9743-db5a370481bc.

Ricks, Morgan. 2011. "Regulating Money Creation after the Crisis." *Harvard Business Law Review* 1(1): 75–143.

Ricks, Morgan. 2016. *The Money Problem: Rethinking Financial Regulation*. Chicago: University of Chicago Press.

Rogoff, Kenneth. 2021. "Don't Panic: A Little Inflation Is No Bad Thing." *Financial Times*, 16 July. https://www.ft.com/content/a7c101be-7361-4307-981d-b8edf6d002be.

Romei, Valentina, and Tommy Stubbington. 2022. "Central Banks Embrace Big Rises to Bolster Currencies and Fight Inflation." *Financial Times*, 17 July. https://www.ft.com/content/d189b2f2-808a-4a9b-a856-234181f98c2f.

Rona-Tas, Akos, and Stefanie Hiss. 2011. "Forecasting as Valuation: The Role of Ratings and Predictions in the Subprime Mortgage Crisis in the United States." In *The Worth of Goods: Valuation and Pricing in the Economy*, edited by Jens Beckert and Patrik Aspers, 223–46. Oxford: Oxford University Press.

Rose, Nikolas. 1996. "Governing 'Advanced' Liberal Democracies." In *Foucault and Political Reason: Liberalism, Neo-liberalism and Rationalities of Government*, edited by Andrew Barry and Thomas Osborne, 37–64. London: UCL Press, 37–64.

Rose, Nikolas, and Peter Miller. 1992. "Political Power beyond the State: Problems of Government." *British Journal of Sociology* 43(2): 172–205.

Rosenberg, Emily S. 1999. *Financial Missionaries to the World: The Politics and Culture of Dollar Diplomacy, 1900–1930*. Cambridge, MA: Harvard University Press.

Sandbu, Martin. 2020. "German Court Has Set a Bomb under the EU Legal Order." *Financial Times*, 5 May. https://www.ft.com/content/79484c01-b66b-4f81-bdc6-fd4def940821.

Sandbu, Martin. 2022a. "Reasons to Think Differently about Inflation." *Financial Times*, 21 July. https://www.ft.com/content/bc369172-328c-483c-947d-6ccf8fced23a.

Sandbu, Martin. 2022b. "The Investment Drought of the Past Two Decades Is Catching Up with Us." 20 July. https://www.ft.com/content/3a8731bc-aad3-42ca-b99e-b3a553974ccf.

Saraceno, Francesco, Willi Semmler, and Brigitte Young. 2020. "European Economic, Fiscal, and Social Policy at the Crossroads." *Constellations* 27: 573–93.

Sassen, Saskia. 2009. "Too Big to Save: The End of Financial Capitalism." *Opendemocracy online*. http://www.opendemocracy.net/article/too-big-to-save-the-end-of-financial-capitalism-0.

Scherrer, Christoph. 1999. *Globalisierung wider Willen: Die Durchsetzung liberaler Außenwirtschaftspolitik in den USA*. Berlin: Edition Sigma.

Scherrer, Christoph. 2014. "Neoliberalism's Resilience: A Matter of Class." *Critical Policy Studies* 8(3): 348–51.

Scherrer, Christoph, ed. 2017. *Public Banks in the Age of Financialization: A Comparative Perspective*. Cheltenham: Edward Elgar.

Scherrer, Christoph, Ana Saggioro Garcia, and Joscha Wullweber, eds. 2023. *Handbook on Critical Political Economy and Public Policy*. Cheltenham: Edward Elgar.

Schindler, Seth, Ilias Alami, and Nicholas Jepson. 2023. "Goodbye Washington Confusion, Hello Wall Street Consensus: Contemporary State Capitalism and the Spatialisation of Industrial Strategy." *New Political Economy* 28(2): 223–40.

Schnabel, Isabel. 2020a. "The Shadow of Fiscal Dominance: Misconceptions, Perceptions and Perspectives." Speech at the Centre for European Reform and the Eurofi Financial Forum, 11 September. https://www.ecb.europa.eu/press/key/date/2020/html/ecb.sp200911~ea32bd8bb3.en.html.

Schnabel, Isabel. 2020b. "When Markets Fail: The Need for Collective Action in Tackling Climate Change." https://www.ecb.europa.eu/press/key/date/2020/html/ecb.sp200928_1~268b0b672f.en.html.

Schnabel, Isabel. 2021a. "The Spectre of Inflation." *ECB blog*. https://www.ecb.europa.eu/press/blog/date/2021/html/ecb.blog210914~a514f7c553.en.html.

Schnabel, Isabel. 2021b. "Monetary Policy and Inequality." Speech by member of the Executive Board of the ECB, at a virtual conference on "Diversity and Inclusion in Economics, Finance, and Central Banking," Frankfurt am Main, 9 November. https://www.ecb.europa.eu/press/key/date/2021/html/ecb.sp211109_2~cca25b0a68.de.html.

Schnabel, Isabel. 2021c. "Reflation, Not Stagflation." Speech at a virtual event organized by Goldman Sachs. https://www.ecb.europa.eu/press/key/date/2021/html/ecb.sp211117~78f0a1f435.en.html.

Schnabel, Isabel. 2021d. "The Monetary Policy Non-puzzle in Bond Markets." Speech at the Bond Market Contact Group meeting, 15 September. https://www.ecb.europa.eu/press/key/date/2021/html/ecb.sp210915~75de3a2dfa.en.html.

Schnabel, Isabel. 2022. "The Globalisation of Inflation." Speech by member of the Executive Board of the ECB, 11 May. https://www.ecb.europa.eu/press/key/date/2022/html/ecb.sp220511_1~e9ba02e127.en.html.

Schnabel, Isabel. 2023. "Disinflation and the Phillips Curve." Speech by member of the Executive Board of the ECB, at a conference organized by the European Central Bank and the Federal Reserve Bank of Cleveland's Center for Inflation Research, 31 August. https://www.ecb.europa.eu/press/key/date/2023/html/ecb.sp230831~c2531 4a3fc.en.html.

Schrimpf, Andreas, Hyun S. Shin, and Vladyslav Sushko. 2020. "Leverage and Margin

Spirals in Fixed Income Markets during the Covid-19 Crisis." *BIS Bulletin*, no. 2. https://www.bis.org/publ/bisbull02.htm.

Schumpeter, Joseph A. 1986 [1954]. *History of Economic Analysis*. London: Routledge.

Searle, John R. 1995. *Construction of Social Reality*. London: Penguin Books.

Searle, John R. 2005. "What Is an Institution?" *Journal of Institutional Economics* 1(1): 1–22.

Semmler, Willi. 2011. *Asset Prices, Booms and Recessions: Financial Economics from a Dynamic Perspective*. Heidelberg: Springer.

Shah, Atul K. 1997. "Regulatory Arbitrage through Financial Innovation." *Accounting, Auditing & Accountability Journal* 10(1): 85–104.

Sharma, Ruchir. 2021. "The Billionaire Boom: How the Super-Rich Soaked Up Covid Cash." *Financial Times*, 13 May. https://www.ft.com/content/747a76dd-f018-4d0d-a9f3-4069bf2f5a93.

Shiller, Robert J. 2000. *Irrational Exuberance* Princeton, NJ: Princeton University Press.

Simmel, Georg. 1978 [1900]. *Philosophy of Money*. London: Routledge.

Sinclair, Timothy. 2005. *The New Masters of Capital: American Bond Rating Agencies and the Politics of Creditworthiness*. Ithaca, NY: Cornell University Press.

Singh, Manmohan. 2017. "Collateral Reuse and Balance Sheet Space." IMF Working Paper No. 17/113. https://papers.ssrn.com/sol3/Delivery.cfm/wp17113.pdf?abstractid=3053196&mirid=1.

Sissoko, Carolyn. 2010. "The Legal Foundations of Financial Collapse." *Journal of Financial Economic Policy* 2(1): 5–34.

Smith, Adam. 1982 [1776]. *An Inquiry into the Nature and Causes of the Wealth of Nations*. Indianapolis: Liberty Press.

Smith, Colby, Jennifer Ablan, Tommy Stubbington, Philip Georgiadis, and Hudson Lockett. 2020a. "Global Stocks, Oil Prices and Government Bonds Tumble." *Financial Times*, 18 March. https://www.ft.com/content/1b1b47d4-68bd-11ea-a3c9-1fe6fedcca75.

Smith, Colby, and Richard Henderson. 2020. "Investors Spooked by Outbreak Seek Safety in Money Market Funds." *Financial Times*, 27 March. https://www.ft.com/content/f86c87dc-764c-4100-b2eb-316020if9e11.

Smith, Colby, Richard Henderson, Philip Georgiadis, and Hudson Lockett. 2020b. "Investors' Retreat to Safety Sees Bonds Hit New Highs." *Financial Times*, 7 March. https://www.ft.com/content/9f94d6f8-5f51-11ea-b0ab-339c2307bcd4.

Soros, George. 2009. *The New Paradigm for Financial Markets: The Credit Crisis of 2008 and What It Means*. New York: Public Affairs.

St. Louis Fed. 2020. "Shares of Gross Domestic Product: Personal Consumption Expenditure." https://fred.stlouisfed.org/series/DPCERE1Q156NBEA.

St. Louis Fed. 2022a. "Central Bank Assets for Euro Area." https://fred.stlouisfed.org/series/ECBASSETSW.

St. Louis Fed. 2022b. "Shares of Gross Domestic Income: Compensation of Employees, Paid: Wage and Salary Accruals: Disbursements: To Persons." https://fred.stlouisfed.org/series/W270REIA156NBEA.

St. Louis Fed. 2023a. "Total Assets." https://fred.stlouisfed.org/series/WALCL.

St. Louis Fed. 2023b. "U.S. Unemployment Rate." https://fred.stlouisfed.org/series/ UNRATE.

St. Louis Fed. 2023c. "S&P 500." https://fred.stlouisfed.org/series/SP500.

St. Louis Fed. 2023d. "Assets: Liquidity and Credit Facilities: Loans: Bank Term Funding Program." https://fred.stlouisfed.org/series/H41RESPPALDKNWW.

St. Louis Fed. 2023e. "Shares of Gross Domestic Product: Personal Consumption Expenditures." https://fred.stlouisfed.org/series/DPCERE1Q156NBEA.

Stafford, Philip, and Richard Henderson. 2020. " 'Intense' Trading Sends Exchange Volumes to Record." *Financial Times*, 3 March. https://www.ft.com/content/de34 a00a-5ca4-11ea-8033-fa40a0d65a98.

Stewart, Ian. 2012. *In Pursuit of the Unknown: 17 Equations That Changed the World.* New York: Basic Books.

Stigum, Marcia L., and Anthony Crescenzi. 2007 *Money Market.* New York: McGraw-Hill.

Stockhammer, Engelbert. 2010. "Income Distribution, the Finance-Dominated Accumulation Regime and the Present Crisis. In *The World Economy in Crisis: The Return of Keynesianism?*, edited by Sebastian Dullien, Eckhard Hein, Achim Truger, and Till van Treeck, 63–86. Marburg: Metropolis Verlag.

Stokes, Doug. 2014. "Achilles' Deal: Dollar Decline and US Grand Strategy after the Crisis." *Review of International Political Economy* 21(5): 1071–94.

Strange, Susan. 1971. "The Politics of International Currencies." *World Politics* 23(2): 215–31.

Strange, Susan. 1986. *Casino Capitalism.* Oxford: Basil Blackwell.

Strange, Susan. 1998. *Mad Money.* Manchester: Manchester University Press.

Stubbington, Tommy. 2022. "Bank of England Says £65bn Gilt Intervention Staved Off UK Financial 'Spiral'." *Financial Times*, 6 October. https://www.ft.com/content /09c43669-18a9-4476-9a95-044a2448d400.

Systemic Risk Council. 2019. "Comment on Federal Reserve and FDIC proposals To Relax Resolvability Requirements For US Regional Banks." 16 July. https://www .federalreserve.gov/SECRS/2019/October/20191008/R-1660/R-1660_071719_134341 _534842034749_1.pdf.

Systemic Risk Council. 2020. "Reigniting Reforms to Ensure a Resilient and Stable Financial System: A Second Phase?" 9 October. https://www.systemicriskcouncil. org/2020/10/statement-by-the-systemic-risk-council-on-reigniting-reforms-to-en sure-a-resilient-and-stable-financial-system/.

Taylor, John B. 2009. *Getting Off Track: How Government Actions and Interventions Caused, Prolonged, and Worsened the Financial Crisis.* Stanford, CA: Hoover Press.

Terazono, Emiko. 2018. "Commodity Trading Enters the Age of Digitization." *Financial Times*, 10 July. https://www.ft.com/content/8cc7f5d4-59ca-11e8-b8b2-d6ceb45fa 9d0.

Tett, Gillian. 2010. *Fool's Gold.* London: Abacus.

Tett, Gillian. 2017. "Janet Yellen Banks on an Aggressively Passive Strategy." *Financial Times*, 15 May. https://www.ft.com/content/8f40a794-50f1-11e7-a1f2-db1957236ibb.

Tett, Gillian. 2019. Central Banks Are Rethinking Their Roles." *Financial Times*, 12 September. https://www.ft.com/content/eb1143fc-d543-11e9-8367-807ebd53ab77.

Tett, Gillian. 2020. "Markets Contemplate a Future In Which Stimulus Does Not Work." *Financial Times*, 13 March. https://www.ft.com/content/of511530-64cd-11ea -a6cd-df28cc3c6a68.

Thatcher, Margaret. 1986. "Speech at Lord Mayor's Banquet." 10 November. http:// www.margaretthatcher.org/document/106512.

Thiemann, Matthias. 2014. "In the Shadow of Basel: How Competitive Politics Bred the Crisis." *Review of International Political Economy* 21(6): 1203–39.

Thiemann, Matthias. 2018. *The Growth of Shadow Banking: A Comparative Institutional Analysis*. Cambridge: Cambridge University Press.

Thiemann, Matthias. 2019a. "Is Resilience Enough? The Macro-prudential Reform Agenda and the Lacking Smoothing of the Cycle." *Public Administration* 97(3): 561– 75.

Thiemann, Matthias. 2019b. "Is Resilience Enough? Why There Is No Anti-cyclical Regulation in Financial Markets Post-crisis and What It Means for Financialization." *Public Administration*. DOI: 10.1111/padm.12551.

Thiemann, Matthias, Mohamed Aldegwy, and Edin Ibrocevic. 2017. "Understanding the Shift from Micro- to Macro-prudential Thinking: A Discursive Network Analysis." *Cambridge Journal of Economics*. doi.org/10.1093/cje/bex056.

Thiemann, Matthias, Carolina R. Melches, and Edin Ibrocevic. 2021. "Measuring and Mitigating Systemic Risks: How the Forging of New Alliances between Central Bank and Academic Economists Legitimize the Transnational Macroprudential Agenda." *Review of International Political Economy* 28(6): 1433–58.

Tickell, Adam. 2003. "Cultures of Money." In *Handbook of Cultural Geography*, edited by Kay Anderson, Mona Domosh, Steve Pile, and Nigel Thrift, 116–130. London: Sage.

Tooze, Adam. 2018. *Crashed: How a Decade of Financial Crises Changed the World*. New York: Viking.

Tooze, Adam. 2023a. "We Are Living through a Trillion-Dollar Rebalancing." *Financial Times*, 31 March. https://www.ft.com/content/4d519cc7-5959-4749-a892-dc8bd5 cf1014.

Tooze, Adam. 2023b. "Chartbook 220 Biden's 'New Industrial Policy': Revolution in the Making, Or an Exercise in Defying Gravity?" 14 June. https://adamtooze.com/ 2023/06/14/chartbook-220-bidens-new-industrial-policy-revolution-in-the-making -or-an-exercise-in-defying-gravity/.

Tran, Hung. 2019. "Repo Turmoil Is a Symptom of a Much Bigger Problem." *Financial Times* 27 September. https://www.ft.com/content/71849166-e02d-11e9-b112-9624e c9edc59.

Treynor, Jack L. 1987. "The Economics of the Dealer Function." *Financial Analysts Journal* 43(6): 27–34.

Tsingou, Eleni. 2015. "Club Governance and the Making of Global Financial Rules." *Review of International Political Economy* 22(2): 225–56.

Tucker, Paul. 2014. "The Lender of Last Resort and Modern Central Banking." In *Re-*

thinking the Lender of Last Resort, edited by Bank for International Settlements, BIS Paper No. 79, 10–42.

US Bureau of Labor Statistics. 2023. "Real Earnings." https://www.bls.gov/news.release /realer.toc.htm.

US Department of the Treasury / Board of Governors of the Federal Reserve System; Federal Reserve Bank of New York; US Securities and Exchange Commission; US Commodity Futures Trading Commission. 2015. *The U.S. Treasury Market on October 15, 2014*. July. http://www.treasury.gov/press-center/press-releases/Documents /Joint_Staff_Report_Treasury_10-15-2015.pdf.

Ugolini, Stefano. 2017. *The Evolution of Central Banking: Theory and History.* London: Palgrave Macmillan.

UNEP. 2021. *Adaptation Gap Report 2021: The Gathering Storm—Adapting to Climate Change in a Post-pandemic World.* https://www.unep.org/adaptation-gap-report-2021.

Van der Pijl, Kees. 2006. *Global Rivalries from the Cold War to Iraq.* London: Pluto Press.

Van der Zwan, Natascha. 2014. "Making Sense of Financialization." *Socio-Economic Review* 12(2): 99–129.

van 't Klooster, Jens. 2021. *The ECB's Conundrum and 21st-Century Monetary Policy: How European Monetary Policy Can Be Green, Social, and Democratic.* Berlin: Heinrich-Böll-Stiftung / Finanzwende.

van 't Klooster, Jens, and Clément Fontan. 2020. "The Myth of Market Neutrality: A Comparative Study of the European Central Bank's and the Swiss National Bank's Corporate Security Purchases." *New Political Economy* 25(6): 865–79.

Vogel, Steven K. 1996. *Freer Markets, More Rules: Regulatory Reform in Advanced Industrial Countries.* Ithaca, NY: Cornell University Press.

Volcker, Paul A. 2008. "Interview by Donald L. Kohn, Lynn S. Fox, and David H. Small, Federal Reserve Board Oral History Project, Board of Governors of the Federal Reserve System." 28 January. Washington, DC: Board of Governors. https:// www.federalreserve.gov/aboutthefed/files/paul-avolcker-interview-20080225.pdf.

Volcker, Paul A., Alan Greenspan, Ben Bernanke, and Janet Yellen. 2019. "America Needs an Independent Fed." *Wall Street Journal*, 5 August. https://www.wsj.com/ar ticles/america-needs-an-independent-fed-11565045308.

von Neumann, John, and Oskar Morgenstern. 1944. *Theory of Games and Economic Behaviour.* Princeton, NJ: Princeton University Press.

Weber, Isabella. 2021. "Could Strategic Price Controls Help Fight Inflation?" *The Guardian*, 29 December.https://www.theguardian.com/business/commentisfree/ 2021/dec/29/inflation-price-controls-time-we-use-it.

Weber, Isabella M., and Evan Wasner. 2023. "Sellers' Inflation, Profits and Conflict: Why Can Large Firms Hike Prices in an Emergency?" Economics Department Working Paper Series.

Weber, Max. 1978. *Economy and Society.* Berkeley: University of California Press.

Weidmann, Jens. 2013a. "Ein Flirt mit Folgen: Zum Verhältnis von Geld- und Fiskalpolitik." *Zeitschrift für Staats- und Europawissenschaften* 11(4): 461–65.

Weidmann, Jens. 2013b. "Eingangserklärung anlässlich der mündlichen Verhandlung im Hauptsacheverfahren ESM/EZB, 11. June 2013." https://www.bundesbank.de/Redaktion/DE/Kurzmeldungen/Stellungnahmen/2013_06_11_esm_ezb.html.

Weidmann, Jens. 2020. "Introductory Panel Statement." Speech at the Institute for Monetary and Financial Stability "ECB and Its Watchers XXI Conference." https://www.bundesbank.de/en/press/speeches/introductory-panel-statement-846034.

Wells, Peter. 2020. "S&P 500 Suffers Its Quickest Fall into Bear Market on Record." *Financial Times*, 12 March. https://www.ft.com/content/d895a54c-64a4-11ea-a6cd-df28cc3c6a68.

Wheatley, Jonathan. 2020. "Surging Dollar, Coronavirus and Oil Slump Hit Emerging Economies." *Financial Times*, 19 March.

Wigglesworth, Robin. 2020a. "The Liquidity 'Collapse' Is a Modern-Day Cobra Effect." *Financial Times*, 6 April. https://www.ft.com/content/6d00a279-d79b-44ae-a7b4-2b65131697a1.

Wigglesworth, Robin. 2020b. "The Week the World Changed: How a Markets Wobble Turned to Mayhem." *Financial Times*, 13 March. https://www.ft.com/content/86f7f914-6536-11ea-b3f3-fe4680ea68b5.

Wittgenstein, Ludwig. 1953. *Philosophical Investigations*. Oxford: Oxford University Press.

Wolf, Martin. 2020. "The Virus Is an Economic Emergency Too." *Financial Times*, 17 March. https://www.ft.com/content/348e05e4-6778-11ea-800d-da70cff6e4d3.

World Bank. 2013. *Global Financial Development Report: Rethinking the Role of the State in Finance*. Washington, DC: World Bank Publications.

World Bank. 2022a. *Finance for an Equitable Recovery*. Washington. DC: International Bank for Reconstruction and Development.

World Bank. 2022b. "Risk of Global Recession in 2023 Rises amid Simultaneous Rate Hikes." Press release, 15 September. https://www.worldbank.org/en/news/press-release/2022/09/15/risk-of-global-recession-in-2023-rises-amid-simultaneous-rate-hikes.

World Economic Forum. 2023. *Global Risks Report 2023*. https://www.weforum.org/reports/globalrisks-report-2023/.

Wray, Randall A. 1990. *Money and Credit in Capitalist Economies*. Aldershot: Edward Elgar.

Wray, Randall A. 2004. *State and Credit Theories of Money: The Contributions of A. Mitchell Innes*. Cheltenham: Edward Elgar.

Wray, Randall A. 2007. "A Post-Keynesian View of Central Bank Independence, Policy Targets, and the Rules-Versus-Discretion Debate." *Journal of Post Keynesian Economics* 30(12): 119–41.

Wray, Randall A. 2008. "Lessons from the Subprime Meltdown." *Challenge* 51(2): 40–68.

Wu, Ethan, and Kate Duguid. 2022. "Fed's Faster 'Quantitative Tightening' Adds to Strain On Bond Market." *Financial Times*, 14 September. https://www.ft.com/content/70e43592-30d0-4348-916b-673910ad7726.

Wullweber, Joscha. 2004. *Das grüne Gold der Gene: Globale Konflikte und Biopiraterie*. Münster: Westfälisches Dampfboot.

Wullweber, Joscha. 2010. *Hegemonie, Diskurs und Politische Ökonomie: Das Nano-technologie-Projekt*. Baden-Baden: Nomos.

Wullweber, Joscha. 2015a. "Post-positivist Political Theory." In *The Encyclopedia of Political Thought*, edited by Michael T. Gibbons, 2932–42. Chichester: Wiley.

Wullweber, Joscha. 2015b. "Global Politics and Empty Signifiers: The Political Construction of High-Technology." *Critical Policy Studies* 9(1): 78–96.

Wullweber, Joscha. 2016. "Performative Global Finance: Bridging Micro and Macro Approaches with a Stratified Perspective." *New Political Economy* 21(3): 305–21.

Wullweber, Joscha. 2019a. "Poststructural Research in International Political Economy." In *Oxford Research Encyclopedia of International Studies*, edited by Marlin-Bennett, Renée Marlin-Bennett. Oxford: Oxford University Press. DOI: 10.1093/acrefore/9780190846626.013.468.

Wullweber, Joscha. 2019b. "Money, State, Hegemony: A Political Ontology of Money." *New Political Science* 41(2): 313–28.

Wullweber, Joscha. 2019c. "Constructing Hegemony in Global Politics: A Discourse-Theoretical Approach to Policy Analysis." *Administrative Theory and Praxis* 47(3): 148–67.

Wullweber, Joscha. 2019d. Monism vs. Pluralism, the Global Financial Crisis, and the Methodological Struggle in the Field of International Political Economy." *Competition and Change* 23(3): 287–311.

Wullweber, Joscha. 2020a. *The COVID-19 Financial Crisis, Global Financial Instabilities and Transformations in the Financial System*. Berlin: Finanzwende/ Heinrich-Böll-Stiftung.

Wullweber, Joscha. 2020b. "Embedded Finance: The Shadow Banking System, Sovereign Power, and a New State-Market Hybridity." *Journal of Cultural Economy* 13(5): 592–609.

Wullweber, Joscha. 2021. "The Politics of Shadow Money: Security Structures, Money Creation And Unconventional Central Banking." *New Political Economy* 26(1): 69–85.

Wullweber, Joscha, and Christoph Scherrer. 2011. "Postmodern and Poststructural International Political Economy." In *The International Studies Encyclopedia*, edited by Robert A. Denemark. Oxford: Blackwell, Blackwell Reference Online.

Wæver, Ole. 2005. "European Integration and Security: Analysing French and German Discourses on State, Nation, and Europe." In *Discourse Theory and European Politics*, edited by David Howarth and Jacob Torfing, 33–67. Basingstoke, Hampshire: Palgrave Macmillan.

Young, Brigitte. 2018. "The Impact of Unconventional Monetary Policy on Gendered Wealth Inequality." *Papeles de Europa* 31(2): 175–85.

Zelizer, Viviana. 1995. *The Social Meaning of Money*. New York: Basic Books.

Zelizer, Viviana. 2005. "Missing Monies: Comment on Nigel Dodd, 'Reinventing Monies in Europe'." *Economy and Society* 34(4): 584–88.

Index

CURRENCIES

New Thinking for Financial Times
STEFAN EICH AND MARTIJN KONINGS, EDITORS